Swimming to Suburbia

Craig Hodgetts

Swimming to Suburbia

AND OTHER ESSAYS

Edited by Todd Gannon

Contents

Introduction

TODD GANNON

FADE IN: *Santa Monica, morning, early 1970s. A junkyard near the beach. Rusted cars, some up on blocks, hoods open, are casually arranged alongside battered appliances and stacks of old television sets. Seated at a makeshift table, an old man tinkers with a radio in the dappled shade of a threadbare awning. Nearby, a small dog scratches in the dust.*

A young man—longish hair, t-shirt, faded jeans, aviator glasses—enters through a flimsy chain-link gate. The old man rises; the young man proffers a few crumpled bills. The old man pockets the bills, gestures lazily toward the cars, then turns and shuffles toward the gate. As the old man drags the gate in a jagged arc through the dust, an engine roars to life offscreen. The young man careens through the open gate in a faded yellow sedan.

DISSOLVE TO: *The young man holds a tattered stencil, off-center, against the hood of the sedan with his right hand. With his left, he shakes a can of spray paint, aims, and presses the nozzle. The can hisses. Colored mist settles on his right hand as the target-like void of the stencil fills with a bright, wet green.*

DISSOLVE TO: *The sedan hiccups over a litter-strewn curb cut into an empty asphalt parking lot. The young man, left elbow jutting through the open driver's side window, spins the wheel with the butt of his right hand. The car skids to a halt across two parking spaces. The young man reaches down and cuts the engine. His fingertips, still green with spray paint, pause for a moment on the key. He leaves it in the ignition and exits the car, slamming the door behind him. Without looking back, he strides purposefully past the car and across the dew-wet grass of a local park. The camera lingers on the green symbol on the hood of the car before pulling away vertically to an aerial shot of the city. The Pacific surf breaks gently around the pier at the corner of the frame.*

FADE OUT.

*

I wrote these lines after staring for a while at a reproduction of an untitled 1970 collage by Craig Hodgetts (see p. 16). The image on the black-and-white photocopy is about four and a half inches wide by seven inches tall and consists of twelve strips of typewritten text affixed to a grainy aerial photograph of Santa Monica. Nine target-like symbols pockmark the image, two of them partially obscured by the strips of text. The photograph is oriented with north to the right and is cropped such that the inland edge of the beach describes a straight line that extends at a roughly forty-degree angle from the upper right corner of the image to a point about two thirds of the way down the left edge. The grid of the city extends from the beach to fill the space beneath the diagonal. Layers of sand, surf, and sea recede back from the line in the triangle left above it. The pier cantilevers out of the grid and over the water, unperturbed by the churning ocean below.

A conventionally modernist interpreter might read this composition as suggesting the inevitable extension of the city grid—the leading edge of manifest destiny—across Santa Monica Bay and out to sea. If the map were oriented conventionally, with north toward the top of the page, the visual weight of the city would bear down ominously on the ocean in the lower left corner, making such a reading all the more convincing. But Hodgetts did not orient the map conventionally. Instead, he rotated it, causing the city grid to appear to recoil from the advancing convexity of the ocean. And just as the layering of pier over ocean might signal to a conventional modernist the triumph of architecture over landscape, the simple act of rotating a sheet of paper suggests, to an unconventional modernist like Hodgetts, that charting a better future often begins simply by changing one's point of view.

Of course, to read this image in this way is to miss much of its point. This photocollage, like Hodgetts's architecture and most of the other texts and images collected in this volume, has less to do with the specific qualities of the artifact itself than with the way that artifact predicts and promotes alternative possibilities for modern life. Thus Hodgetts's impatience, early in his career, with traditional building, and his gravitation toward portable electronic and mechanical equipment that more effectively accomplishes tasks traditionally assigned to built form. Thus his preference, as his practice matured, for cinema's choreographed dynamism over photography's composed stasis as a way to represent the roving eye of the modern urban denizens for whom he writes and builds. Thus his enthusiasm for the work of James Stirling, whose irreverent postwar reinterpretations of the language of modern architecture first revealed to Hodgetts architecture's unique power to invigorate the human spirit, and of Charles and Ray Eames, whose distinctly American, do-it-yourself modernism provided a template for his own design practice. Thus his lifelong fascination with Los Angeles, a city that derives its coherence not from the coordinated arrangement of built form but instead from the cacophony of thirteen million individual futures improvised simultaneously at the edge of Western civilization.

And thus Hodgetts's tendency, in the essays that appear in this volume, to eschew the strident manifesto form adopted by his early modern forebears and to avoid as well as the academic, jargon-laden prose of so many writer-architects of his own generation. Such writing quite simply cannot touch the particularized ambitions that lie at the heart of Hodgetts's project. Instead, hints of the engaging, immersive style of the New Journalists, that loose band of unorthodox writers who reshaped the popular press in the 1960s and '70s, echo in these pages. Think Tom Wolfe, but stripped of his smugness, or Hunter S. Thompson, minus the gonzo excess, or Joan Didion, relieved of her resigned fatalism but still gripped by a deep fascination with the technologized fragmentation that constitutes modern life, particularly as it plays out under the clear blue skies of Southern California.

Like the New Journalists, Hodgetts is a first-class noticer and an expert describer. He constructs his *mise-en-scènes* from overlooked castoffs of technological society, and his protagonists, sometimes in the guise of professional colleagues, mentors, and friends, deftly rearrange the fragments with care, originality, and wit. Throughout, they privilege one-off improvisation over abstract planning, seductive performance over rote function, and immersive pleasure over sober efficiency. The aggregated results of their individual labors cohere to orchestrate a new kind of city, one still scored for modernism's familiar technological accoutrements but arranged to produce a distinctly new feeling, as if the city we thought we knew were played in a different key.

*

After training in automotive design, theater, and fine arts, Hodgetts made a name for himself as a precocious graduate student at Yale in the mid-1960s. Following a brief collaboration with his mentor James Stirling, he launched a small New York-based practice with his classmate Lester Walker in 1968. The next year, he relocated to Los Angeles, where he commenced his celebrated teaching career, first at CalArts and later at UCLA, and launched a fruitful, if sometimes tumultuous, collaboration with Robert Mangurian. When that partnership ended in 1983, Hodgetts briefly left architecture for dalliances with fiction and the film industry only to be lured back by the energetic young architect Hsinming Fung. The two launched their award-winning collaboration in 1984, and have lived and worked together since.

Amid this frenetic professional activity, Hodgetts regularly carved out time to write, publishing some 100,000 words since 1970, and squirreling away probably as many more in the form of unpublished essays, plays, and other musings. All but the earliest of the texts collected here were written in Los Angeles, and often are directed at the problems and personalities most closely associated with that city. The Eameses figure strongly, as do many of Hodgetts's friends and collaborators including Mangurian, Coy Howard, and Frank Gehry. Given the well-known reticence of many Los Angeles architects of Hodgetts's generation, these texts provide a rare, first-person account of a crucial period in LA architecture.

Other texts focus on the nature of the city itself. In Los Angeles, Hodgetts glimpses tantalizing visions of the future in the present. Typically, he finds them the idiosyncratic nooks and crannies that punctuate the city's unruly sprawl. In "Swimming to Suburbia" of 1987, he deploys a canny musical analogy to encapsulate his understanding of the city. LA's urban organization, he proposes, is akin to the indefinite arrangement of composer Terry Riley's *In C*, which turns over significant control of the shape of each performance to the individual musicians who play it. The aleatory coherence that results strongly contrasts both the tightly controlled intensity of the renaissance city, which Hodgetts aligns with Beethoven's *Eroica* symphony, and the coordinated unanimity of the medieval city, which he equates with a Gregorian chant.

If, for Hodgetts, "Swimming to Suburbia" constitutes something of a theory of the city, proposals like "Useful Ideas for a Future LA" (1989) and "La città pulpa" (1996, with Hodgetts + Fung) demonstrate that theory put into practice. The latter scheme, an extended comic strip Hodgetts + Fung contributed to the 1996 Milan Triennale, imagines the improvised appropriation of what's left of a near-future Los Angeles in the wake of a devastating earthquake. "Notes for *La città pulpa*," a sort of speculative sequel to "Swimming to Suburbia" prepared in tandem with their Triennale proposal, is included here, as is the full theatrical script Hodgetts and Fung devised to structure the graphic presentations they exhibited in Milan.

Of course, Hodgetts's reach extends well beyond Los Angeles. His longstanding commitment to integrating mechanical, digital, and media technologies into architecture provides a unique foundation for his examinations of the recent history and probable futures of the field. Particularly in essays dating to the 1970s and '80s, when technological questions associated with early twentieth-century modernism often were overshadowed by the more historical and theoretical rhetoric of postmodernism, Hodgetts's foregrounding of technology provides a crucial counterpoint to much of the literature of the period. His friendship with Stirling, with whom Hodgetts remained close until the British architect's death in 1992, led to "Inside James Stirling" of 1976, still one of the most informative treatments of Stirling's iconoclastic early work, and spurred an illuminating series of later reflections on Stirling's life and legacy. Taken together, these texts form an important point of entry into the growing but still insufficient literature on a seminal figure of late twentieth-century architecture.

Though the texts collected here are replete with profound insights into the nature of architecture and the workings of the contemporary city, Hodgetts would resist being labeled a theorist. Nor, despite his careful presentations of the work of Stirling, the Eameses, and other key figures of twentieth-century architecture, would he consider himself a historian. Given his trenchant commentaries on contemporary work and the contexts in which it operates, he might begrudgingly admit to having occasionally assumed the role of a critic, but he'd likely chafe at that label as well. This is because Hodgetts, first and foremost, writes as an architect. For him, writing is but another medium, akin to paper, pixels, glass, or steel, through which to project his design sensibilities, to illuminate his many disciplinary and extra-disciplinary interests, and to articulate his vision of a better future.

For this reason, Hodgetts sees little reason to cleave to the familiar habits of architectural writers or to limit himself to publication in the usual disciplinary venues. In addition to such periodicals as *Progressive Architecture, Log, and The Architect's Newspaper,* Hodgetts's essays have found their way into popular publications including *New York Magazine, Ms., Glamour,* and the *Los Angeles Times*. As initially published, many of these writings were accompanied by his own architectural drawings. Some, like those in "The Birth of Individual Architecture," straightforwardly illustrate the specific architectural proposals Hodgetts outlines in his texts. Others, like the collages that accompany "Inside James Stirling," attempt to capture visually the design sensibility that drives the work he describes. Others still, like the suite of production-design vignettes Hodgetts produced for a never-completed film adaptation of Ernest Callenbach's 1975 novel, *Ecotopia*, augment the imagination of others with his own speculative designs.

Sometimes, Hodgetts sees fit to more radically reimagine the conventional relationship between text and image, as in the photocollage described at the outset of this essay, the "Useful Ideas for a Future LA" broadsheets, the Città pulpa comics, and the complexly interwoven lines of text that comprise "The Synthetic Landscape," which Hodgetts composed as a graduate student at Yale in 1966. Drawing on his early studies in playwriting, Hodgetts even has turned to the theatrical script as a vehicle for his ideas. With its focus on characters and dialogue, the form allows Hodgetts to foreground his interest in the social consequences of architectural design, as demonstrated here by *La città pulpa* and by *Purity*, his amorously charged staging of a fictitious 1930s encounter between Eileen Gray and Josephine Baker at Gray's famous modernist villa at Cap Martin.

For all this, the central character in this collection is Hodgetts himself. Whether speaking as a restless technophile, a committed futurist, or a concerned citizen, his unique voice resonates through these writings with boundless enthusiasm for the immediate future and unparalleled passion for the discipline of architecture. Throughout, Hodgetts attends to architecture's myriad analog and digital inflections with formidable intelligence and relentless curiosity, choreographing on nearly every page provocative tensions and productive opportunities between tectonics and information, between the monumental and the ephemeral, and, ultimately, between free individuals and the increasingly sophisticated technological environments they inhabit.

Part I
Polemics

City Peace,
House Peace

DESIGN QUARTERLY 78/79,
CONCEPTUAL ARCHITECTURE (1970): 34–36

In 1970, John S. Margolies edited an influential issue of the
American journal, *Design Quarterly*, on the topic of "Conceptual
Architecture." The issue featured contributions from young
architects, artists, and designers including Ant Farm, the
Archigram group, Archizoom Associati, François Dallegret, Peter
Eisenman, Haus-Rucker Company, Craig Hodgetts, Les Levine,
Onyx, Ed Ruscha, and Superstudio.

Hodgetts's contribution, developed in collaboration with
Peter de Bretteville, comprised two collages which offered three
proposals for architecture by other means. Each reimagines
traditional notions of individual property, with two encouraging
shared resources (cars, homes) and one short-circuiting urban
efficiency by parking a car on the freeway. Importantly, the
cars, but not the homes, were to be marked with "an identifying
symbol." For Hodgetts, if technology was to offer a new medium
for architecture, it had to be conspicuously identified as such.

CITY PEACE I

BUY A DISCARDED AUTOMOBILE WHICH STILL OPERATES FROM A JUNK DEALER AND PAINT AN IDENTIFYING SYMBOL ON IT.

PARK IT IN A PUBLIC PLACE LEAVING THE KEYS IN THE IGNITION.

CITY PEACE II

BUY A DISCARDED AUTOMOBILE WHICH STILL OPERATES FROM A JUNK DEALER AND PAINT AN IDENTIFYING SYMBOL ON IT.

LEAVE IT ON THE FREEWAY SOME MORNING.

IF POSSIBLE FLATTEN THE TIRES.

34

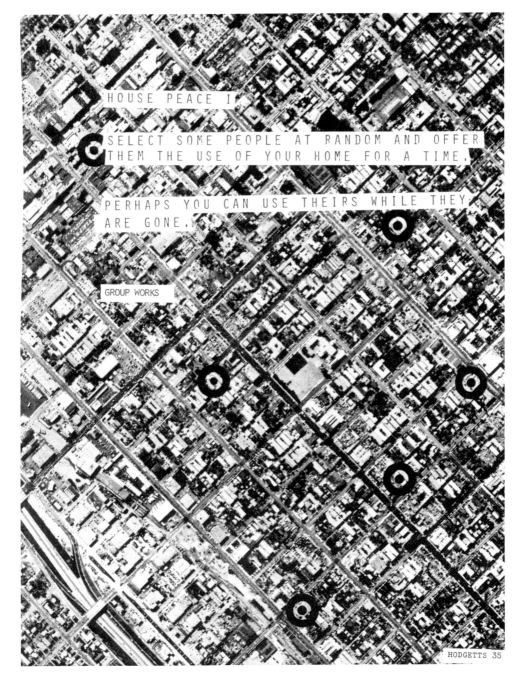

HOUSE PEACE I

SELECT SOME PEOPLE AT RANDOM AND OFFER
THEM THE USE OF YOUR HOME FOR A TIME.

PERHAPS YOU CAN USE THEIRS WHILE THEY
ARE GONE.

GROUP WORKS

HODGETTS 35

Designers create iconographic objects which, if they
Men like Lindbergh, who fixed a
don't hum, or whirr, or buzz, still pursue an elusive
borrowed mirror to the bulkhead
"presence." Architects like Robert Venturi and Peter
with chewing gum in order to see
Millard, denied the metaphor of movement, opt for a
his compass; St.-Exupery, whose
The onslaught of mini-cars,
sentient presence which underlines the impassive sym-
which eschew the voluptuous
bolism of an hierarchical order. Even John Glenn, a
form to which Harley Earl*
"capsule hero, expendable and replaceable, like a
married them, seem to gain
superbly machined part of an automatic process", was
anonymity by the very loss
styled to conform to our own primitive science-fiction
of mammalian characteristics,
imagery, yet, during docking manouevers in the Gemini
so that, like insects, they

avoid the narcissistic image

we need for empathy.

Mumford's fear of a "machine

fetish" becomes more and more

irrelevant as machines become

less and less like animals.

Mustang, FORD MOTOR COMPANY

VING SHELVES. YOU WON'T BE SHORT OF CUPBOARDS. YOU COULD HAVE AN OFF-WHITE PILE LINEN RUG,   A...

A PURPLE MUSTANG IS AN INTENSLY EVOCATIVE SEXUAL IMAGE.

A PURPLE VOLKSWAGEN IS ONLY A VOLKSWAGEN PAINTED PURPLE.

002.1
Craig Hodgetts, original manuscript page from "The Synthetic Landscape,"
written while a graduate student at Yale University, c. 1966.

The Synthetic Landscape

ARTS IN SOCIETY VOL. 7, NO. 3, CALIFORNIA INSTITUTE OF THE ARTS: PROLOGUE TO A COMMUNITY (FALL–WINTER 1970): 126–32

In the fall of 1970, the editors of the University of Wisconsin's arts journal turned over editorship of its Fall–Winter issue to Sheila de Bretteville, Barry Hyams, and Marianne Partridge, who used the issue to showcase writing and projects from the faculty and staff of the newly formed California Institute of the Arts. Contributors included Allan Kaprow, John Baldassari, Dick Higgins, Nam June Paik, Ravi Shankar, and Hodgetts, who was a founding Associate Dean of the institute.

Hodgetts's contribution, a complexly typeset interweaving of multiple narrative strands, was developed from a paper he had initially written as a graduate student at Yale for a course taught by Vincent Scully. Garnished with lines borrowed from Alain Robbe-Grillet and Harold Pinter, the text offers a poetic meditation on the nature of objects—and humanity's altered relationships to them—in a technologically advanced society. In it, Hodgetts lays out many of the themes he would develop in later writings and foreshadows the paradoxical tensions involved in the technologically progressive, experientially immersive, and erotically charged humanism to which he has been committed since the late 1960s.

We stand on the threshold of a post-organic landscape we already know but cannot see, with induction hums instead of mechanical rattles, the secret interiors of solid-state diodes instead of the livid glow of the vacuum tube, the seamless box instead of the bolted contraption.

An orchestra recorded without an audience and made perceptual to individuals from time to time through the medium of loudspeakers is an evolution of the concert hall situation, while the

The Slow evolution of natural forms and materials characteristic of an organic order has been supercharged by conceptual abstraction and the synthesis of fundamental bits. In a synthetic environment, abstract and electronically generated and revolutionary, the relationship of man to the organic system may be recorded compositions of viewed as constant (i.e., we must still breathe an oxygen-inert gas mixture) Stockhausen are more nearly While that of man to his surroundings is a constant variable. synthetic. Consequently the tonal

Already painters like Rauschenberg have recognized that wrenching an and rhythmic patterns associated object loose of its systematic use and projecting it into harsh conflict with with traditional musical forms, other objects and images no longer produces the intense dislocation which are dependent on human characteristic of surrealism, but instead mutes the identity of each object, dexterity, are absent from merging it with the overall structure. There is no implicit outrage in the Stockhausen, with a corresponding manipulation of objects which are programmatically reproduced since increase in conceptual their character is non-assertive and open-ended. The object, by

sublimating identity to context, needs only the smallest persuasion to

become an integer in a new fabric.

clarity. There is no transposition

from system to system—we hear

precisely what we were meant

to hear—An ersatz symphony reels

from an ersatz cabinet. We wear

ersatz woolens and imitation

uppers in our comfortable fake

sponge chair, nibbling on pseudo-

cheese crackers. Around us,

counterfeit sunlight silhouettes the

pretend lace of the curtains as a

child on a sham motorcycle pedals

into the room—

It's a retreat. It's a place to go for rest and peace. So you want quiet decoration. For instance … this room.

This room you could have as a kitchen. Right size, nice sun comes in. I'd have teal blue, copper, and parchment

linoleum squares. I'd have them echoed in the walls. I'd offset the kitchen units with charcoal gray worktops.

Our senses plug into high-speed printers and gauges for the latest.

decoded state-of-the-world before retiring to contemplate Ford and

Le Corbusier and the world that was.

"Through these halls, these galleries of another century, this enormous, luxurious, baroque lugubrious hotel—overloaded with a dark and cold ornamentation of woodwork, stucco, moldings— marble, black mirrors, dark paintings, columns, heavy hangings …"
— *Last Year at Marienbad* by Alain Robbe-Grillet

"Everything is or can be" says Cesar Vivaldi—the scars of research, the pock-marks of technology have disappeared. At a stage of systemic probability

the great accomplishments of
The synthetic object is, after all, capable of rapid and revolutionary
science and engineering have been
change, during which man and nature alike effect only rudimentary and
in the creation of devices with no
evolutionary changes.
physiologic analogue. Our

conceptual models, metaphors for

a secret universe, line eyes, ears,

hands, to atomic interstices—the

mechanical parallel with our own
The junk sculptors of the fifties recognized the found object, but their
bodies has been short-circuited
work, particularly that of Stankeiwicz, sought to amplify an animism only
into an electroencephalic
latent in the form. It was comforting to think of the rusted automobile parts
reproduction of our nervous
as satyrs, gnomes, and assorted hobgoblins; to be reassured by totems of
system.
our own making when technology lurched out of our control, and seemed

aimed at the atomic disintegration of the entire race; to fondle a

mechanistic icon in a time of technological oppression rather than a

human idol in a time of human oppression.

If you look closely at a brass

elephant from contemporary

Ceylon you might see a leit-motif of

Coca-Cola trademarks woven into

the authentic Oriental engraving,

or an obscure but still legible "U.S.

Army Ordnance" pressed into the

base of a bronze vessel from

Korea. I told my friend who had

bought such a vase that I would be

happier with the shell casing

itself than with its handmade

Doppelgänger. He did not agree.

The Peruvian native who constructs

a dwelling in an electric

transmission tower precisely as he

would in a tree and taps the lines

for power as he might tap a tree for

latex demonstrates an awareness

of systems-overlap which we have

yet to grasp.

We'd have a small wall cupboard, a large wall cupboard, a corner wall cupboard, with revolving shelves.

You won't be short of cupboards … You could have an off-white pile linen rug, a table in … afromosia teak

veneer, sideboard with matte black drawers, curved chairs with cushioned seats, armchairs in

oatmeal tweed, a beech …

— adapted from *The Caretaker* by Harold Pinter

We see, smell, taste, touch, and hear only remnants and by-products of

systems born of the reunification of sub-microscopic, non-corporeal

particles. Chemistry and physics are the new midwives, delivering

parthenogenetic objects on a geometric timetable.

Men like Lindberg who fixed a

borrowed mirror to the bulkhead

with chewing gum in order to see

his compass, or Saint-Exupéry whose

night mail flights were poetic

exploration of man and machine,

of Le Corbusier whose architecture

explicitly outlined the heroic acts

of the twenties, were succeeded by

The quality of each part of

Saarinen's G.M. Technical Center

as a perfectly machined, integral,

but anonymous systems imposes no   the anti-heroes of the '60s.
Fuller's hypothesis, that man is in effect carrying his own evolution forward
fixed, pictorial limits to the
by technological advances is valid only if he can assimilate the change.
organization. The building might

extend indefinitely along its axis

according to demand, pushing,

extruding hallways deeper and

deeper into action. Those hallways,

lucid, pragmatic, and vital, are the

avenues of what is happening, not

the rambles of boredom. They

rush from room to room,

demountable, hermetic,

A purple Mustang is an intensely evocative sexual image. A purple
self-contained.
Volkswagen is only a VW painted purple.

The organs with which we

understood the operation of

devices which were the "ablative

absolute" of our bodies are dead

appendages. A vast fissure splits

senses from concept. We might

learn to intuit the malfunction of

a mechanical device, but the solid-

state computer must tell us. Our

relation to a growing lattice of

autonomous systems is defined by

nodal links which avoid kinesthesis

and replace sensuality.

Paper dresses, microminiature electronic circuits, cera-metallic cooking
ware, three-dimensional holographic projections, and instant igloos signal
the end of an era in which we desperately picked, cut, cleaned, twisted,
and wove natural materials into useful configurations.

The onslaught of mini-cars: like
insects, they avoid the narcissistic
images we need for empathy—

Mumford's fear of a machine fetish

becomes more and more immanent

as machines become less and less

like animals—

A poet in San Francisco gave his

long medieval refectory table to the

Designers create iconographic objects which, if they don't hum, or whirr,
Salvation Army. He now eats from
or buzz, still pursue an elusive "presence." Even John Glenn was styled
a plastic and chromium dinette
to conform to our own private science-fiction mystique, yet during
set with his son, who is named
docking maneuvers in the Gemini program the televised coverage of a
Aluminum.
near catastrophe in space was not so interesting to the television

But the machine, being recognizably mindless, or at least soul-less, must
audience as the fake gunning of artificial heroes. The California boy who
be demonic if it is animate. The extension of self-awareness to an object
stayed aloft for some seventy hours in a carnival Ferris wheel was closer to
supposed to be animate is a gesture which prompts even McLuhan to
Yankee heroism than our team heroes.
call us the sex organs of the machine.

Concentrating on Ecology

LOS ANGELES TIMES (19 APRIL 1970): R11

In this review of three recent books on environmental concerns, Hodgetts criticizes the emergence of Establishment, big-business, and, in his view, ultimately superficial tactics and valorizes more effective action that starts with a radical rethinking of consumerism, growth, and humanity's domineering relationship with "spaceship earth."

THE ENVIRONMENTAL HANDBOOK,
edited by Garrett De Bell (Ballantine)
ECOTACTICS, edited by John G. Mitchell
with Constance L. Stallings (Pocket Books)
S.S.T. AND SONIC BOOM HANDBOOK,
by William A. Shurcliff (Ballantine)

When I left California in 1965 for the big city lights on the East Coast, the FSM at Berkeley had just had its first big bust. Mario Savio, Mike Rossman, and others were beginning to describe a new kind of education without hierarchy, without authority, without even buildings. A great consciousness of the interrelatedness and integrity of students all over the world was beginning to spring up. A sense of community, sharing, each other began to flow, full of energy, hopeful. From my perch in New Haven, busy with the business of the Establishment, it seemed remote and even irrelevant. Our problems of alums, housing, jobs, welfare, graft, crime—the list of "the" problems of the '60s is endless—were too urgent to deflect for the luxury of community. It was too convenient to turn to technology for an answer. After all, wasn't the nation committed to landing a man on the moon by the end of the decade?

LITERARY ELITE. When people talked about Ecology Action, I found their notions preposterous and reactionary. The literary elite, I thought, had always been afraid of the machine and its obvious benefits. The American Space Age plastic cowboy had the obvious answer to environmental problems and, like the Man from Glad, or the Lone Ranger, or John Wayne as a Green Beret, he was sure to have some gadget or other hanging around his Bat Belt to boost the standard of living and free the subjugated peoples of the world.

I wasn't around when Stuart Brand, publisher of the *Whole Earth Catalog*, was running around with Ken Kesey and the merry pranksters either, but Tom Wolfe says, "Brand took LSD right after an Explorer satellite went up to photograph the earth and as the old synapses began rapping around inside his skull at five thousand thoughts per second, he was struck with one of those questions which inflame men's brains: Why haven't we seen a photograph of the whole earth yet?"

And that was it. The beginning of a cosmological consciousness that is only now emerging as the one issue big enough to hold all the radicals, and leftists, and Birchers and, yes, the Ku Klux Klan, because it's the only issue that deals in the common currency of all our paranoias, and that's survival. We had all known, all along, that the earth was round and surrounded by a transparent blanket of air, and the rest of high school geography classes, but it took that portrait of a tiny, radiant earth, somehow nobly alone in the vastness of space, to fully realize the awful corollary of Adlai Stevenson's remark to the U.N. that "we stand together, passengers on a little spaceship, dependent on its vulnerable resources of air and soil, all committed for our safety to its security and peace, preserved from annihilation only by care, the work, and, I will say, the love we bestow on our fragile craft."

So it's chilling to open *The Environmental Handbook* and find a book full of essays from a new coalition of theorists, student leaders, and preservationists talking about ecology, which I'd only vaguely heard of and which had something to do with tide pools, and discover that, ecologically, our fragile craft is mortally sick. Suddenly, a concern for the environment had become big business, and it's all over the billboards for power companies, and in all the advertising for oil companies, and even headlining issues of *Look*. It's as though the manufacturers had put up with about all they could take from the poor, the young, and the black, and in the spirit of a true national issue, jumped on the nearest *Kulturwagen*.

After all, concern for the environment is clean-cut, healthy, and idealistic, and when better pollution control devices are built, Buick would build them. Business as usual is the recurrent theme, as the advertisements picture boys and girls accompanied only by (appropriately controlled) trail bikes and a 200-horse-power van, and assorted frozen and pre-digested foods (cyclamates removed) camping "out" in beautiful American forests, only occasionally marred by the thundercrack of the SST on its way across the country; and the SST was the Sierra Club's business, not theirs.

RUSSIAN ROULETTE. They don't seem to realize that this vision of ever-increasing consumerism is a game of environmental Russian Roulette in which we all pay the consequences whether we play or not. The issue is not to clean-up, paint-up, fix-up, in the comfortable sloganese of the Silent Majority, with cans of aerosol bug spray, buckets of detergents, and power lawnmowers, because this is the very lifestyle which is killing our planet. Neither is the issue the "preservation" of some far-flung retreats favored by a few wilderness freaks, or of some picture postcard view marred by a set of power lines, because these are fragmentary symptoms of the disease and not the cause. The issue is that, for the most part, the very fabric of our highly industrialized, technocratic civilization depends on the systematic destruction of our natural life-support system.

We had all taken growth for granted. No one seriously thought that the economy itself was inevitably turning the dream into an affluent swamp.

"Drugs," according to Mike Rossman, "have had profound cultural consequences. One of them is that kids ... are starting to become conscious of their physical selves. The hippie movement is turning toward the care and feeding of the body, to natural childbirth, to a reinvestigation of ourselves as animals on this planet, rather than as a conquering, domineering man, distinct from the rest of the system."

Perhaps the Judeo-Christian injunction that man "have dominion over the land and subdue every living thing" can be finally arrested in this century. As the essays in the *Environmental Handbook* detail the wreckage of our planetary ecology, it becomes abundantly clear that we can replant the forests we've carelessly destroyed, and bury the power plants, but we cannot reverse the damage to the chemistry of the sea and the air and that without those two oceans the earth would be lifeless.

In short, we've gone too far for merely cosmetic remedies. Two sister books, *Ecotactics* and *SST*, are essentially primers for action. Like scores of movements in the past, the issues strike at many of the cherished myths of American supremacy by challenging the wisdom of competition in the air, or national pride as motivation. The SST is clearly a blunder. It is another link in the line that reaches through the Edsel, the F-111, the Cheyenne, and now the C-5A. In many ways it symbolizes the imperious and unquestioning use of technology to further highly questionable ends which are now finally, tragically being acted out in our century. We have a choice: either be the bad guys and hold onto our piece of the action regardless of what happens and go down with the ship: or, to turn off the switch, de-escalate our frantic game of consumerism, and look toward the future. As Ehrlich points out, "Nature bats last."

004.1
The Founder.

Biography of
a Teaching Machine

ART FORUM (OCTOBER 1973): 77–84

Shortly after his exit from the post of Associate Dean at
California Institute of the Arts, Hodgetts penned this portrait of
the Disney-sponsored school as one of modernism gone off the
rails. The emancipatory freedom he clearly prized was traded
here for sanitized efficiency. Where the Institute's temporary
home in a former convent in Burbank seemed conducive to the
indeterminate flux of artistic creation, the Valencia campus
by Thornton Ladd comes off as overly corporate, risk-free,
guaranteed "feasible," and managed to the point of asphyxiation.

For a time the California Institute of the Arts seemed to be the community of the arts Walt Disney had originally proposed. But that was an accident. The construction of the promised campus in Valencia, California, which had helped to persuade over 600 faculty, staff, and students to help realize Walt's Dream and act out their own, had been set back by a series of monsoons and strikes for more than a year. The temporary campus in the aerospace belt of Burbank was a derelict convent school called Villa Cabrini. Its quaint Mediterranean-style buildings were surrounded by the giant L-1011 transport project and were vibrated regularly by 727s as they jetted up from Burbank's short runways. But the series of loosely connected courtyards, surrounded by arcades and gardens, seemed to filter students through a mesh of opportunities, while providing light, intimate spaces for meetings. It had been designed, after all, for people who shared deep convictions, and the environment reflected their faith by a confident lack of formal organization.

All right, sometimes it was more like an East African bazaar than a school. It was a cacophony of sounds, from power saws, Moogs, cellos, and aircraft, and of disciplines from touchy-feely to Grotowski. But spirits were high, and in spite of the appalling lack of facilities, serious work was going on.

The students simply possessed the space. They slept, made love, and bargained for food in the organic grocery installed in the basement of the humanities building—itself once a dormitory for prepubescent uniformed little girls. Students produced video extravaganzas, dotting the hills of Burbank with coordinated strobes and firing salvoes of electronic sound at passing aircraft. They wrote. They danced. They repaired automobile tailpipes with the same enthusiasm and the same tools each would use later as a sculptor or designer. The experience was total, fetid, generating.

The abrupt dismissal of Maurice Stein, Dean of the School of Critical Studies and a radical sociologist, was a harsh blow to our confidence. But even then our basic feelings remained whole: there had never been a school like this one. It was unthinkable to retreat into an office with office hours, or the sinecure of faculty tenure at some other institution. One could learn to endure and eventually celebrate the world of freeways and franchises, Mark C. Bloom and Tastee Freeze, with the art we were then inventing.

Few of us at the time thought the structure in Valencia would be anything other than a necessary relief from the problems of facilities and space. True, there were horror stories about the dormitories and the corridors, and Paul Brach had insisted that he would dismiss anyone on his faculty who lived in a tract house in Valencia. But what was a little inconvenience in return for marvels like the modular theater, a three-million-dollar box in which the entire floor was mounted on variable height air pistons, or the sophisticated sound systems and electronic controls packed into the multimedia lab. Of course, after the earthquake we had no choice.

We are stacked up over Newhall, California. The heat is almost incandescent, like a huge autoclave filled with NOX and water vapor. As the wing drops and we bank into the northwest leg of our circle, a flurry of brown Army helicopters, Sikorskys, scuttle through. Looking as far as one can see through the granular atmosphere and the streaming Cessnas and Tri-Pacers, I realize where we actually are. The scale is superhuman. It looks as though Godzilla might loom over the Santa Clara Mountains, wade into the Pacific Tie Line electrical complex, and disappear through the pass where the Golden State Freeway plunges north to still hotter, still more deserted frontiers like Bakersfield and Death Valley. And then, there, still partly covered by the wingtip, there it is: CalArts, Walt Disney's extravagant legacy to the art world. There is that legendary thirty-six-million-dollar community of the arts that Walt's brother Roy held together with financial baling wire and gaffing tape until it exploded a year after it began.

I turn to our pilot, "There's your building, Thornton!" It looks plenty good from up here. An enormous flayed rectangle, Pentagon sized, with rank upon rank of skylights and stages, studios and galleries, bulging through a vast shopping-center flat roof like carburetors on a super dragster. Strewn around the skirts of the thing are fast-moving figures darting out of the desert black shadows cast by the overhangs and sprinting the last fifty yards across the parking lot to their cars. It is a scene straight from *Destination Moon*, just before the final long haul across the tundra to blast off. This land, too, is naked as a test range; with a torpor that seems almost evacuated.

A little town is building around the base of the thing. The lumber is piled systematically by each plot and erected time-lapse fashion into rows of houses with swimming pools and carports.

In the old town, Newhall, men still wear Stetsons. I remember that, and I remember that Hopalong Cassidy made his first Western in some of the canyons that sport fifty-thousand-dollar homes these days. It's motorcycle country now, except for the new subdivision. There's a passion these days for building in the deserts if you think about it: Soleri, Bucky Fuller, NASA. It is almost *de rigueur* for a certain brand of avant-garde imagery to start with nothing and put your stamp on it without having to put up with the messy constraints that would dilute the message. The constraints out here are elements, not politics. It's the kind of territory where contractors unroll PERT charts and wear ties and tell you, to the day, when the tile will be installed.

The Newhall Land and (euphemistically) Farming Company has been busily developing the desert tract immediate to CalArts into a "new town," picaresquely called Valencia. With some imagination, I suppose, there is something Spanish

004.2
Gallery with student painting.

about the terrain—dry-baked ochre, spaced with knotted shrunken little trees and flaking hills. But to the cynical it seems more like Aerospace Corporation Country, now dotted with orderly, monochromatic houses in various states of completion, getting ready for some executive transferred from the Midwest to cycle through on his way up the corporate ladder. The Golden State Freeway invites the visitor to ignore the old town set back into the hills, with its peeling frame houses and weathered natives, and brings us to the feet of the self-advertising pitch-and-putt course buffering the town from the freeway. Valencia boasts, with flags and billboards, a bedroom community where children can grow up protected from the imaginary population crush and the imaginary difference in the smog level of the city thirty miles to the south.

From Valencia, like Hans Hollien's collage of an aircraft carrier in the desert, the CalArts building simply overpowers the landscape. From the pass five miles up the highway, lit up Parthenon-style as it is at night, it is awesome. But on arrival, a visitor might find the building curiously inconsistent with either image.

The scale *is* monumental, with giant balustrades picking out the rectilinear lumps of theaters and libraries and classrooms at two-story intervals. Bricks twice the size of ordinary bricks course up in acres of unbroken wall surfaces. The image of buff-colored cantilevers overhanging those walls is staggering. The entrance balustrade, four feet high and cast in indestructible concrete, does seem to run to infinity. But the aluminum rails which flank the monumental entrance staircase quiver alarmingly if touched, and threaten to collapse if asked to bear weight. Under a massive entrance portico, six aluminum doors bat around in the wind like the screen door on a squatter's porch, giving the impression that at any moment the carefully stuccoed imitation cast concrete painted fascia will begin to shake, rattle, and roll. An architect friend visiting the building said simply, "Cheapo."

This is Thornton Ladd's building. He is perhaps Southern California's most prominent "artistic" architect. Among other buildings, he is responsible for the serpentine Pasadena Art Museum and a look-alike, but green, shopping center in Thousand Oaks. Ladd was chosen for the CalArts job in that peculiar tribal fashion which seems characteristic of the Southern California Power that gave us H.R. Haldeman and John Ehrlichman. An institution like CalArts was, to them, not for experiments. The building they wanted to build would confirm the status quo.

Thornton's building lies symbolically under one roof, to emphasize the unity of the arts, one supposes. A blob, then, as opposed to a grid. Static rather than interactive. It occupies the center of a giant asphalt parking surface, which in turn is placed on the scrub and sun-scorched dirt which extends as far south as Van Nuys, which was itself scrub and sun-scorched earth.

One might quibble with the cosmology, but the ambition is clear. In long view the asphalt tilts into a black moat, separating the dung-colored houses in Valencia from the school at the top of the hill. Like a well-designed castle, CalArts allows access to its activities from only a few well controlled points, and effectively creates a no man's land between the school and its immediate environment. Revisionist attempts to restructure the curriculum were to meet, not the administration, but the building.

ERA, Economic Research Associates, was chosen to perform the feasibility study. Their fame in development start-ups could be traced to their confident financial analysis for the original Disneyland when Orange County's remote orange groves frightened most investors. As members of the Valencia planning team as well, ERA proposed that a CalArts campus on the edge of the tract would boost Valencia's cultural aspirations and fill the gap now occupied by a rerun house and the Saugus Speedway. According to ERA's plan: 1) CalArts would purchase fifty-five acres of "undevelopable" land by the freeway at half the going price of thirty-five-thousand dollars per acre; 2) faculty housing would be accommodated by Valencia's own stock of nifty pseudo-villas with twelve-foot-high entrance ensembles and green night lighting; 3) a future shopping center across the street would provide for sundry student needs; 4) Valencia residents would have the opportunity to become friends of the school by attending student concerts and exhibitions; as if that weren't enough, to elaborate the tuned-up economics of the situation, 5) ERA argued that still another client, Magic Mountain, would be ideal for the development since they could offer the students reasonable wages as carney hustlers for rides and amusement features. Where else could visiting parents go with their scions after a busy day touring CalArts? Everything slotted together. Valencia was managed on the same thesis as the moon shot, and CalArts was part of the booster assembly.

The components, when construction began in May 1968, were to be the Chouinard Art Institute and the Los Angeles Conservatory of Music. Disney support had kept both afloat for years during which their steady decline had gone unmourned by everyone but a slick coterie of alumnae. By the time Walt's brother Roy decided the time had come to corner the art-school market, the two faculties had no energy to fight the move. The dying schools would merge, under Disney tutelage, into an Art School Extravaganza. ERA looked around at other art schools, surveyed the market, and engineered the final assembly of what the publicists tagged "Walt's Dream." "It is the principal thing I want to leave behind when I move on to greener pastures," as Walt himself so touchingly put it.

At the time, Chouinard and the LA Conservatory had highly motivated faculties, but ERA found no evidence that their experience with the LA scene was valuable. ERA focused on a fresh start completely overlooking the existing assets of downtown location and talent. ERA also managed to overlook the fact that most art is city-generated. Certainly fifty-five acres of land could have been found within the LA basin, or failing that, the school could have been designed for a smaller site.

Thornton Ladd, who was then on the board of the Conservatory and incidentally a fine musician, presumably knew more about the ways of artists and students than anyone from ERA or Walt E. Disney Enterprises (WED). Exhibiting some real foresight, he proposed a campus near the Hollywood Bowl, but that plan was rejected in favor of the desert idea. But just to be safe, the Disneys buttressed the Valencia choice with the solitary participatory gesture of the entire enterprise to date: a questionnaire distributed to students at Chouinard and the LA Conservatory which asked if they would be willing to drive thirty miles to their new school if it were to have "well-equipped facilities open twenty-four hours a day, seven days a week." Since both schools were on budgets limiting access to eight hours, and students were hardly enthusiastic over the broken down, one-time

004.3
A gallery with two drinking fountains and one painting.

concert grands and moribund machinery they were expected to use, that sort of blackmail produced the desired response: seventy percent of the students said, in effect, "anywhere, as long I can do my work." ERA therefore concluded that the students could fend for themselves.

As ERA saw it, the school could do pretty good business, a kind of art mecca for tourists where, for a fee, they could observe industrious students in smocks, berets, and white tuxes, playing Mancini-like music, painting, and singing their way into the hearts of America. (At least that's the way the promo film pictured it.) And although ERA's surveys are models of restraint, they thought the art-student market was bullish, especially in Southern California where simply everyone wanted to be an artist or a star in the time-honored tradition of Hayley Mills and Annette Funicello. Why didn't they just go ahead and dub it "Art World?" At any rate, Disney Enterprises was excited. The synergism was truly astonishing: CalArts would produce animators, composers, actors, technicians, and illustrators, and Disney would have the pick of the best, the cream of the cream, and Valencia would have a focus, and Magic Mountain would have an audience, and what's more, the whole thing would pay for itself in ten years.

004.4
Standing 400 feet from C block.

In other words, the Disney interests who have been bringing the public clean fun since Steam Boat Willie saw the California Institute of the Arts as a coup for clean art. Disney builds empires on cleanliness. A short *tête-à-tête* with any Disneyland exec, for example, reveals a marked pride in having designed a pure-profit environment which encourages "guests" to behave well. The immaculate park itself makes a littering guest feel as if he were tracking mud on a white carpet. Recent press releases on the latest Disney phantasmagoria in Florida crow that they have finally succeeded in amassing enough land to control not just the immediate area surrounding the enterprise, which is fair enough, but to control and benefit the entire area they perceive to be "influenced" by Disney World. This is the most concrete statement to date of a feudal philosophy which characterizes the growth of Orange County as "stimulated" by Disneyland and the Disney empire as the much-abused generator of other people's business. With area control to execute the Disney World Philosophy, the success of huge projects is nigh insured.

However, there was a serious problem. Even with big names like Henry Mancini, the composer, and Millard Sheets, the muralist, and Chuck Jones, the animator, on the board of trustees, they were unable to find a president. The academic types they wanted simply refused to see the educational value of the carefully imagineered commercial aspects of the plan. Besides, the educators they encountered tended to believe in academic freedom, causing the men from WED to fear for the Disney image itself. The artists they had in mind like to paint old boats on the beach and write songs about love's sweet anguish. Only a real star with recognizable charisma and an acknowledged reputation could attract faculty and guide the would-be stars down Fortune's path. Because on the other hand, viewed as an exercise in management, a school must have appeared elementary; the men from WED were, after all, masters of cueing and control. They had done it all before. Compared to the horrors of Disneyland on the Fourth of July, the Berkeley Free Speech Riots of 1965 must have seemed small potatoes.

Nonetheless, the Disneys suffered from limited experience with real stars. They had never before had to work *with* a star on anything, at least not one complete with prima-donna tendencies, passionate about his or her artistic/ creative integrity. The Disneys had always created their own stars in the form of animated mice and ducks or had bought dated stars for movies or Disneyland band bashes; those stars did as they were told. Or best yet, Disney sent real star person- alities, willful ones like Lincoln, to the "imagineers" to be re-realized with their highly sophisticated audio-animatronics techniques. For the first time they needed a few imaginative men who had developed careers and reputations independent of the Disneys so the latter could fade into the managerial background when the time came. But rather than dwell on the issue, they concluded that to get a star, you had to have a property to attract. Students and faculty would come later when, at least in the shopping-center theory, the "magnets" were in place and functioning. Ergo, the building came first as the solution to the personnel problems.

The Disneys have always believed in strict hierarchy—they were infamous in the '30s for opposing unionization of animation artists and writers. Today the repeated 16" x 20" portrait of Walt which tacitly monitors each executive is never upstaged by the 8" x 10" of Brother Roy. It has always seemed to me that there is a variety of covert fascism which is inevitably built into large-scale real estate developments. Somehow the sidewalk *belongs* to someone; and there are those insidious bronze plaques, the fine print of American private property set flush with the concrete, which informs you that permission to pass is revocable at any time. Of course at Disneyland, by paying admission a guest establishes a psychological set which validates his temporary and revocable status. One hardly feels coerced by long lines and orderly queues – after all, it is *their* castle.

The Disney World Philosophy runs deep into the foundations of that Valencia teaching machine. The architectural concept is based on a plan in which the organizational tree has explicit branches, formidable connections, and an unavoidable sequence of events. In plan it looks like a puffed-up version of an office organization chart. This sort of form was the foundation of the Industrial Revolution. The constant, easy flow from station to station makes repetitive work highly efficient. Since Disney's success as a filmmaker was largely based upon the application to film of production-line principles (as opposed to team principles), it is no surprise to find the halls lined with official-looking doors and a number of studios outfitted with what seem to be foreman's offices. The overall impression is one of efficiency, secrecy, and strict order.

The animators at Disney's original studio used to complain about their "backroom" status. A Disney animator tells of the knot hole decorated with glasses, hair, and ears, which was between the animation studio and a hallway to Disney's office. When Disney's visitors arrived, one of the boys in the "back room" provided a nose and moustache by poking his phallus through the hole. Curiously, most of the CalArts board missed the connection between sophomoric stunts like these and what seemed to them the profoundly obscene and perverted erotic art that students began taping to the walls of their new quarters.

In theory, students and faculty would encounter one another while perusing the de Kooning retrospective, or passing through on the way to the cafeteria in the Student Activities wing, or the Multimedia lab in the Music wing, or one of the other magnets dusted helter-skelter through the complex. Generous corridors, often fifteen feet wide, would provide smooth motoring for the student population hurrying from place to place, filling their busy schedules with ceramics, fashion design, and etching, though occasionally diluted with a fast coffee break in the coffee shop with one of their handsome profs. And zap! the world has yet another grown-up version of the Hollywood High we all suffered through with the endless versions of Archie and Veronica, Sandra Dee, and Room 222.

Predictably, no one thought to involve potential faculty or students in the design process. Or, if that were impractical, to question the design of a facility so closely tailored to a then thoroughly discredited style of instruction. An early planning meeting, for instance, centered around the question of buzzers for clocks, with collateral insight into educational management. Several strategies were available, ranging from the design of a more flexible space which could adapt to a variety of teaching styles, to an evolutionary program which might best accommodate the faculty's teaching plans. However, evolution precludes control. And in balmy Southern California, where the only speculation is on the deal, fast answers get results.

004.5
Discretion: student-modified directory map.

In what seemed like no time, announcements of CalArts' ground-breaking, color-coordinated with Valencia's Helvetica Medium advertisements began to turn up in the hands of the right people. Word was out that Bob Haldeman of Nixon Administration fame would make the introductory speech. Shortly thereafter Valencia's full-page newspaper advertisements began to feature, not houses, but the CalArts campus—cultural hub of the upper valley. Prospective home-owners saw careful renderings of the soon to-be completed campus tarted up with trees, wandering coeds, and a tweedy, pipe-smoking professor clucking over an academic problem. A middle-class constituency was lured into a vision of their tract as the home of a classy institution that Walt himself had sired. Now, of course, the mostly middle Americans shine their Hemi-sportboats and tune their ATV's most weekends, and don't seem to miss the esoteric happenings at the school on the hill.

It was not as if the Disneys didn't realize that the Week-N-Der folks in tract houses were not generally interested in fine arts. Rather, it was their under-standing that they could engineer an art school, disguise it with walnut veneer and gracious lobbies, in order to produce the blue-chip stamp aesthetics which appeal to the same people who depend on Disney to provide them with "Family

Entertainment." When the promo film for CalArts was finished, it was sent out on the road as a trailer for Mary Poppins, implicitly promising a place where young people could go and learn the techniques for making healthy movies, nice movies like the one just seen.

Chairman Buzz Price, an ERA man, once told a group of deans that he would not say the word "nipple," for instance, in mixed company, and one is reminded of those screaming confrontations on the picket lines between nice girls who used naughty language and the cops whose sense of decency was offended. Paul Brach, the new Dean of the Art School, replied that he refused to act as censor. Allan Kaprow had already suggested a nude happening on the Valencia strip, until finally a strategy was suggested by the new president, Robert Corrigan's assistant. Why not, Julie asked, uniform a group of neat-looking music students, and pay them as tour guides. They could divert visitors from the seamier facts of life at CalArts.

As a visitor it must be hard to believe there could be seamy activities in that building. One's initial impression is of those factories in industrial parks with clean, pretentious office space nearest the road, blocking the view of some more expedient, practical structure. But if Ladd is ever expedient, he tries hard not to let you know. The design takes great pains to protect the appearance of importance, order, and sanity. The open relationships established by the students at Villa Cabrini—the ability to pinwheel across a courtyard and intersect a flute ensemble or a seminar on low energy building systems on any given day—simply disintegrated in the careful pattern-making and judicious assignment of space in A block, B block, and C block, nomenclature which has stuck precisely because no one created a more persuasive landmark than those signs designating those areas.

When compared to other Disney exercises, the poverty of conception truly boggles the mind. At least Disneyland's Main Street preserves interest and relationship in human scale by designing the buildings to two-thirds scale. But nothing is underscaled about CalArts' new home. The preoccupation with magnifying the scale of the building controls the exterior where balconies are twice normal height and overhangs ranging from fifteen to twenty feet are not exceptional. The effect, in renderings and models, was to reduce the sheer bulk of the building and make it look positively domestic. In reality it is perversely ponderous. Perhaps Ladd and the Disneys expected the artists who would study there to be, not only ... well, smart, and creative, but physically formidable like those raygun-toting space heroes who lurch across landing pads wearing some kind of exotic leather underwear. For it is, in some way, simultaneously suburban and extraterrestrial. For all its connection to the ground—and they excavated hundreds of thousands of

004.6
Design school office.

cubic yards to set this baby in—the most conspicuous connection to reality is the Golden State Freeway curling back to LA like an extended umbilical.

Once inside, the sensation is curiously—subterranean—but like a space station. Locked off from outside light and views of the spectacular mountains which surround the valley, one must navigate the building on instruments. Small colored diagrams, covered with tiny numbers, allow the visitor to decode his or her position, range, and bearing, and proceed to the next orientation point. On either side of the corridor, the doors must spring shut automatically as a precaution against fire and remain closed to preserve the space for escape. The visitor cannot see the space he or she is traversing and must risk embarrassment if the numbered door does not correspond to his or her information. Infrequently, at irregular intervals, paintings blazon the white concrete, or a series of photographs of infinite highways stick indecorously to the wall with masking tape. Moving figures hug the wall. The silence, the hush pervading the structure is medicinal, antiseptic, subterranean blue. Your privacy is assured. Anyone who makes it down those halls and identifies his or her room correctly obviously belongs there.

This is Thornton's building, conceived to integrate the arts and involve artists in a community of interchange and practical cooperation. In fact, his solution opts for the image of unity rather than the complex, often contradictory, reality which might have produced a genuine unity. Any suspicious Easterner, and most of the school's staff consisted of them, immediately recognized that characteristic in the building, even if they found Venturi's *Complexity and Contradiction in Architecture* irrelevant to their pursuit. Ladd must have meant to create awe and perhaps even accommodation, but never communication. The metaphor broke down in execution and the Community became an incoherent maze with maximum impediments to communication.

Students quickly recognized the need for supplementary communications like video links and closed-circuit broadcasts. For a time, the prospect of having a vast model of an even vaster LA as guinea pig for media experimenters like PULSA and Ant Farm and Raindance Corporation generated a lot of enthusiasm. *Radical Software* was a major text for the electronic transformation of community. PULSA installed a matrix of five video feedback stations at crucial corners throughout the building to identify where the action was and discovered that if there was any, it was not happening in public. To be fair, there was a group who used the video link as a kind of theatrical platform, a stage with no whereabouts. Students showed paintings with it, exhibited themselves, photographed themselves photographing. But generally the picture was consummately bleak, relieved only occasionally by furtive-looking students who never paused or waved. Mostly they seemed bent on getting wherever they were going and avoiding whatever experience lay between studio and parking lot. It looked like all those halls and galleries and public spaces are part of some vast commuter terminal for way-out artists, who for reasons of their own prefer to drive thirty miles or so each morning to their studio in the desert.

And so, Parents' Day at the new building arrived. The suspicious elders were treated to a tour of the teachers and examples of the work they paid for. Sparsely dotting the building were organic cookie stands, dance and film performances, painting exhibitions, and of course, the inevitable white-draped flute and drum players. Bizarre sounds lured the curious to one of the many airless, windowless studios to witness a multimedia performance. The perplexed parents wandered into a black-lighted room filled with improvised electronic-sitar-feedback sounds illuminated by the undulating patterns from an awesome number of colored video monitors. The control room itself, crammed with shiny, expensive technology, was integral to the exhibit. One handsome gray-haired liberal type standing in the center of the experience finally burst out laughing, turned, addressing his irony to no one in particular, and asked, "Do you guys wanna know what really killed Roy?"

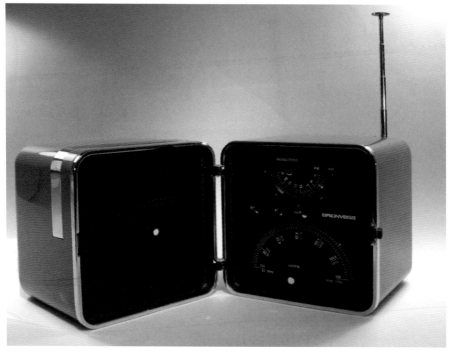

005.2
Marco Zanuso and Richard Sapper. Brion-Vega
Cubo radio, 1964.

Object Lesson: Four Short-end Views

PROGRESSIVE ARCHITECTURE (NOVEMBER 1973): 77–80

In four short parables, Hodgetts makes a case for flexible, pragmatic performance over the niceties of specific form and customary style. If architecture is always about facilitating communication and communicating a culture's collective ambitions, in Hodgetts's view, better media for that work exist, and architects need to catch up. Radios, televisions, and custom hot rods offer clues.

THE M.O.S.F.E.T.[*] **AND THE BIBLE.** Nowadays we must recognize that physical organization is the least powerful means of structuring relationships. The machine-object, the fundamental icon of orderly process for more than 200 years, is today the weakest link in the cultural economic system. Since the Industrial Revolution, the purpose and character of the machine aesthetic have dominated our planning to such an extent that one must consider whether the modern city is more than an eclectic antique founded on a superseded system of logic.

According to the technologic myth of industrialization, the linear organization of physical process made possible the production and distribution of goods for the popular market. This specialization of workers and tools in the factory served as a model for the separation of roles in society itself, shaping our conception of the layout of city and house. Special districts in the metropolis correspond to the structure of production and management of the assembly line. In the service of a now superseded technologic efficiency, boundaries are provided between districts assigned to various uses without reference to the activities of those traveling between them.

Buildings and environments once seen as elements required to structure relationships must now be seen as elements for the neutral support of unspecified activities. Phenomena like Woodstock I and II illustrate the power of even a casual turn of attention by the media-public, placing a demand on resources which even the most careful planning could not accommodate. Our use of tools can now coincide with our needs. No longer must we plan production and transportation with a fixed trajectory. Data processing and the electronic conditioning of the environment render one-shot planning obsolete by selective feedback and programming of individual operative requirements.

Thus the separation of production and individuals—of industry and housing—forced by cumbersome processes becomes a matter of choice. A new kind of community, bounded by communication, may develop without regard for geography or geometry. In a wired nation, production and distribution are diffuse and polyfocal. Without the need for heavy traffic from point to point, it becomes possible to support the activities of individuals in our society without recourse to the nineteenth-century separation of home and work, husband and wife, child and factory.

[*] Metal-oxide–semiconductor field-effect transistor

DRAGGING THE BRION-VEGA. When the directors hauled the Cisitalia and a bunch of other cars into the Museum of Modern Art in the early '50s, kids had just begun to chop and channel their Detroit iron into a mean Mafioso kind of look, and the Studellac went to the drags with a swapped Caddy engine under the well-tailored skin of the Loewy coupe. It was already too late for the craft and breeding of the Italian line (or the International Style for that matter), because Americans had discovered performance. The kids called anything that was pretentious, overweight, and underpowered a *shot rod*. In short, all show and no go.

Their parents may have been suckers for Detroit's slogans, but since four-barrel carbs and streamlined headers were the way to get the most out of your mill, everyone knew you couldn't cruise the drive-ins and shopping centers looking for a little competition if all you had going for you was "torsion-bar luxury." They had discovered performance. Not the balanced, almost architectural response of Ferraris and Alfas, but a violent, head-wrenching explosion of power more like the mega-wattage of super groups like the Jefferson Airplane. The svelte, disciplined fuselages on the Italian machinery didn't look *right*—they didn't somehow express the American fascination with machinery as an instrument of change. But in no time, the kids found just the thing to hop up all that classy Italian machinery. They removed the engine, a marvelous construction of polished manifolds and mono-grammed bolts, and replaced it with a domestic v-8. The resulting machine, with a super light chassis and tuned-up power plant, was the prototype for most of the avant-garde architecture of the '60s—and a lot easier to maintain than the twenty-four overhead valves that came with a Ferrari.

The American scene, after all, was based on improvisation. The time frame is right now. It is no coincidence that American automobiles are somehow always photographed moving in the great outdoors, surrounded by trees and mountains; while their European counterparts are shown parked on moist streets, in front of flower shops. Getting there is at the very heart of the American machine. Being there—being born there—is the *raison d'être* of its European counterpart.

Twenty years later, the Museum of Modern Art offered a second look. The principles are the same: discreet, beautifully crafted envelopes for ingenious mechanisms—like little buildings—with all that connotes of premium art and stability. Folding tables. Folding houses. Folding radio. Everything accomplishes something, somehow. Seemingly infected by the American way these elegant objects promise performance European style, without the gee-gaws and prehensile devices offered up by our domestic stuff. A little radio designed by Sapper and Zanuso seemed to have all the qualities of portability, utility, and graphic clarity lacking in our domestic models. Its neat rectangle and soft corners are pure architecture compared to our automobiles and clock radios. All of that has to do with what you see, not what you hear. But the Brion-Vega makes polite coughing sounds as though to excuse its older role as transducer. The voice of a radio, whether it comes from a plastic fantastic or an imitation RCA Victor dog, is always up to date. We don't care what a set looks like when it's on. We want to be overwhelmed with cassette decks, instant replay, and 120 watts RMS per channel of undistorted sound. We want a no-holds-barred opportunity to change our lifestyle. We want the medium to disappear in a vivid connection to another reality.

ALL NEWS ALL THE TIME. Long after midnight, on a stretch of highway hundreds of miles from architecture, you turn a small knob on the dashboard of the automobile and flick casually from rhythm and blues, to all-night talk, to classic oldies but goodies. The "no there" that Gertrude Stein used to refer to is now a place quite capable of originating a program linking like places around the world. This "place" needs nothing more, architecturally, than an appropriate black box to be the operative nucleus of a metropolis. No wonder the city center dies of inattention. The distribution of information, once motivation for cathedrals, halls of government, and great libraries, is no longer dependent on proximity. A pervasive nostalgia for the form of these things makes contemporary architecture falsely hierarchical in an autonomous landscape.

The urban environment is seen as perhaps it always had been—as information intensive rather than location intensive. The old landmarks have been replaced by movable distributors of economic-cultural information, which are as portable as the objects that repeat, store, and relay it. The new geography has as many centers as points. Everything originates everywhere.

Archigram's Walking City, telescoping extended legs to touch perhaps lively spots in the old skyline nearby, is not half so responsive as Ma Bell, and nowhere near as cheap. Visions of the city to come begin with unlikely collections of generators, coders, and peripherals, linking in unseeable, unmeasurable ways with satellites and neighbors. The exquisitely graphic organizations of gravity and flow which characterize modern architecture from freeways to shopping centers has become no more relevant than Le Corbusier's dictum that architecture is the full and magnificent play of light and shadow. Architects who continue to play at the aesthetics of ebb and flow, light and shadow, have their hearts set on a history which has just ceased to be.

The autonomy produced by instant access fields of information and

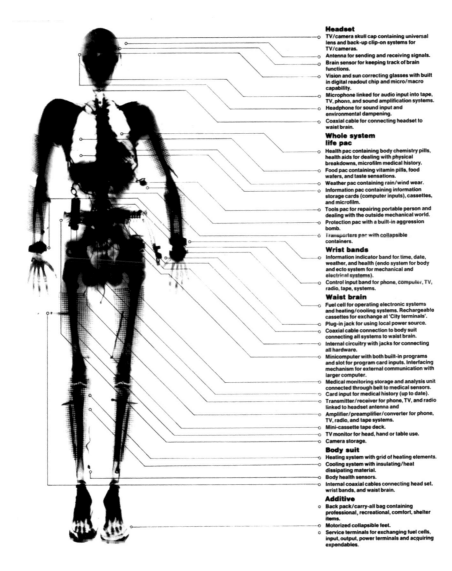

Headset
- TV/camera skull cap containing universal lens and back-up clip-on systems for TV/cameras.
- Antenna for sending and receiving signals.
- Brain sensor for keeping track of brain functions.
- Vision and sun correcting glasses with built in digital readout chip and micro/macro capability.
- Microphone linked for audio input into tape, TV, phone, and sound amplification systems.
- Headphone for sound input and environmental dampening.
- Coaxial cable for connecting headset to waist brain.

Whole system life pac
- Health pac containing body chemistry pills, health aids for dealing with physical breakdowns, microfilm medical history.
- Food pac containing vitamin pills, food wafers, and taste sensations.
- Weather pac containing rain/wind wear.
- Information pac containing information storage cards (computer inputs), cassettes, and microfilm.
- Tools pac for repairing portable person and dealing with the outside mechanical world.
- Protection pac with a built-in aggression bomb.
- Transporters pac with collapsible containers.

Wrist bands
- Information indicator band for time, date, weather, and health (endo system for body and ecto system for mechanical and electrical systems).
- Control input band for phone, computer, TV, radio, tape, systems.

Waist brain
- Fuel cell for operating electronic systems and heating/cooling systems. Rechargeable cassettes for exchange at 'City terminals'.
- Plug-in jack for using local power source.
- Coaxial cable connection to body suit connecting all systems to waist brain.
- Internal circuitry with jacks for connecting all hardware.
- Minicomputer with both built-in programs and slot for program card inputs. Interfacing mechanism for external communication with larger computer.
- Medical monitoring storage and analysis unit connected through belt to medical sensors.
- Card input for medical history (up to date).
- Transmitter/receiver for phone, TV, and radio linked to headset antenna and
- Amplifier/preamplifier/converter for phone, TV, radio, and tape systems.
- Mini-cassette tape deck.
- TV monitor for head, hand or table use.
- Camera storage.

Body suit
- Heating system with grid of heating elements.
- Cooling system with insulating/heat dissipating material.
- Body health sensors.
- Internal coaxial cables connecting head set, wrist bands, and waist brain.

Additive
- Back pack/carry-all bag containing professional, recreational, comfort, shelter items.
- Motorized collapsible feet.
- Service terminals for exchanging fuel cells, input, output, power terminals and acquiring expendables.

005.1
Studio Works (Craig Hodgetts and Robert Mangurian) with Jeffrey Hannigan. Portable Person, 1973.

twenty-four-hours-to-any-point-on-the-globe goods distribution is independent of form and style. Functional accommodation is assigned to equipment, not configuration, reversing the roles of architect and engineer. For it is the engineer who devises controls for a comfortable environment, the engineer who produces televisions, lighting systems, and smokeless Bar-B-Q's. In deploying these articles in a fixed relationship, the architect often subverts the user control implicit in the increasing portability of the object. The architecture of efficiency, as proposed by the Bauhaus, is a cumbersome reminder that brick and mortar cannot produce more, with less, than a printed circuit.

The building as a highly configured machine-object, as rigidized form, must be seen as the historic records of a singular activity traced in form. Bolting down a fireplace or a bathtub makes no more sense than bolting down a vacuum cleaner. We don't because, before vacuum cleaners, the brooms were always kept in the closet.

Yet Le Corbusier, though able to propose the generosity of the Dom-ino House, was unable to resist artfully wrapping static walls around otherwise portable furniture. In love with form, and the dialectic which determines the final, tailored shape, architects have been unable to put down the needle and thread and take up the loom. They understand the design process to be the painstaking cut and fit of a well-tailored skin to the well-tempered environment when the environment is quite able to take care of itself.

IF THE POPE WORE NEON. Technologic imagery hardly guarantees a sophisticated object. Mickey Mouse watches and injection molded, imitation carved TV cabinets opt for a populist imagery, but are themselves sophisticated products of industrialization and distribution. The imagery of pop rainbows and sentimental re-creations are strategies for a marketplace increasingly worried about imagery yet peculiarly confident of performance. The formal references that were once difficult to separate from functions, references that forced Gropius to reassert that form followed function, have become straitjackets for political and ideological conformity. In an environment defined by "state-of-the-art" performance, the canons of formal appreciation—proportion, consistency, balance—are seen to be semantic devices for communicating the responsible *intentions* of the designer rather than necessary aspects of function. The President—or the Pope for that matter—can make formal appearances from the bedroom, if he wishes, since the frame of reference is not the long, glorifying perspective of St. Peters, but the Vario-Switar lens of the image orthicon TV tube. Formal constraints, and the corollary mandate to select the single best form for a given function, are absurd at best when the context is fragmented in hundreds of home TV screens. The point is not to set out a new hierarchy of cans and cannots, but simply to try to point out the existing context in an effort to define our expectations for serviceable environments.

The presence of "architectural" qualities of composition does not offset poor performance. Venturi's dissertations on beautiful ugliness are the scholar's rationalization of the historically "ugly" forms of billboards and moon landers which outperform objects with a more conventional organization. The performance features once integral to building form—acoustics, iconography, temperature control—have been co-opted by high performance objects, which accomplish their work without necessary inflection of the built form.

The high spaces and careful window placement of classical architecture once functional entities, have become mere symbols of humanist concern. Biomorphic, technomorphic, and socially symbolic forms must be replaced by an environment whose content is described by performance. There are no models for such forms, they are by necessity composite, pragmatic, and ambiguous.

The pragmatist employs one set of objects to ventilate the space, another to light it, and a third to fill it with atmospheric sound with the proper reverberation time. His buildings have the erasable qualities of magnetic tape. Always adjusting image to content, configuration to information flow, his buildings are conceived as a field of environmental controls, supporting a range of activities in a loose-fitting matrix, rather than fitting a single activity into a customized mold. The luxury of exclusively formal constraints, like the luxury of couturier clothing, is only for those who can afford it.

Unlike past cultures, ours does not have to print aspirations on buildings. Film and magnetic tape are far more efficient. Buildings in the shape of ducks and elephants, as well as recent adventures like the Pepsi-Cola, Lever House, and Seagram buildings in New York, have an uncomfortable habit of turning up, finally, as residual graphics on a package somewhere in the supermarket. Postmodern architecture should recognize that the media and technology available today can be responsive to individual patterns of life *without aesthetic intervention at any level*. The plazas and courtyards which served to locate and provide definition for an opera house or a bank have their counterpart not in the setback of an office tower from Sixth Avenue but in half an hour of the *I Love Lucy Show*. The limited utility of architecture as an instrument of corporate or state enterprise reflects nothing more than the values of a post-industrial culture which measures only results, not intentions. Specific forms, in this view, serve only to limit change and close options. Generalized forms, enriched with temporary user identity and fleshed out with functional objects, increase long-range utility by increasing the range of response. The value of television, after all, is that it allows the sponsors to be bullish on violence one day, nostalgic on sex the next—something that can't be said for the Parthenon.

A
REPORT
ON

THE
STATE
OF
ECOTOPIA

NOVEMBER
1999

A Report on the State of Ecotopia

ARCHETYPE VOL. 1, NO. 1 (SPRING 1979): 11–13

By the end of the 1970s, Hodgetts had grown weary of the slow progress of his architectural practice and embarked on a series of extra-disciplinary projects. With the help of the literary agent Richard Kahlenberg he secured a 5,000-dollar advance on a science-fiction novel. The novel, which involved a nineteenth-century rocket ship designed by Prince Albert, husband of Queen Victoria of England, was never completed. Around the same time Kahlenberg enlisted Hodgetts to produce a series of images to drum up interest and investors in a film version of Ernest Callenbach's 1975 novel, *Ecotopia*, on which Hodgetts was to serve as set designer. A cult classic, particularly among the environmental movement, Callenbach's novel narrates the first visit by an American to a new, environmentally conscious nation formed out of the secession from the United States by Washington, Oregon, and Northern California. The film was never completed, but Hodgetts's visualizations of Callenbach's environmental utopia, complete with descriptive notes by the fictional Agent Hunsaker, were published in the premier issue of *Archetype*, an architectural journal launched by the architect Mark Mack and others in 1979. The images were accompanied by the following byline:

After saturating West Coast sensibilities, Ernest Callenbach's inventive Ecotopia will be made into a movie. These images by Craig Hodgetts, the set designer, portray the modification of the environment after the secession of the West Coast from the United States. The rendering of a futuristic utopia has allowed Hodgetts, who is perpetually innovative anyway, to work with an unencumbered imagination.

The Confidential Report reprinted here is the Anti-Ecotopian force appraisal of the capabilities and design discoveries of the Ecotopian nation. We publish them at some risk, in the shadow of Three Mile Island.

OFFICE OF INTERNATIONAL SECURITY

SOLAR COLLECTORS ARE EMPLOYED TO CHARGE   NATIVES CITE SKI-LIFTS, SKY TRAMS
THE CAPACITANCE- DISCHARGE CELLS WHICH   AS NORM.
POWER THE MAGNETIC TRANSPORTATION SYSTEM.
EXCEPT FOR THIS FEATURE, FUNCTION IS
SIMILAR TO OUR SIDE BOS-WASH CORRIDOR -
THEIR SIDE PORTLAND TO SAN FRANCISCO IN
TWO HOURS PLUS.
THE ELEVATED PORTION OF THE SUBJECT
SYSTEM GUIDES LIFTING BODY VEHICLE
WITHOUT A RESULTANT DYNAMIC STRESS ON
THE STRUCTURE BUT RESULTS IN A PECULIAR
SWAYING OF VEHICLE UNACCEPTABLE TO OUR
SIDE.

AGENT   ASSIGNMENT   LOCATION

3993505

SUBJECT VEHICLE HAS NO FIXED SEATING
FOR EXTENDED TRIPS, FORCING RIDERS TO
DETERMINE ADJACENCY; PHYSICAL CONTACT
IS THUS UNAVOIDABLE IN EVEN MODERATE
LOADING.
NATIVES CLAIM BENEFITS IN COMFORT,
LESSENING FATIGUE, HIGHER EFFICIENCY.
THIS INVESTIGATOR ATTRIBUTES THESE CLAIMS
TO STEMS STRATEGICALLY PLACED IN SUBJECT
VEHICLE TO DISPENSE LIQUIDS, SMOKE AND
SOUND ON AN INDIVIDUAL BASIS.
SIMILAR TO ANTIQUE " PAD ".
POSSIBLE FOR THE CORRECT OPERATIVE TO
ESTABLISH BASE CONTACT THEIR SIDE

AGENT	A SISTI GLOMPED NAT TRAVELLER.	LOCATION
Hunraher	*Scotopin*	*Stetten* 399 505

OFFICE OF INTERNATIONAL SECURITY

WINDMILL GENERATORS LIKE THESE ARE
IN USE THROUGHOUT THE COUNTRY. EACH
IS MORE THAN ONE HUNDRED FEET IN
HEIGHT, WITH A PROPELLOR ARC ESTIMATED
TO EXCEED FIFTY FEET.
PRELIMINARY CALCULATIONS INDICATE
OUTPUT COULD AVERAGE TEN THOUSAND KILO-
WATTS PER UNIT, SUGGESTING THAT SYSTEM
EFFICIENCY IS FAR BELOW THAT OF OUR
NUCLEAR BREEDERS.

NATIVES CLAIM THE VISUAL EFFECT,
EDUCATIONAL VISITS, PICNICS ON
THE 'MILL ARE SUBSTANTIAL SPIN-
OFFS, OFTEN CITING THE ANACHRON-
ISTIC CABLE CAR AS PRECEDENT.
AGAIN, NO PARITY WITH DELOREAN
VEHICLE OUR SIDE.
ELEMENT IN FOREGROUND ACCOMODATES
SIX PERSONS FOR " MAINTENANCE. "
THERE IS NO CONTROL OVER ACCESS.

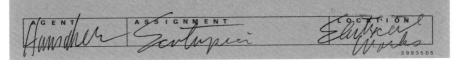

AGENT   ASSIGNMENT   LOCATION

3993505

CONSTRUCTION OF THE GENERATORS FOL-
LOWS THE NATIONAL PRACTICE. WOOD
AND LOW TEMPERATURE ALLOYS ARE EX-
TENSIVELY EMPLOYED. WEIGHT PENALTY
BY OUR STANDARDS IS SEVERE, BUT IN
THE SUBJECT CASE OFFSET BY FEEDBACK
VENT LOOP TO CONSERVE ORIGINAL
CHARGE.

" KEEPER" IN YELLOW JACKET IS
USUALLY AN ARTIST OR WRITER WHOSE
DUTIES ARE CONFINED TO GENERAL
MAINTENANCE AND OCCASIONAL ATTIT-
UDE CORRECTION, BUT MAY SERVE AS
HOST TO ROUTINE VISITS OF SCHOOL-
CHILDREN AND SIGHTSEERS.
LOW EFFICIENCY HERE SUGGESTS RE-
PLACEMENT OUR SIDE BY AUTO-
ELECTRONIC DEVICE.

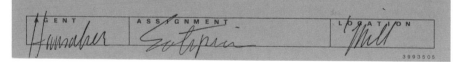

AGENT	ASSIGNMENT	LOCATION

3993505

OFFICE OF INTERNATIONAL SECURITY

THIS PORTION OF THE BUILDING IS CONSTRUC-
TED OF CALIFORNIA REDWOOD. TYPICALLY ROUGH,
AS THESE "RETROFITS" TEND TO BE, IT
NEVERTHELESS AFFORDS TO MS. FAIRCHILD THE
OPPORTUNITY TO RELAX WITH FRIENDS IN A
SETTING WHICH IS SYMPATHETIC TO HER
NATURE.
NATIVES EXPECT SUCH STRUCTURES TO BE
ENDLESSLY MODIFIED THROUGHOUT THEIR PER-
IOD OF USE AS DIFFERENT PERSONS SEE FIT, AND
TO BE UNCEREMONIOUSLY REMOVED FROM THE
BASIC BUILDING IF THEY ARE NO LONGER
USEFUL.
OURSIDE, OF COURSE, SUCH STRUCTURES MUST
BE RIGOROUSLY SEALED.

AGENT	ASSIGNMENT	LOCATION
Hunsaker	*Ecotopia*	*Pres-Suite*
		3993505

OFFICE OF INTERNATIONAL SECURITY

ECOTOPIANS BEGAN ALMOST IMMEDIATELY TO
RETROFIT OLDER BUILDINGS LIKE THIS ONE
FROM THE EIGHTIES WITH ACCESSORIES TO
ENHANCE THEIR LIFE-STYLE.
THUS THE WINDMILL LOCATED ON A PLATFORM
JUST BELOW THE PRESIDENTIAL SUITE
DRIVES A PUMP FOR THE COMMUNAL HOT TUB
PRESIDENT FAIRCHILD INSTALLED UPON
TAKING OFFICE.
THE USE OF EXCESS FLOOR AREA AS A GAR-
DEN FOR THE PRODUCTION OF PERSONAL FOOD-
STUFFS ON THE FLOOR BELOW REFLECTS A
NATIONAL POLICY UNENFORCEABLE OUR SIDE.

TRAFFIC IN THE SUBJECT BUILDING
IS VARIED. THE BY NOW UBIQUITOUS
SCHOOL CHILDREN FAR OUTNUMBER OF-
FICIAL VISITORS AND THE FEW
STAFF MEMBERS FAIRCHILD CHOOSES
TO EMPLOY.
AS WITH MOST FACILITIES THEIR SIDE,
THERE IS LITTLE OR NO CONTROL
OVER ACCESS.

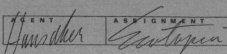

AGENT	ASSIGNMENT	LOCATION
Gunsather	*Ecotopia*	*Presidential Bldg.*

3893505

OFFICE OF INTERNATIONAL SECURITY

SUBJECT STATION IS ENTIRELY <u>UNDERGROUND</u>
WITH THE EXCEPTION OF A SMALL HOUSE AND
THE LASER ALERT SYSTEM WHICH SEALS OFF
THE ENTIRE BORDER. SYSTEM ANALOGUES OUT
SIDE ARE IN OLD FLORIDA WHEN THE " HAUNTED
HOUSE " WAS A FEATURE IN WHAT WAS TO BECOME
THE U.S. CAPITOL.
PROCESSING UNDERGROUND IS EXPECTED TO
INCLUDE BACTERIAL DECONTAMINATION, ORAL
TESTING, BIOGRAPHIC SCREENING, AND SOMETHING
CALLED " VALUES EVALUATION " BY THE
NATIVES.

AGENT	ASSIGNMENT	LOCATION
Hunneker	*Ecutopia*	*Border Station*

OFFICE OF INTERNATIONAL SECURITY

SUBJECT AIRCRAFT IS AERODYNAMICALLY
SIMILAR TO SO CALLED " HANG GLIDER " AS
THE HYDRAULICALLY STRESSED MEMBRANE
FORMING THE WINGS CAN BE MODIFIED TO
OPTIMIZE SPEED AND ATTITUDE. COMBINED
WITH A REFLECTANCE TARGETING SYSTEM FOR
ITS LASER ARMAMENT AND MAGNETIC DEFLECTORS,
THE MANOEUVERABILITY THUS ACHIEVED ENSURES
STRATEGIC SUPERIORITY THEIR SIDE IN
TYPICAL COMBAT SITUATIONS. PILOT AND
FAMILY ASSUME RESPONSIBILITY FOR
MAINTENANCE — THUS DUAL SEATING HAS
MORALE MOTIVE AS WELL AS FUNCTION.

AGENT	ASSIGNMENT	LOCATION

Time to Reboot Ecotopia

2016. PREVIOUSLY UNPUBLISHED.

Nearly thirty years after Hodgetts completed his set designs for *Ecotopia*, he returned to the theme in the wake of the 2016 presidential election. This piece, which he circulated privately to friends and colleagues, is published here for the first time.

Prompted no doubt by the events of the '60s and '70s—Vietnam, oil, Watergate, the prohibitions on abortion and marijuana, and extreme misgivings about the social and political trajectory of the country he loved—a San Francisco writer imagined a better world. He called it *Ecotopia*, an amalgam of ecology and utopia. It would be, he mused, a nation-state carved out of the body of the USA. A nation-state no longer subject to the whims and wiles of a corrupt and loveless federal government. A state able to stand on its own principles of sustainability, progressive social policies, and gender equality. It would be a state where solar power, electric vehicles, and vegan vendors roamed streets full of community, craft fairs, and gentle entrepreneurs, all under the benign leadership of an elected council of women.

His name is Ernest Callenbach, and the book became a cult sensation, tapping into the idealism and yes, naiveté of the beats, the hippies, the airy-fairy artists, and long-haired professors who were his cultural models. It was 1975, well into the reign of the Haight, but it was more than that.

Callenbach's thesis was that the citizens of the state of California had had enough. That they had no choice but to secede from the United States to protect their culture from an assault from the right. That they had enough sense to get while the getting was good and establish a government built on what he saw as an important and necessary fact: that the globe we live on needed an example of how to get things right. So his nation-state, his overture to peace and prosperity, was simple. Cut the cord that binds and reset the goalposts.

It is now forty years since Callenbach's manifesto captured my imagination, and it is remarkable just how prescient it was, and how ironic that the bubble we call California is still tethered to a country that would follow a leader who denies global warming, who extolls the virtues of policing, and revels in controversies concerning sex, gender, and a woman's right to choose.

California is the world's fifth largest economy. Bigger than England, more productive by far than Spain and Italy combined, with the world's most advanced factory producing the world's most advanced electric vehicle, farms that supply the world with agricultural produce, and home to companies like Google and Apple whose global social and technologic networks are transforming culture around the world and yet ... and yet it plays second fiddle to an East Coast hegemony that can't quite grasp the source of its creative culture, and is just beginning to wake up to the synergy of its industrial/entertainment/scientific infrastructure.

If Callenbach were here to fan the flames, he'd be preaching revolution. I'm sure of it. He would ask why we Californians are suddenly worried that a new administration might attack Roe vs. Wade. Why we worry that new immigration policies might gut families who are integral to our way of life, and why we Californians find a trade war, or any war for that matter, so distressing. Because all we need to do is say "no!" You mind your business and we'll mind ours. Just as we carry on with our so-called sanctuary cities, we can declare ourselves a free-trade zone. We can be to the world what a duty-free shop is to an airport. As a free zone, California would attract manufacturers, research entities, and distributors, further expanding both our financial resources and the depth and diversity of our culture. Without dependence on the department of education we might be able to at last forge a truly twenty-first-century educational system. We can leverage our own health care, originate our own protections for intellectual property, create a twenty-first-century financial system and tell Wall Street what to do with their cigars.

Just think what we could do as a nation-state. If those tax dollars that go to fund war machinery were to find a way to stay right here, in our pocket, we would have our wineries and *mercados* but have great cities and visionary transit and neighborhood centers as well! It would be a far cry from asking for handouts from a congress that sees California as a political thorn in the side, yet here we are, forty years after Callenbach's wake-up call, with less-than-meager federal support for a high-speed train, housing for the homeless, restoration of the Los Angeles river, or truly progressive education.

With a growth in GDP of 3.2 percent against the remainder of the nation (which remains at a sub-par average of 1.5 percent) it could be argued that California's tax dollars are keeping the central government afloat.

Of course, such a focus on self-interest might be construed as un-American, and if it were only about tax dollars one might cede the point. But concerns about the environment, the rule of law, and the equal treatment of all our citizens are more than enough justification for serious consideration. To some, it's a moral imperative with profound implications to nurture one of the world's foremost incubators of social and technologically sustainable innovation. The world needs that, and so do we.

008.1
Hodgetts + Fung with Robert Mangurian. Venice Interarts
Center, Los Angeles, 1980.

Behind the Action: Architecture and the Vision of Reason in the Age of MTV

DESIGN BOOK REVIEW 24, "CINEMARCHITECTURE" (SPRING 1992): 12–15

Hodgetts makes a case for a cinematic—as opposed to photographic—architecture that trades the statically composed single image (what he refers to as "the money shot") for carefully choreographed sequences of often oblique views that cater to the roving eye of the mobile observer. The contemporary culture of MTV, he claims, operates this way and, he continues, citing the Acropolis and Le Corbusier's Carpenter Center as examples, so does the best architecture throughout history. Illustrating his text with sketch sequences of his own design work, Hodgetts takes direct aim in this piece at strains of postmodern architecture then in fashion, advocating ephemeral experience over kitsch pastiche.

On the sound stage, artists and technicians often work for months to paint the backings, ready the practical structures, and attend to period details that will distinguish the fourteenth, say, from the twenty-fourth century. Like most construction crews, they measure prodigiously, confer with the designer, curse inconsistencies, and whistle at girls. True, the hollows of their cornices and moldings gape vacantly at the kliegs and translux panoramas of the fictive city without, but no effort is spared to create the patina of age, abandonment, or luxury in the replica towns and buildings created for the lens. Illusion is rampant: the vanishing point accelerates to a point only a few meters above the floor; mirrors and miniatures blend seeming incongruity into a seamless reality.

Now alive with people, the actors, costumers, grips and gaffers, script supervisors and supernumeraries await the director. Lights are focused, reflected, diffused. The frame is established as a ripple of adjustments turn this chair, that table, waft a breeze through a window toward the greedy lens. Lines are rehearsed; an arc of motion is inscribed on the floor; everything is ready.

The "hero" cola can is removed from its package. (The term "hero" on the film set is reserved for the prop or architectural element that is the focus of the shot, in this case a specially prepared can of cola that has been printed without the usual overlay of ingredients, government admonitions, and copyrights in an effort to strengthen the graphic qualities of the design – much as architects swing out the airbrush whenever an offending power pole is in evidence.) A red, white, and blue logo glistens through corn syrup permafrost and Krylon matt finish. A hovering prop man balances it delicately, inserting a straw as he places it before the camera and aligns its position with a silhouette on the preview monitor.

It fills the screen, obliterating the set, the lighting, everything!

I think, "This is a sobering experience for an architect."

008.2
C. A. Doxiadis, Acropolis III, Athens, after 450 BCE.
Perspectival reconstruction.

FAST REWIND. A little bit before the birth of Christ. Masons and sculptors chipping away at the lintel and elements of what is about to be the Temple of Athena. Depictions of extreme violence transposed to a great 3-D still in marble, about to be hung like a giant Kodachrome over the entry. Phideas, a.k.a. Cecil B. de Mille, studying arrested motion with the only means at his disposal: the human eye. Centuries later Leonardo will travel much the same path at a microscale as he attempts to decode the fractal dynamics of a breaking wave. And yet later everyman will endlessly slo-mo images of the perfect slam-dunk-rehearsing mind, and body, and sinew—literally able to calibrate the distance between the backboard and the magic Nikes from the comfort of a Barca-Lounge.

We can remember other momentous stills: the image of a shock wave surrounding a speeding bullet, the sweat exploding from a prizefighter's brow, or the staccato arc of a Louisville Slugger. Our planes fly faster and javelins sail higher because of that ubiquitous "click" of the shutter as it "freezes" the action.

But to freeze the already frozen? Architectural form shares immobility with geological formations and very little else. It is revealed by animation rather than fixed examination. The information to be gleaned from the surface of a building, no matter how seductive the glints of surface detail, remains locked in the realm of the image plane—thus the obstinate coincidence of traditional representation, such as that of Piranesi, Palladio, even Hugh Ferriss, and the essentially pictorial experience of classical form. Referenced only to itself, and lacking the dynamic element of *motion by the spectator*, such a depiction is at best an independent work of visual art, and at worst just another family portrait of the sort that clogs the walls of aristocrats eager to show off their acquisitions. Architectural excursions into the realm of pictorial form, such as the Teatro Olimpico, further frustrate architectural discourse by mandating a passive observer. Simply stopping time (click!) often illuminates the structure of a dynamic action that could otherwise defy analysis, but the same cannot be said for architecture, and Phideas, AKA de Mille, knew it!

Thus the *mise-en-scène* of the Acropolis, as analyzed by Vincent Scully in *The Earth, the Temple, and the Gods* (Yale University Press, 1979) broke with the well-established tradition of axial planning, and relinquished the control implicit in monumental compositions. "Here, you hold the camera" is a surefire way to make friends, suggesting a place in which familiarity evolves through personal vision in concert with a refined visual order, inherently anti-hierarchic, rather than *ad hoc*; the success of the architect, like that of the film designer, is defined by the accumulation of visual and spatial opportunities, rather than the painterly power of a single image. As described by C. A. Doxiadis in *Architectural Space in Ancient Greece* (MIT Press, 1972), it becomes apparent that the images conveyed by each structure on the Acropolis—caryatids, fluted columns, and narrative reliefs—are merely props, while the progression of framing devices, long shots and angular transitions provide a "cinematic" visual structure, rather than a monumental "architectural" order.

The oblique views thus engendered deny frontality with all the vigor of a far-right front row seat at the cinema, savoring the distortion of perception even as we are swept from vignette to vignette. (Interestingly, the technical term for the view from a side front-row seat is "Keystone," after the resemblance of an image which is projected off center to the shape of the architectural element of the same name.) To thus confuse the viscous progression of formal spaces in Egyptian, Mayan, or even Chinese monuments with the limber joinery of the Acropolis is like comparing the stationary camera of early film directors like Georges Méliès to the casual mobility of Wim Wenders or Orson Welles. Neither suspends the discipline of formal relationships. Neither do they sacrifice visual clarity to a convenient blur. The proscenium/frame is a convenient container rather than a formal reference.

In fact, clarity and formal discipline provide the visible text for the development of a convincing montage in both architecture and cinema. An exposition of Sergei Eisenstein's architectonic approach to montage suggests that the dynamics of visual activity on the picture plane itself—right/left, in/out, up/down—combined with variations in rhythm and scale, definition, and contrast, provide the structural matrix for narrative content.

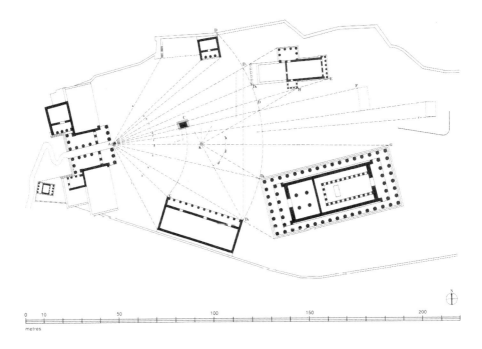

008.3
C. A. Doxiadis, Acropolis III, Athens, after 450 BCE. Plan.

Similar abstract compositional principles apparent in the work of well-known Constructivist artists of the time lack only serial development to be, well … *filmic* in nature. Walter Gropius, László Moholy Nagy, and others often employed rhythmic series of circles, squares, and rectangles as a notational basis for choreographic sequences essentially cinematic in nature. Moholy-Nagy's short films, based on investigations of a rotating, "architectural" object, clearly yearn for a cogent, yet malleable medium that could render time with the plasticity of clay.

The battle between "representational" and "structural" models of cinem-(a)-rchitectural theory suggest a mirrored universe of ideas, in which media, content, and ideology share a parallel but dyslexic destiny. For many, the vision of a cinema devoid of story, politics, and recognizable imagery is as distressing as that of an architecture devoted exclusively to historical reference.

Compare, for instance, the studied "architectural" compositions of *Ben-Hur* to the fluid, eclectic, thoroughly convincing, but ersatz border sequence in Welles's *Touch of Evil*. In the latter, patched together on a corner of Abbot Kinney's Venice of America (itself a rather elaborate "set"), the opening shot begins in a congested street. The camera adroitly singles out a tourist couple as they emerge from an auto, cranes up to scan the texture of buildings, rooftops, and a flash of dark horizon, then scuttles down to reveal a darker transaction, before following the couple's progress across the border. *Ben-Hur*, with a fixed camera, frames the famous chariot race within a telescopic visual field dominated by a sandwich of near and far architectural ornament. Without total replication, the sequence in Ben Hur could have been just another R. G. Canning monster truck show. In *Touch*, the essence of the Mexican border is established by motion, props, and scenography in spite of the dominant Venetian decor of the place.

Like a skeletal strobe of the crane shot in *Touch*, the entry ramp at Le Corbusier's Carpenter Center offers visitors a similar transposition of time and space, compressing reflections, artifacts, and function into a single, unbroken movement. Jammed between rather dour brick bookend buildings, the entry begins on a bit of lawn, ramps up to offer a lectern-like rail to the elbows, suddenly jerks it away, then plunges though a glassy cavern as the surrounding undulations stutter toward gridlock, and the sky is replaced by a broad gray concrete slab. Throughout, the horizon, the varying rhythms of the mullions and steelwork, the incendiary up lights like strange luminous crows, and the transit from grass to a river of smooth rock affirm a tactile reality that proclaims, "You are here." Were the visitor a ten-year-old customer and the ramp a guide rail, one might imagine the ghosts of Disney's Haunted House inhabiting the space beyond Corb's walls, and whirling mechanical illusions at work in the studios beneath the ramp.

Control is the key. The spectator, in film as well as in an arena event, is the static observer of a (hopefully) moving image. In architecture, the spectator is the mobile observer of a (hopefully) static image. Vision flicks from deep to shallow space, zooming for texture, meaning, or context. Such a sidelong glance is generally disparaged by architects, who will settle for nothing less than an adoring gaze, but it is typically controlled and amplified by the filmmaker.

Imaginative control of the context, particularly in the construction of convincing replicas of long-ago places or never-to-be fantasies, permeates the creation of an ephemeral world which often supplants the "architectural" backdrop. There are no exceptions. Automobiles, window displays, street signs, reflections, even the trash on the street, become active design elements in a filmic tradition that requires the designer to consider every item within the pictorial frame.

In today's cities, a vast compost of transit lines, merchandise, landscape, and advertisements camouflage urban form. The origins of vehicles, costumes, and materials are increasingly, terminally, diverse. Buildings and parking kiosks duel on every corner. Rap and hip-hop echo convincingly from the margin.

This view from eye level is not going to go away. All the City Beautifuls and

Lady Birds, and romantic theoretical postulations will not, in this writer's opinion, bring back a coherent vernacular. Architects, like composer John Cage, need to discover a way to exploit the accidental setting within which they work. MTV, raves, and Generation X already have.

Back on the set, the klieg lamps lie in neat rows on the floor. Coils of wire, junction boxes, and folded velour drapes cast long shadows under the work lights. Cut strands of manila line dangle from far overhead. There is no trace of the city that was just here.

009.1
T. Lux Feininger, *Mensch und Architektur,* c. 1928.
Gelatin silver print. 6 ½" x 3 ¼".

Heretical Remarks on Architecture and Photography

ARCHITECTURE CALIFORNIA VOL. 14, NO. 1 (MAY 1992): 57–63

In contrast to the cosmetic and static depiction of buildings in most architectural photography, Hodgetts advocates a dynamic realism which registers the passage of time and reflects the necessarily collaborative nature of architecture. Tropes borrowed from cinema such as sequential images and evocative props, he proposes, might bring architectural photography closer in line with the lived experience of architectural space.

There is a narrative attached to every architectural photograph. It may be buried and need decoding, but it *is* there. I think of the architectural photographer as a *balladeer*, like Annie Leibovitz, the chronicler of Rock and Roll, and I strongly disagree with the notion that the photograph must simply *record* the design concept. I am much more attracted to Piranesi's approach to depicting architecture, a more romantic, contextual approach that suggests all the uses, abuses, and realities that the structure has endured with the passage of time. The demands of 'image' and 'visualization' have the same effect on buildings that they do on film stars: they are only allowed to be photographed in light that eliminates all their wrinkles, to such an extent that all evidence of the passage of time is erased, the image becomes an abstract conception, untainted by time, and the building (or star) is pushed toward a purely *cosmetic* reality.

Essentially, architectural photography runs a gamut of intentions from flattering, to exposing, to depicting, to penetrating, but architectural photographers are seldom 'free agents.' All of their operations are strongly oriented toward meeting the objectives of clients—architects or editors. There is also the issue of empathy: the photographer must empathize sufficiently with the architect's intentions so that the pictures resonate with it rather than with a personal photographic style. Inevitably, there are architects who want to deal with their buildings as immaculate objects. I think that it has to do with the fact that architects haven't been able to define what they do as a *collaborative* art.

Such operations are in league with the social notion of protected and defensible space: I see the depiction of buildings according to such exclusive principles as an intensely political – and especially capitalistic—practice, one that extends beyond the photograph itself to the rightwing side of the barricade. Some architectural photography is clearly self-referential, and then one must respect the photographer's intentions. But as a *medium for transmitting a message* about buildings, or cities, or the body, I consider photography to be highly questionable.

As a professional practice, architectural photography is driven by a couple of things. One is tradition: in painting, 'portraits'—of people, dogs, horses, or even estate gardens—have historically functioned as the visual signs of the power of ownership. Architecture—when it was lucky enough to be depicted, which was very rare—could only be *painted* in such an extremely labor-intensive way that it fell victim to that imperial tradition of portraiture. With few exceptions—like Eduard Gaertner in the nineteenth century, or Edward Hopper in the twentieth century, both of whom aggressively confronted the vernacular and the ephemeral—painters haven't taken the trouble to render vernacular architecture as a foreground element.

009.2
Henri Cartier-Bresson, *Hyères, France,* 1932.
Gelatin silver print. 7 ⅞″ x 11 ⅝″.

In photography, it is equally unusual to find building 'portraiture' that is *not* in the imperial tradition. I like Tim Street-Porter's attitude, for example, because he is highly conscious of the role that photography can play in *foregrounding* buildings as opposed to relegating architecture to its proper place—behind the action.

Today, too much published architectural photography perpetuates the imperial tradition rather than advancing other tendencies that emerged in the nineteenth century. Early documentary photographers like Henri Cartier-Bresson established the fact that photography is an instantaneous art. What photography is most agile at, what it is uniquely capable of doing, is capturing the single moment.

Filmmaking provides the most suggestive model in this regard. In film, there is a symbiotic relationship between the framing of the scene, the action taking place within the picture, and each and every pictorial element that makes up the image you finally see. Each aspect has a creative destiny of its own—whether it be a weird postcard on the wall of a dark interior, a building in the background, or figures lurking at the margins of a scene. The 'prop' person who sets the scene has done so with empathy for the script, for the terms of the set design, and for the personalities of the actors – paying close attention, for example, to what would look good *in Laura Dern's hand* as opposed to randomly choosing something for her to hold. What you have is a kind of *creative mesh* at that moment when the camera rolls, something which the cameraman tries very hard to step back from and capture. One of the greatest cinematographers, Néstor Almendros, once said that cinematographers make very bad directors because they are best at just snapping images out of bus windows or on street corners with total spontaneity. An aesthetic energy is at work in the apprehension of such immediacy, one that defies all conventions of premeditation.

In architectural photography, props work like subtexts, like footnotes. They don't simply embellish; they supply an essential dimension of the final image and very often occupy a more prominent place than the architecture, because they are *things* with which one can have a direct empathetic relationship.

A vase of flowers, a negligée tossed over the back of a chair: those are *things* that we emotionally relate to on a different conceptual level than we relate to buildings. Props are like actors in a scene with no actors. Whereas in film, the prop person is a respected member of the larger team, in architectural photography there is a certain disdain for the 'stylist.' But photography has to be a passionate intervention in reality in order to make reality *read*. In *The Spirit of Saint Louis*, Jimmy Stewart gets into the plane and says "Oh, my God, I can't see how much fuel I have," and his girlfriend says, "Here, use the mirror in my compact." Suddenly he has a mirror but also a romantic talisman. The photographer must find the right position on the emotional scale in order to deepen the response to whatever is being displayed, to set the stage for it. And very often the odd object can do that. Manipulations of scale—again, thinking of what Piranesi achieved—can also produce effects that have tangible emotional appeal.

This phenomenon of intersubjective appeal is brought home by the recent print ads for clothing by Calvin Klein and Kenneth Cole, where the suggestiveness of the expensive Klein campaign need only be *referenced* to have powerful effect in Cole's ironic retort. In the United States, the public depiction of subjectivity, the layers of implicit agreement in public discourse, the assumptions about the literacy of the audience, are absolutely staggering. The highest compliment you can pay your audience is to assume they are *quick*. With that you win a kind of intellectual battle; you make them yours. Rather than presenting an object for contemplation, you present the aura of the process but cut the process short before delivering anything, like selling the sizzle without the steak.

In this connection, there are important differences between photograph-ing existing buildings or urban situations and photographing *new* architectural designs: with new buildings, you are dealing with a one-of-a-kind object that has had a lengthy gestation characterized by complex interactions of possibilities,

009.3
Raphael Soriano, *Hallawell Nursery and Garden Center, San Francisco*, 1941-42. Lath plant booths.

constraints, and compromises, so that the completed but often compromised building is somewhat like a wounded soldier. The photographer is asked to resurrect the architect's vision, to somehow refresh and restore it—not from the abuses of use (because it hasn't had any yet), but from the scars of its birth. The unnerving thing about photographs of a new building is that they capture the moment of birth: they become the building's baby pictures.

The flurry of glossy magazines in the late 1970s corresponded to the façadism of the postmodern vocabulary, producing a coincidence between architectural thought and static photography. The picture was all you got—even if you were physically standing in front of the building. Architecture that is more complex demands a series of representations in order to be understood. The most interesting buildings today don't have a preferred point of view. I don't know what the preferred point of view is at the Loyola Law School, or the Schnabel House, or even in some of our own work. There is no longer that one, archetypal, sum-it-all-up photograph. This heightens the need for key events in architectural representation —action or props, for instance. Architectural photography just isn't meaty enough for our minds any longer. In comparison to the mass of intellectual, conceptual, visual, sensual, and emotional information that bombards us on a daily basis, it feels like we have come to a full stop in our ability to refer to architecture. Stepping away from architecture, for example, in the new Subaru television ad campaign, the various dimensionalities of an automobile are rendered with layers of text moving over the image of the car. When you come upon a General Motors commercial, with the same old car going down the same old road, it's more like the typical architectural photograph: "Well, here's your building, folks."

There are lots of things about photographs that have very little to do with human visual perception: most photographs are in focus throughout their whole frame, which is impossible for the human eye. And, the eye cannot compare, the way a photograph allows it to, the pinpoint resolution of a nut or bolt as a discrete element deployed on a flat field. One of the effects of such extensions of human capability is a kind of obsessive orientation to detail that is actually promulgated by photography. Photography suddenly competes with drawings as a tool for the teaching and learning of technics. The photograph reduces design elements to a point where one can appreciate relationships at a slightly more abstract level [007.3]. It coheres all those things into one plane, so that even a vase of flowers is just another detail. The architectural photograph is an amazing tool, but in fact, it is *biased* toward technics, toward a kind of clinical scrutiny that gives it enormous pedagogical power. If, on the other hand, photographs become stand-ins for other forms of experience of buildings, the appreciation of architecture is driven further and further from consumer desire and back into the laboratory.

Artists working with photography of buildings are continually extending the parameters of the field. Barbara Kasten, for example, creates her pictorial abstractions from shards of buildings, often using intensely colored lights. Jayme Odgers uses photography as a narrative vehicle for his own musings. In work like this, the photographer actually pays the architect the compliment of being inspired by the building and using it the way musicians have used musical compositions, like Ravel orchestrating Mussorgsky's *Pictures at an Exhibition*. This approach doesn't compromise the building; it just gives the photograph new *autonomy* and delivers it from a hierarchical structure wherein the photography is the foot servant to the building. It grants the vision of the photographer its full license.

When the architect seeks to control every element of the image-making process, the overall creative energy is diminished and the playing field open to others is drastically limited. Again, it's like aging movie stars insisting on absolute control of every photograph of themselves, as compared to the actress who is confident enough to say, "Like it or not, this is what I'm doing, this is what I look like."

This may sound heretical, but I think architecture will start to improve only when photography starts to *move*. Based on my view of the vital role of architecture in life, taking into account the fairly low resolution of video or film compared to still photography, and also because without arresting the image, the eye cannot easily focus on details, I would propose that moving images would reduce the fixation upon *image*. Iconic images would give way to the realm of cities, medieval cities, for instance, where the buildings are the wallpaper around the urban space. They are not objectified; they are part of a continuum of urban fabric. For me this has more to do with the way people use space than does the current representational idiom.

The still photograph does reveal things to us that are inaccessible in any other medium, like the final arc of the basketball before it plunges through the net. Half a millennium ago, Leonardo went to unbelievable lengths to understand what happens when a wave breaks, watching it repeatedly, until he was finally able to make a sketch that made visual what he thought happened. Still photography now reveals even more subtle phenomena, only far more easily, but it has not succeeded in liberating architecture from its fixed nature. It merely chains it to a state lesser than itself. We can measure the changes brought about in sports by still photography and electronic instant playback technologies, which allowed high jumpers to jump higher, runners to run faster, javelin throwers to throw further: what experiential qualities of architecture could we unlock by applying the same technologies to the perception and study of the built world and by investigating how space operates *dynamically* as opposed to pictorially?

Rubbing Out the Craft: Architecture and Fabrication in the Age of Information

ARCHITECTURE CALIFORNIA VOL. 16, NO. 1 (MAY 1994): 7–11

Hodgetts meditates on the architecture's maintenance of seemingly anachronistic affiliations with material craft and speculates on the possibility that technology affords the opportunity to craft not just physical objects, but also experience itself. That experience and lifestyle can be more effectively designed with virtual communication than brick-and-mortar building has been a topic throughout the twentieth century, Hodgetts argues, and the achievements of Le Corbusier, Conceptual Art, the New York Five, and others have demonstrated the productive possibilities of breaking the bond between the discipline of architecture and traditional material.

Someone jokes, "Pretty soon everyone with four eyes will have a pair of these!" Someone else responds, "And that will include everybody!"

I finger the bridge of the lightweight, liquid crystal goggles and watch as 2-D becomes 3-D, then smile appreciatively as the raked image of an automobile fills my view and bursts into a multi-colored flurry of pistons, valves, and pure internal combustion.

My student is presenting a thesis—a virtual shopping mall with elaborate graphics and a premise designed to infuriate those who equate architectural meaning with physical presence. Why, he asks, must we expend the enormous effort required to build a retail complex, park all those cars, replenish all that stock, heat and cool the space, guard it, maintain it, lease it, and market it—just to consummate the production cycle? Isn't there an easier way? Couldn't one simply design a virtual space for display and transactions, pump it out over the information highway, and let Barry Diller and his cronies handle the cash and shipping?

Indeed!

In the same way, we might ask about the priorities of making other 'stuff' in the age of information. Are we, as architects, to become the guardians of an arcane tradition, to define our role in the evolution of the new city solely in the realm of technical virtuosity? We may admire the beauty of an array of fasteners ceremoniously deployed across the face of a structure, but even the most obsessive among us can recognize the widening gulf between a vernacular, which has become increasingly driven by expedience, and the admirable joinery of an architecture that reflects our passion.

Certainly 'making things' well is both socially responsible and personally rewarding, but where is the line drawn?

A new fabric of visible social priorities has imposed a complex, often obstinate network of 'clients' on a professional system heretofore structured only to deliver well-crafted buildings for well-defined goals. The end user, who generally lacks both voice and motivation, has been traditionally excluded from participation. Certainly serious consideration of the wishes of those with little or no professional knowledge would have been unthinkable even a few decades ago.

Or would it?

Isn't it simply that the spectrum of desires and diversity of lifestyles now impels each designer to seek out and articulate the centroid of need as carefully as one might have explored the natural terrain of a hillside in the halcyon days of aristocratic patronage? What we as architects make is increasingly a range of decisions that aim to optimize highly defined constraints. Very often, in fact, we expend the lion's share of design effort on the 'solution' to the puzzling, mostly fractal outlines of a project's aspects, then skate through the 'technical' problems of specification and construction. As for the 'finishing' work, the matters of surface and detail, it is increasingly difficult for us to attain any satisfaction without breaking the ever-shrinking cost-envelope. The craft turns out to be something no one can pay for.

What is potentially reinvigorating is that the means now exist to bring not only materials and fabrication but the purpose to which they are dedicated within the design process. In short, the potential exists for a redefinition of the craft of making architecture to include the craft of making experience itself.

In nineteenth-century England, cast iron revolutionized the production of machinery. It was rigid, easy to cast into a limitless array of shapes, and far more accurate than the wood and brass it replaced. Some engineers saw its value for erecting large enclosures, and proceeded to build greenhouses and exhibition halls. Most architects fixed only upon its implications for surface. We can almost hear them thinking: "What a great substitute for terracotta!"

Computers, simulations, and interactivity are tools that may speed the production and display of design products, but are far more significant as necessary complements to a dramatically expanded, and massively detailed architectural agenda. The greater the number of constituencies affected by an architectural problem, the greater the demand that solutions be portrayed convincingly in advance. Garnering public, private, or institutional support, or gaining community-based approval is virtually impossible now without the most advanced tools of visualization. Stress on the informed opinion of Everyman demands more than a gauche rendering and a site plan: when the 'message' is made so palpable in venues like advertising, architecture is under the gun to comply. The architecture of feed-back, back-talk, and cross-talk has already been defined.

"Let your fingers do the walking" was more than a clever advertising jingle. It forecast what would become the deep structure of cities such as Los Angeles, in which information is processed, decisions are made, and transactions are consummated on the phone. And it puts into grim perspective the hierarchy of nanoseconds, digital gates, and fiber optics that overlay the traditional city of stone, metal, wood, and asphalt. Simultaneous cities such as this, governed on one hand by the speed of light, on the other by the squeal of brakes, are simultaneously infinitely expandable and multi-centered, acrobatic and ponderous, spontaneous and inertial.

What began as an application of craft-based knowledge to the enclosure of space has in effect become a service profession on the fringe of a vast (cut-rate) construction industry. What architects do to redefine priorities now will determine whether hard-won skills will find applications above the line, where decisions are made, or below the line, where they are simply packaged.

Is it possible to pinpoint the moment of passage—that is, when the realm of architectural making re-calibrated its trajectory, and formed a new pact with concept over craft, gray matter over grout and mute blocks? Wasn't it 1914, when a young French architect better known for brash statements than adherence to the party line unveiled his latest salvo: a house, or rather, a precarious collection of planes and spindly legs he dubbed the Dom-ino, which embodied the essential elements of houseness yet brilliantly sidestepped the conventions of making anything at all? This thing seemed to imply—did imply—that it *didn't matter* what it was made of; that there was a deeper reality than that of the shingles and copings that were the subject matter for most architects. His disdain for—and indeed impatience with—the preoccupations of a craft-based architecture had finally found expression in the purely cerebral world of support and platform.

When he declared in *Towards a New Architecture* that "The architect is above all an engineer ... profile and contour are a pure creation of the mind," it followed that the intellectually embarrassing (and irrefutably material) bricks and concrete of the Villa Savoye had to be purged in a campaign to suppress any evidence of craft or its partner-in-crime 'honest labor.' It wasn't until the 1960s that such an absolutism found expression in the United States when a circle of so-called 'conceptual' artists including Sol Lewitt, Donald Judd, and Carl Andre stripped sculpture bare of figural imagery (even), and suggested that a box, a grid, or even pavement possessed the ingredients for artistic expression. Holding oneself at a palpable distance from the craft of making took on political/aesthetic meaning as the artist sought to appropriate generic form, invest it with cultural meaning, scrub off the fingerprints, and walk away without a trace of dirt under (his) (her) fingernails.

It was a new role for artists who had been stigmatized as passionate Bohemians unable to distinguish between physical pleasures and artistic product. It turned the tables on the conventional, though unstated, celebration of the artist's labor ("Oh, I wonder how long it took to do that?" "Oh, I wonder how he did that?") in proposing that the true artistic act lay in the creation of intellectual property—and then in the fierce protection of one's property rights.

The game played to capacity houses in New York. Architects like Peter Eisenman, never far behind, seized the moment to launch ideas for a conceptually beautiful—if practically disadvantaged—series of projects, and, in some cases, fully realized propositions that startled by their brave disregard of worldly phenomena like snow and ice.

Whether by accident or design, Conceptual Art also drove a wedge into arguments for the nobility of labor itself, mostly of the Marxist variety, though both Abe Lincoln All-American Self Sufficiency and 1930s-Style American Ingenuity had supported similar theses. From now on, simple labor was a thing to be avoided at all costs, and the politics of guilding an upscale version, namely the craft-labor of a skilled artisan, gave way to street-fairs and the patronage of blue-haired old ladies.

Certainly we cannot dismiss the simultaneous efforts in Menlo Park and the Jet Propulsion Laboratory that gave us the 'wire frame' as a stand-in for the walls and floors of computer-generated designs, or the picaresque designers a few years later who created the frivolous surfaces identified with the Memphis Group. All of these adventures helped to articulate a single message: The manipulation of space and structure need no longer be dependent on an exclusive palette of materials, or even a physical manifestation for there to be 'architectural meaning.'

Architects, of course, have always inhabited the virtual environment of the imagination. Since the beginning, the three dimensions of even the most banal structure were first encoded in graffiti or on linen. The monumental drawings of Boullée and Mies and Kahn were 'immersive' in the modern sense—they only lacked the fitful illumination of the electron beam. Virtual reality, it would seem, is only the latest consummation of our perpetual longings for a poetics of space. It's not the final bell.

So it is no surprise that architects who inhabited the fashion curve have taken to supporting their practice by the sale of drawings—sketching enticements in a vellum surround rather than building them on hard rock—or striving to achieve professional dominance on the basis of graphic representations. Such images are easily absorbed, transmitted, and reproduced, and *mirabile dictu*, can be consumed and appreciated fully without the messy circumstances of excavation, waterproofing, and engineering.

After all, if a discerning visual appetite can be satisfied by a stew of micro-processors juggling the refraction index of a bunch of mathematically defined surfaces in order to ray-trace a perceived journey through time and space, can any of us (except perhaps Pevsner, Lynch, Rudofsky et al.) be so peevish as to main-tain that it really matters? Is the ephemeral Information Superhighway a genuine replacement part for those heavy concrete ones that develop potholes, expansion cracks, and tawdry roadside attractions?

Architects, with the conviction that physical presence is an inevitable part of the equation of supply, demand, and transaction, have been slow to recognize the impact of communication technology on the environment, to identify the cluster of innovations that define a new agenda for the built environment, and especially to *react*.

But what if we begin to speculate on the potential of an architecture unbound by physical constraints? Computers linked to models linked to cutters linked to quarries linked to distribution nodes linked to erection mechanisms are proving that the extravagant curves of Gehry's design for Disney Hall are not only plausible, but rational and even affordable. Himmelb(l)au proposes building-size objects fabricated in the shipyard and delivered whole to a site on a barge. Is our mission to continue to elaborate the built world becoming more and more fractured in our effort to define the material aspects of a building's physical presence?

As these processes trickle through our technical culture, it becomes apparent that formal dexterity per se is an unlikely candidate for future celebrity. The very do-ability of new-age technology, from model-scan to final product, will inevitably draw it out of the experimental studios of the avant-garde and deliver it whole to the purveyors of the basics. While superior art will doubtless retain its prestige and inherent value, 'me-toos' will have the means to produce less disciplined work with less effort than ever before and in ever-more slick formats. Alternatively, if the technics of construction have been largely resolved by suppliers (and they have) then Buckminster Fuller's observation that the architect of the future would function as a catalogue buyer is already a *fait accompli*.

In either case, the history of architecture is in for a jolt.

011.1
Craig Hodgetts (in turtleneck) reviewing graduate student
work at UCLA, April 1978.

Role Reversal

CONTRACT (2 FEB 2005)

In this short piece, Hodgetts ruminates on the difference between speculative student work and professional practice. His assessment is colored by optimism for the future, justified by technological advances and the heart with which his students approach their work.

It's after 10:00 p.m., and the lights are still glowing from the second floor of UCLA's Perloff Hall. Laden with pizza, I buzz through the studio door and take in the scene. The acrid smell of Zap Kicker. The sultry hum of laptops. The crisp return of a plotter. Strains of hip-hop and Debussy leak from earbuds.

Tomorrow is the presentation for my Vertical Studio. About twelve young architects are finishing a project that would never find a real-life client. But there they are, pushing the boundaries beyond reason. I scan the plots. What variety: blobs, vectors, the occasional Platonic solid, a nervous hive of tiny spaces. Each one bristles with enthusiasm, even the ones that reside in the "under no circumstances" category.

I remember the passionate debates, the how-tos of the past ten weeks, and mourn qualities that don't easily make it to the business of architecture, in which decisions about delivery systems, staffing, and quality control often outgun aesthetic debate. However, after more than thirty-five years at it, I have found that there's a surprisingly productive balance between practice and teaching.

A small firm, such as ours, which seeks out unique projects, must cultivate intellectual curiosity and an appreciation for cultural change. It is axiomatic that the nature of our projects deserves the most informed perspective. It is critical that the projects interact with the public in a meaningful way—one that is informed not simply with the appropriate technical response, but with a deeper, more meaningful understanding of the intertwined roles of our culture and the architecture that serves it.

It's astonishing to realize that in the minds of students, the trajectory of the role of architecture is becoming more tangential to its fellow design arts, while we professionals are still trying to guard the henhouse. Students talk easily about branding, prefabrication, and gender roles. Architectural thinking is now thoroughly infused by the worlds of commercial art, industrial design, fashion, and film! With sweat (and occasional blood), students validate approaches that have sunk far below the horizon in a professional context.

Students also are harsh critics. Since they are most often driven by idealism, I'm sometimes acutely aware of the compromises we've been forced to make in our work, and uncomfortable with the combination of economics and professional commitment that quell my impulse to simply pull the plug. Often we are able to take heart from the knowledge that our approach is "in tune" with a younger, less bruised and battered outlook, and reaffirm our resolve. On occasion, the habits of academia strengthen my determination to do the research—to photograph Main Street, graph the relationships, or diagram the timeline. Sometimes this can be incredibly persuasive during a presentation, but I've found most potential clients are simply interested in the product, rather than the nuances one might bring to the table.

"Enjoy the conceptual freedom of your studio work," I tell them. "Exercise your creativity to the fullest," I admonish, knowing full well that most will never find themselves in a position of authority, nor have the good fortune to find and nurture an understanding client.

And yet, there is a great appetite on the student's part to confront reality, especially the technical reality and experience gathered in architectural practice. The sure knowledge that the drawings, no matter how comprehensive, will raise questions, or that the carefully dimensioned proportions of a project will morph incrementally the moment the foundations are poured, speaks volumes to them. And, for my part, their ability to nonchalantly "print" a model from their Rhino file on a rapid prototyping rig demonstrates how completely our profession will transform in the next decade or so.

It's clear from my contact with students, that in the near future, even the most exotic ideas will be explored with relative ease. The patience and commitment required to build an Eiffel Tower—or even a Bilbao—will have been largely eliminated by software that seems to transform at a logarithmic pace. The technical demands of our profession will be so highly evolved that, budgets and clients excepted, there will be few, if any, limits on form.

My question to students, and indeed to my staff, is: "What now?" Architecture is not simply about exploring possibilities and realizing personal fantasies. It's about a continuous and never-ending search for the right thing at the right time in the right place.

It's those of us with a few miles on the clock who understand that a great designer brings a sensibility that transcends technical virtuosity. And the greatest gift a designer can bring to a project is humanity. And that's hard to teach. That's something you have to be.

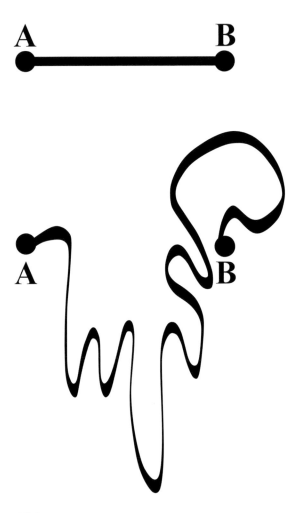

012.1
Craig Hodgetts, *Two Paths for Getting from Here to There,* 2005.

Analog + Digital

LOG 6 (FALL 2005): 107–114

In Hodgetts's view, architects' interest in digital technologies has been too technical and symbolic and insufficiently social and experiential. These qualities have been Hodgetts's concerns for the bulk of his career, as has his humanistic understanding that despite advanced technology (digital or otherwise), human interactions with the world are analog. To truly immerse ourselves in the digital, Hodgetts claims, architects need to understand it as an augment of analog existence.

In a Paris gallery, just after the collapse of the Kaiser's war, a young Erich Mendelsohn prepared for what would become his signature exhibition. Using a chalk line, he snapped a gridded pattern onto the walls, and then, consulting miniscule sketches that he had brought back from the front lines, proceeded to plot, grid line to grid line, the coordinates of each drawing, until the room was overtaken by vast shapes capturing every nuance of his vision. In effect, this was nothing new. Artists and craftsmen had been enlarging two- and three-dimensional images for centuries in order to navigate the void between concept and finished product. Highly systematized operations utilizing perforated delineation and powdered charcoal enabled the precise transfer of imagery to surfaces as varied as blocks of marble slated to become the friezes and architraves of classical temples, or the curved ceiling of the Sistine Chapel. In our own era, billboard artists used an electric spark rather than the barb of the pointer's wheel to trace the contours of brand names, even as Pong and its successors were invading the video game arcades.

Architects, meanwhile, labored in the vector world of Cartesian coordinates. Navigating point to point, they produced plans, sections, and elevations conditioned by an extreme economy of information. It could be argued that information management was the defining force in the development of the planar geometry that has dominated Western architecture since the Renaissance. Building materials, for instance, are overwhelmingly vector-based. A four-by-eight-foot module presupposes a set of orthogonal relationships regulated by those dimensions, in contrast to the infinite range of shapes the computer is capable of generating, which might (in theory at least) go around the world before passing through the next control point. Simple, direct, requiring no mediation, the Cartesian system has been equally efficient in cubits, yards, centimeters, and even inscribed in the sand, thus requiring no special training to use. If the role of digital design were limited to this sort of operation, the only thing it would do is fatten the pocketbooks of designers, since frankly, it would have zero impact on the field otherwise.
So what is the point?

Precisely this: in the digital realm, it makes no difference whether a line is curved or straight, ragged or smooth. The information required, on a pixel by pixel basis, is identical. Couple that with production machinery guided by those same pixels, and it becomes plausible to trace any shape, even the implausible tracery of Louis Sullivan or the tendrils of art nouveau architect Hector Guimard, within the economic framework of *fabrication* rather than the excesses of artistic production. This leaves just the issues of functionality, appropriateness, constructability, and emotion. As we witness the inevitable transfer of mercantile and creative resources to an ephemeral, volatile realm in which the ebb and flow of information transcend the boundaries of space and time, one might well question not the digital design process itself, but the role of architecture in the digital age.

Will the art of building emerge as sideshow or mainstay? Will the forms of cities and buildings come to resonate with experiential qualities achievable only through the use of digital computational tools, or will architecture simply keep wireless hot spots dry and comfortable? Will users look up from their laptops and PDAs long enough to appreciate the material world that envelops them, or fixate more and more on the lifestyle accessories with which they surround themselves? Can our buildings become as ergonomically responsive and rich with information as an automobile, for instance, or must we regard them as frozen information, high-viscosity components of an increasingly volatile environment?

The answers to these and other questions hinge on architecture's ability to adopt the technology of production itself, rather than attempting to emulate the forms and surfaces of digital imagery. Technology has only recently become a partner in the production of architecture: In times past, adventurous architecture had only a passing acquaintance with the developing technology of its time. A few hundred years ago, while Leonardo was musing about helicopters, submarines, and spring-powered vehicles, and Jacques de Vaucanson was building a clockworks-driven robot, buildings were still being constructed by piling stone upon stone, and the big deal was Brunelleschi's use of a chain to rein in the tension forces of his dome. In fact, given what we know of the pyramids alone, it could be argued that through the end of the nineteenth century, every building could have been constructed within the technological parameters that existed before the birth of Christ.

Consider that the protean curves of Mendelsohn's Einstein Tower and the taut surfaces of Le Corbusier's Villa Savoye represent diametrically opposed architectural propositions, yet share the common technology of a thin plaster skin troweled over a crude brick core, and it is tempting to conclude that we might dismiss technology altogether from the canon of architectural discourse. Architecture has always been a technological wallflower, binding architects to static arrangements based on gravitational attraction and surface elaboration. But the explosion of computational tools and visualization devices has invited architects to join the party of industrial designers and manufacturers who employ advanced production techniques for use in the aerospace and automotive industries.

There is a dream today that architecture will join the mainstream of production technology—that craft-based elements will be phased out of architectural making, and that the agony of fabrication will someday take place in a digital kingdom where the click of a mouse will cause a machine "somewhere" to extrude, wrap, punch, and deliver a fully realized building. But there is a huge gap between "printing" a 3-D model and assembling a full-scale, functioning environment. The conjunction of design, tooling, fabrication, and assembly has never been more seductive, nor, for that matter, more elusive. For while the impulsive path of information, lifestyle, and meaning seems to trace an ever-ascending trajectory, that of less volatile disciplines such as architecture seems mired in the viscous tar of thwarted potential. Are we doomed to rote emulation rather than true innovation? Are we destined to opt for the *appearance* of the digital rather than the substance? Are we basically embellishing the same, more or less mundane contents with snazzy new packaging?

Looking back, it is easy to see that the Citrohan House had more to do with clever marketing than mass production, much as Peter Eisenman's polemical exercises in extreme Cartesian conflict had more to do with visual rhapsody than intellectual theory. Looking ahead, do Neil Denari's visualizations of a digital environment, for example, transcend those examples? Do their sleek surfaces *embody* or simply *represent* the seamless, vacuum-formed environments promised by the computer? And does this methodology advance the digital design agenda?

Here, there is a fork in the road. The environments of Denari, Hariri & Hariri, and others are unequivocally beautiful, and go the extra mile in projecting a manifest digital destiny, but they must still be produced with the painstaking artisanal labor that has not substantially changed since the days of Louis XIV. Astonishingly, trading *fleur-de-lis* for precision, the plumb bob for laser levels, and linseed oil for acrylics has done little to remove the hand of the laborer from the enterprise, while a true digital translation, say, of a design for an industrially produced module, would result in a sea of joinery at odds with the conceptually pure realm of cyberspace. So we find ourselves caught between the evidence presented to our senses and the theoretical gap between artifice and truth.

Are we back to clay, or the devolution of the designer's tools to "primitives" with little, if any, built-in discipline? This is the case if "prophets" like Greg Lynn and Bernard Cache are to be believed. Disciplined renditions of "intuitive" forms can now be routinely achieved by digital means, thus opening the door to the technical documentation that is still a prerequisite of fabrication and construction. Are we at the tipping point? Is there now a preponderance of dispersing technology that will continue the flattening of global hierarchies? Or are we still on the cusp of a new paradigm, with a seductive, but still largely speculative future to be determined?

The computer is arguably the first "business" tool that does not require a specific physical environment in order to be useful. Using a laptop produces no extraneous matter. Every transaction up to and including instructions to the fabricator, merchandiser, and end-user can be accomplished without any physical support. Calling this a "paperless office" does such a revolution a great injustice. It is actually an "office-less" office, allowing creative transactions to take place literally worlds, or at least continents, apart. An essay I wrote for *Progressive Architecture* in 1973 explored this potential,[1] and we expanded on the idea in an installation for the 1976 Venice Biennale, in which remote workplaces redefined the American suburb. "*La città pulpa*," an installation designed for the XIX Milan Triennale in 1996, further pursued this theme by exploring its implications at the level of urban design.[2]

Even our shared expectations of the future seem now to be so diffuse that there is no clear trajectory. Where once, say at the 1939 World's Fair, there seemed to be robust consensus about what future we wanted to unfold in the Western world, there is now only a fragmented, almost apologetic future-phobia. And yet, a future now being constructed on a motherboard somewhere will ultimately be far more pervasive than any we have envisioned in the past. Like a garden where once there were only weeds, the computer is not yet fully "established," although there are already pockets in prevailing quarters that have set themselves up as resistant to change. But change they will, inevitably.

We have duly noted significant signs of the seismic impact cyberspace is having on formerly stable patterns of life. Stock market manipulations, the rise of global terrorism (sometimes wrought with devices as simple as the cell phone), burgeoning third-world economies, the blurring of intellectual property lines, extreme obsessions and pursuits, and the undertow of analog reality all owe their ascendance to the computer and its operational networks. At the other end of the spectrum is the hybrid DNA of a cultural transformation in which the prize is nothing less than a redefinition of the world's cultural and economic landscape. Authorship itself is at stake. The Renaissance ideal of the arts as the ultimate shaper of our thoughts has given way to something far more subtle. And with that has gone the notion of the originality of the work art.

In the digital world, we learn from others, sample, and modify, often seamlessly. We grow new systems from the old, graft new limbs onto old systems, update and repackage traditional forms. Those who believe that the accident of "reproduction" grants them "possession" had best look to history books to review the litany of

1   See "Object Lessons: Four Short-end Views," 45–51 in this volume.
2   See *La città pulpa* and "Notes for *La città pulpa*," 260–269 and 131–139 in this volume.

examples of the many who have beheld and embraced a new idea as their own. As the idea is more easily distributed and emulated, the differentiating factors have become brand, image, and marketing strategy. This is no less true in so-called creative enterprises, such as architecture and fine art, than it once was in smokestack, hard-goods production. In fact, the marketing of elite goods, from clothing to plastic surgery, from champagnes to sea salts, is increasingly dominated by brands whose products differ little, if at all, from those of less "desirable" or less carefully defined producers. Among the reasons for this, one suspects, is that desirability is easily induced by means of image and packaging. This is certainly true in architecture, as the complexities of place, culture, and purpose that once provided a challenging framework, the complexities of program, and even the technology of production are often subordinated to the desire to project a compelling image.

Curiously, the architectural avant-garde seems blissfully unaware of the cultural and emotional resonance of the digital transformation, and instead remains focused on technical production rather than the projection of a radical new culture. For Western culture, this suggests the rejection of more than 2,000 years of spatial evolution. Ever since the discovery of the right angle, with its equal—though not always *democratic*—division of space, Platonic geometry has been the hallmark of Western building—materials, tools, techniques—and also consumer goods and packaging. Interestingly, a glance at a similar catalogue of items from the Middle Ages shows that there was nothing like the present unanimity. In fact, it wasn't until the advent of mass production that the idea of a compatible geometry took hold, and then only slowly.

Major architectural projects have so far managed to avoid the functional and formal innovations that might usher in a transformative paradigm in favor of the kind of solitary, iconic presence that has defined the field's pecking order since its beginnings. New projects by a glittering array of designers are simply the avatars of old formulas in new clothing, with architects performing their customary duties in servitude to wealth and power. Little more than a decade into the hegemony of the digital, with a fully digitized apotheosis just around the (virtual) corner, it is still difficult to assess its impact on architecture. We swipe our cards and pump our own gas, communicate incessantly and shop online, but there seems to have been little change in our expectations of the role of the built environment. Predictions about a pervasive digital environment have largely come true, with wireless hot spots, global information access, and hyper-individuality. But anomalies persist, to such an extent that while first-run motion pictures are increasingly viewed at home rather than in theaters, compelling arguments for working at home (even though buttressed by the twin homilies of energy conservation and family values) have not gained wide acceptance.

Contrary to all architectural expectations, the digital revolution appears to be manifest in every which way *but* spatially or environmentally. Lacking the direct response of Stirling and Foster to a technological era, or the analogs of Venturi or Eisenman, the "utopian" architecture of the digital era strains for relevance, but achieves only symbolic reference. Mostly ducks clad in plumage glistening with LEDs or multihued frits, with expedient if not utilitarian programmatic development, this architecture surrenders to the eye rather than the body, miming the emanations of the plasma screen rather than the human pulse.

This sort of representation, privileging affect over effect, is particularly pervasive in the paradoxical realm of digital design, where, overwhelmed by an infinity of textures and seduced by the friction-free feedback of a glowing terminal brimming with pixelated images, it's "only natural" to defer substance to the moment of "save." It is also only natural to surf the cascades of design alternatives and imaginative excursions via a kind of ultimate Xbox, in which the inhibitions of "real" action are sublimated to the visceral joy of hand-eye coordination. Weaned on instantaneous change wrought by minimal effort, and seeking to explore expansive, multiple pathways, the dictums of digital gaming have already demolished conventional narrative structures, and threaten to set expectations for next-generation commerce as well as lifestyles.

The digital era, like a digital game, requires an analog interface. Like it or not, the human body is an analog device. We can neither see, hear, nor touch digital information without a prosthesis—a screen that translates a stream of 0s and 1s to produce an image, or a speaker cone driven by an analog signal derived from those 0s and 1s. Our world, it turns out, is unremittingly analog. We navigate, communicate, and create in a universe of analog perceptions and fields. Our first-person encounter with the world around us, unmediated by interpretive devices, defines our experience, and will, well into the foreseeable future.

The impact of the digital on technology, design, and lifestyle cannot be overstated, and it is mesmerizing to think of the degree to which it promises to liberate architecture from constraints that originated with the repetitive order of the industrial revolution. In a brave new digital world, animated by pulsing facades and RID transactions, surrounded by the sheen of merchandise, and lulled by thousands of invisible eyes, it will matter little to the digital urbanite whether the surroundings are faux nineteenth-, twentieth-, or twenty-first-century, so long as there is an agreeable mix. Equipped as they will be with standard-issue analog sensory equipment, they will taste, feel, hear, smell, and touch their way through that environment, just as they have always done.

Part II
Projects and urban prognostications

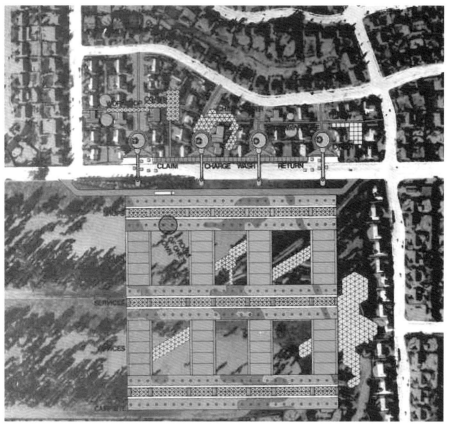

013.1
Craig, Kent, and Vicki Hodgetts, The Community
superimposed on suburbia. Photocollage, 1972.

The Birth of Individual Architecture

MS. MAGAZINE (PREVIEW ISSUE, SPRING 1972): 90–91, WITH KENT AND VICKI HODGETTS

In Hodgetts's view, social patterns are always linked to technology, though not always in a good way. Here, the automobile has produced an isolated and isolating suburban milieu, which Hodgetts and his collaborators propose to counter with a campus-like enclave offering alternatives to the car-dependent, consumerist, nuclear family. In their proposal, traditional architectural and social structures are dissolved by communication technology and replaced by an individualized, accommodative, and flexible community which promotes personal freedom, individual choice, and ad hoc, fluid social relationships (even for children) through clever architectural arrangements.

In the beginning, there was Eden, the wall-less wonder. Then came dwellings—basic living units that didn't change drastically for thousands of years. There was plenty of social upheaval that should have revolutionized architecture, but not enough technology to do the changing.

Once the Industrial Revolution got under way, architecture became much more fluid and sensitive. Since then, virtually every change in social patterns has registered its attendant technological response, so that the whole American landscape is littered with a physical record of our social development.

The car gave birth to the suburbs, ever more distant and more sprawling; to highways, to cities with no centers, and to families with absent fathers. Suburban tracts were oriented mainly toward children. The mothers had little in life that wasn't child-centered, the fathers were gone, and the children had few models of working adults. Being a child became a profession that, in the 1950s and '60s, extended to the age of twenty or thirty. (After that, you couldn't be trusted.) The suburban tract society was wedded to the idea of private property and to the perpetuation of a nuclear family that was isolated from the community, and even from itself.

The liberated community—the logical next step in our architectural evolution—will be built on the site of the suburban tract. It will extend the communal life of children to include adults, and bring individuals of all ages back into communal relationships.

The university campus—with its constantly fluid population and its living and working areas adjacent to each other—is the closest existing model for liberated communities to come.

But, in contrast to campus life, in the new community all people will be equal. All options will be open. Each person's uniqueness lies in the particular configuration of time and events (real or imagined, existential or cerebral) of her or his life. The community will free us to express that uniqueness. We will need to own nothing permanently—no houses, cars, objects, or clothes; no children, mothers, fathers, husbands, or wives. A person's immortality will no longer descend vertically through the generations, and therefore it will be independent of children and family pride. Communications systems will now spread fame and accomplishments horizontally across the contemporary earth. There will be no need for possessiveness of people.

We will spend our lives writing, directing, and producing our own movie: the movie that is our life. Our architecture will be our stage set. It must be demountable, reusable, changeable, flexible. Imagine a room with walls, bare ceilings and

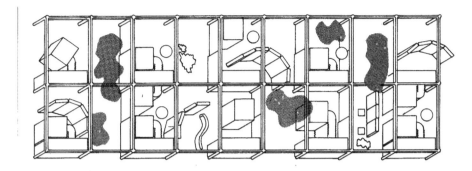

013.2
The campsite.

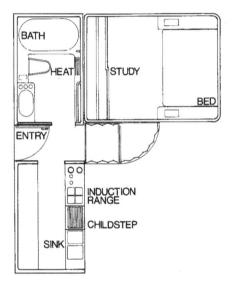

013.3
A room of one's own.

floors, a slide projector, and vast communal libraries with records of the earth's peoples, places, objects, and events.

But that is only part of the non-genitive society. All the components will be present, but no one will be forced to live either hermetically or communally. The system can easily encompass either preference.

Below, we see the overall view: the way that a mobile community would fit into an existing suburban tract [013.1]. Individual units cluster together or move apart to make new forms. Factories are run by remote control from cybertowers in the cul-de-sac. Computers replace commuters; downtown offices dissolve into a million crossing circuits; garages turn into galleries, metal-working shops, and organic restaurants. Fences come down and backyards are plowed and planted. Single-family houses become food co-ops, child care centers, and half-way houses for people who are changing their family units. New foliage grows in dead-end streets, and electric cars that belong to everybody are parked, awaiting the convenience of any residents, or washed and recharged in garages along the boulevard.

In "The Campsite" [013.2], people attach their units in corridors that intersect with laboratories, studios, theaters, classrooms, and computer centers. The community is a field, with everyone having equal access to everything; nobody lives in "the better part of town."

The new community provides every man, woman, and child with a private bedroom and study, connected by a hallway to a private kitchen and bath. On this page, the unit plan is viewed both in floor plan and in three dimensions [013.3 and 013.4]. The private "campsites" float free in a large communal area, a sort of giant corridor separated from a parallel corridor by a sky-lighted arcade of shops, infant and child care centers, public places, patches of green, and trading posts for toys, books, clothes, or friends. Along the ceiling of this corridor run grips, and walls can slide along them in a variety of ways to provide as much open or enclosed space as is desired. Kitchens are accessible from the outside or the inside: for those whose greatest joy lies in preparing and sharing food, the corridors can be walled in and converted into a giant kitchen and dining area; for others the space becomes a child care center, or an office or a recreation room. Bed canopies fold down for privacy or roll up to convert a bedstead into a living room couch. Those who wish to may keep possessions permanently, but for those who wish to be unencumbered, trading posts and lending libraries of every description provide the props.

This system does not oblige children to live either with or without their biological parents. Microwave ovens (which never get hot) are safe for the child who lives alone, and the "childstep" makes the equipment accessible to small people. There are no dangerous streets to cross on the way upstairs to rooftop gardens or downstairs to shops, labs, classrooms, etc. Children can move about as freely as adults.

Very small children are cared for either individually or by one or two people, in households of ten or twelve, or in kibbutz-like nursery schools. It's a choice of the parent, based on the atmosphere in which the child flowers best. Beyond the age of six or seven, each member of the community is autonomous. A man and woman who wish to live together might rent adjacent rooms and wall off the area between them, making a private house beyond the corridor. Three or four men, women, and children can do the same.

This plan is visionary, but not impossible or even unlikely. We may see the beginning of individual architecture.

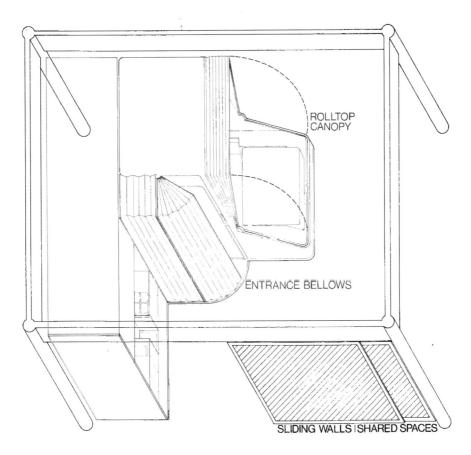

013.4
Connecting units, seen from above.

014.1
Studio Works (Craig Hodgetts and Robert Mangurian),
Palazzo Gagosian, Venice, CA, 1981. View of atrium.

Palazzo Gagosian

ARCHETYPE (FALL 1982): 15–17

A sense of loss, of absence, permeates this description of Palazzo Gagosian, the gallery residence Hodgetts and Studio Works partner Robert Mangurian designed for the curator Larry Gagosian in Venice Beach. This Venice is not Venezia, these forms are not their forms. The project and its context are haunted by ghosts. Technology remains a part of the discussion, but this is ancient technology at work—tiles cut and set by hand, pictures hung and regarded without mediation. At Palazzo Gagosian, timelessness, if just barely, trumps timeliness.

A Palazzo! On a neglected, strictly linear side street in a West Side version of Venice, in the reactionary hush of the '8os. Where today runs deeper than yesterday.

An art gallery. Uniquely defined by the uses of the past. A genuine antique.

Neither hanging pictures nor looking at pictures has needed to change. The technology and perception are genuine holdovers from another age—before Telstar and ITT; before the so-called "Age of Information" reduced the genuine to computer-enhanced types and colored them any color you wished as long as it was rainbow.

The building has a sister in the real Venice. The old Venice. Another palazzo only this time on the Grand Canal. With stone steps plunging into the water for tradesmen's deliveries, and a close quartet of marble columns supporting the vaulted cellar.

A fading rock star occupied the penthouse, unable to afford the whole spread any longer, so the rest was swathed in cobwebs and muslin. There were few lights. Dust swirled about the feet of those who made the pilgrimage. Yet, through the obligatory aroma—beyond the dusty gold records propped in cracked frames on carved marble—one could imagine that noble and austere structure in finer times.

The roller skates rush by. Everyone wears earphones. The cast-iron stumps of a forgotten arcade march down Market Street to the Pacific Ocean. It's not the Grand Canal but it will have to do.

There was no Walkman in Venice of America, maybe no sensimilla in old Venezia. Things change. Black dudes with good definition didn't roll by with slim blondes on fluorescent polyurethane wheels when this palazzo took shape. So now they stream past as though it's always been there, failing to notice a symmetry more than a little like early Corb. Or was it Palladio? The artificial thickness of the three-eighths-inch stucco is silent. The doors are always closed.

Beyond, in the passage, murky light filters in from a glass-block aperture. In the diminishing perspective, a visitor can just see a barred portal, make out various niches. To the right, a steel staircase for the resident butts up to a hole in the wall above. Light might stream down. Then, through twin alcoves, a sliver of sunlight cants across a wall. Subterranean echoes swirl from a broad, high room. Like a tomb.

It is possible by now to imagine that this place is below the ground. It is time to put away memories of the surface. Of the inevitable discotheques and motels. Neat squares and rectangles, draped muslin, great sheets of figured paper line the walls. The single opening frames the visitor. Notes his presence. The footsteps recede.

014.2
Palazzo Gagosian. Street façade.

Then the cold steel rail of a staircase leans upward. Again to a hole in the wall. Again for the resident.

Bare metal gleams through worn paint. Above, a luminous antechamber grids the space as the visitor ascends.

Overhead, intersecting jet streams fade across a sky crisscrossed by kites and clouds. A perforated wall beats a crusty rhythm around the edge. Windows like slits and squares glint down. One expects a green tinge from ancient algae, a ghost metaphor from Euclid, a star-map—*putti* at the very least.

The sound of bongos on the beach seeps over the rim. It's 1981. The Madrigal is no longer in fashion.

Even if one steps over the ribbon of water to the gray marble disc at the center, the bongos do not similarly evolve. The sudden Platonic alignment of the solar plexus with some celestial axis fails to rend reality. There is no music of the spheres. No Romeo climbs to the tiny porch which interrupts the perfect radius.

The ellipse of the sun's shadow crawls around the circumference. Two feet per hour at solstice. Less than an inch as one mounts the jigsaw steps to the little porch, wondering if there is any need to *say* anything. Wondering if an elegy is required. Staring at the gridded gray surface below, veined and mottled like a mysterious planet, and understanding at the same time that it's been cut and fitted by ordinary labor. As it has for millennia.

A presumptuous resident might feed on the contrast. Might ogle that round blue cookie like a kid in a commercial, looking for the label, never realizing it's been there all the time.

That the clouds and the kites and the stars are enough.

014.3
Palazzo Gagosian. View of atrium.

015.1
Swimming to Suburbia, 1987, cover.

Swimming to Suburbia: Some Thoughts on the New City and How It Came to Be That Way

LOS ANGELES FORUM FOR ARCHITECTURE AND URBAN DESIGN, *FORUM NEWSLETTER* NO. 1, 1987.

In this text, based on a 1987 lecture at the Getty Center for the Arts and Humanities and later published as a stand-alone pamphlet by the Los Angeles Forum for Architecture and Urban Design (of which, Hodgetts was a founding member), Hodgetts ruminates on his adopted home, Los Angeles. The text is colored by his trademark frustration with the status quo of architecture and urban planning, as well as with his equally trademark optimism of better futures produced through thoughtful design. In LA, he argues, the old rules of city planning—stone structures that symbolize authority—no longer apply. This city is "quasi-electronic," even "cybernetic." Where others see a mess, Hodgetts sees a template for an alternative future.

To make his case, Hodgetts charts a history of cities in which rigid stone gives way to fluid electronics as the primary medium of communication. Along the way, conventional symbols become obsolete.

LA, particularly in the tumultuous, anonymous fabric of its sprawl (Reyner Banham's Plains of Id, not his freeways), provides a look into the future. Here, there is no need for simplistic "correspondence between physical form and tradition." Rather, it is "perfectly suited to generative movement." A "grab-bag of style, convenience, and opportunity" which "surrounds each individual."

Characteristically, Hodgetts questions his own premises along the way but ultimately comes down on the side of Los Angeles and its opportunistic accommodation and celebration of the individual.

LA's streets and avenues are stitched together from a mosaic of discrete city grids which are discontinuously linked by dislocations, swerving axes, and polar rotations. These grids open vistas, frame trivialities, and reveal anomalies. It is a system of altercations and inconsistencies; of thoughtless breadth and pragmatic anticipation, which has bred, albeit carelessly, the culture of cruising, hatchbacks, and convenience corners which exemplify the present vision of the future city.

In short, the city grid is the medium from which all other media emanate. People do things with it: they plan excursions and funerals, meditations and trysts, with the abandon of an action painter. The city is perhaps less an artifact than a benevolent flux in which to pursue individual destinies. Yet it seems that our ability to understand and modify urban destiny has in both theory and practice been hopelessly mired in the cramped space of our most elementary perceptions. In other words, given the universe of energy and its corollary matter, we are only able to measure and perceive the "physical" world, and consequently have developed systems of architectural "order" related to the ability of various urban objects, buildings, and so on to reflect light. Because of this fixation, the planning of most cities is still at the toy block stage, while much of the rest of the world has discovered electricity.

We generally see walls and roofs as shaping our cities, but there are those of us who are frustrated by the limits of construction and its control of making and memory, and there are others who recognize the inconvenient weight and the permanence of stone as a natural way to dominate the culture as a whole. I would propose that our idea that the stone image confers status by its simple existence must be re-examined in light of the relative effort required for its realization.

Imagine, for a moment, the ponderous task of coordination in the times when even basic size and shape could only be communicated with difficulty. A world lacking FAX and stats, limited to messengers toting papyrus rolls in boats up the Nile, could hardly be blamed for the rigid geometry which came to signify civilization. That geometry was a useful tool. It got things done, enabling legions of people to work on a single product, even a simple, elemental one: there was a necessary symbiosis between the monolithic communications network and the task at hand. So it comes as no surprise to find the design for the network itself carefully incised into the rock, in effect memorializing the "chain of command" which may have been the real invention of such a culture. Thus the definition of power and rank came to reflect the rigidity of the medium in which early civilizations worked (imagine the consequences of *People* Magazine in stone), with the resulting geometry inferring a like status at some future time.

By the late Middle Ages, the routines and sub-routines of city building inherited from the Romans had become the structure by which urban life was evaluated. The medieval city became a familiar artifact, so much so that Giotto's toy-like depiction of formerly monumental edifices as tilted, colored, even charming objects-at-play defies their status, reducing them to the engaging companions to urban life that they had become. Buildings themselves became entertaining pleasure objects, as plentiful as Walkmen; they made you feel good, dressed up your life, and provided a defined context in which you could relate to others.

The city, like a good host, was where it was happening, and the creative nature of man was not only supported, but even exemplified in the complex structures of its plazas and streets. Henceforth, the synthesis of man and city was to become increasingly reciprocal, evolving steadily away from the paternalistic patterns of imperialism to the point where it became a complex communications organ capable of extending the dynamic interchange of man to man, man to institution, and man to his work. It became the *"communitas"*: a place which, in my view, functioned as a kind of media center, where the grand and the accidental could find appropriate accommodation, while the exchange of goods, information, and judgments could multiply indefinitely.

Free interchange characterized the city center. But by the time Sixtus V had re-erected the obelisk at what was to be the Basilica of St. Peter, the Roman in-crowd had moved on. And in cities throughout the world, with the rise first of widespread publishing, then of railroads, telegraph, radio, and telephone, the essential function of communication began to operate without particular reference to its center. Suddenly, the now-meaningless symbolism of place and adjacency was seen to be less compelling than the complex symbolism inherent in a gigantic task, whether it be the building of pyramids, cathedrals, spaceships, or even cities themselves.

The society which discovers a stimulant such as this task, which, after all, requires extraordinary talents and diverse communication, has no need for the puffery of conventional symbols. Thus the waning of architectural symbolism in the recent past makes sense. By engaging ourselves in the creation of a symbolically charged and represented task, we have finally devised a way to make an object, a symbol, and a center which requires the most diverse creative energies ever assembled. This object realizes the potentiality of our technology to take us beyond the realm of the city and of architecture: it is the Apollo. The Apollo is a monumental object by the measures of profile and height, but when compared to the static mass of a pyramid it is sufficiently buoyant to be tossed at the moon. While the pyramid required grunts, lots of them, not eurekas! the Apollo is about eurekas! which are the social lubricant par excellence.

The Apollo is a locus of creative thought, not a geographic center. It suggests that our civilization is busy evolving uses for traditional architectural implements which reach beyond static celebration to the pursuit of performance itself. Norman Bel Geddes alludes to a similar translation of values in his famous comparison of a rose window to a radial aircraft engine, but stops short of the suggestion that the engine in fact "is" the twentieth-century rose window (or was, until the digital display).

Now it is not at all convincing to argue that the central structure and hierarchic patterns which once wove houses and shops into what was known as a city have more than a tedious utility. Gridlock, rot, and the telephone have taken care of that argument. But what about Los Angeles? It is, they say, a non-place, an obese sprawl masquerading as an urban cliché, a city in which the City Hall is just another off-ramp, where, if you are looking for the "real city," you might just as well go to the beach.

The beach is benign, providing equal accommodation for all—so long as you've got your umbrella, your radio, and your suntan oil. As a city metaphor, it suggests a benevolent framework which replaces hierarchies, haves and have-nots, towers, and centers, with a uniform network of services and delights. It provides an invisible structure without visible corollaries to the activities which it is able to sustain. The beach and, by extension, Los Angeles, is a new city, frustrating to architects and planners who seek correspondence between physical form and tradition, but perfectly suited to generative moment.

Los Angeles is frustrating because the ways in which we have studied cities in the past—analyzing their solids and voids, their bumps and valleys—is no more relevant today than are the fingers of phrenology which attempt to "scientifically" plumb neurological depths by describing the surfaces of the skull. This is because cities have become as quasi-electronic as the brains they house. Any analysis must address this reality. As Keith Jarrett has remarked, "There's electricity in all of us!"

Similarly, if Los Angeles is reduced to a Nolli map, it seems opaque and uninspired when compared to its European cousins. Yet we must remember that the functional shape of the new city is best described by the flux of its electronic network. The city is made up of variegated, constantly changing rhythms of bookings, orders, transactions, and contacts too rich in information to be subject-ed to holistic analysis. The "skull" of the modern city cannot be cleverly sliced for diagnosis and cure: It is an entity requiring the sophistication of a brain-scan rather than the ministrations of a triple-o pen. Los Angeles is a holographic city.

Let me give an example of the implications of such an analysis by comparing three musical compositions: a Gregorian chant, the *Eroica* symphony, and composer Terry Riley's *In C*.

In the chant, we are offered a vision of unanimity: a single melodic line thick with voices of every timbre, without so much as a rhythmic defection, reflects the quality of Medieval agrarian society.

In the music of Beethoven, a marked tension is apparent as themes and sub-plots vie for attention, yet the whole is clearly dominated by a single powerful idea—much, it would seem, like the Renaissance city.

Finally, in the work of Terry Riley, each of a series of three- and four-note phrases is played as often as each member of the ensemble chooses, producing a slowly evolving field of harmonic events often characterized as non-music. In fact, as is the case in a holographic image, the relationship of each unit of the piece to the whole is absolutely typical. Each moment is the whole at the same scale, even though the whole is articulated in its parts.

I believe that Los Angeles has the qualities of the Riley piece. Here, a grab-bag of style, convenience, and opportunity surrounds each individual like a microcosm of the whole city, offering short-range choice from tacky to flamboyant, catering to lifestyles from monkish to raffish, creating opportunities even a champion self-stylist could never exhaust.

Consumptive, competitive, and creative, the mythic avenues of this city, lined with trees of all species and kaleidoscopic homes, have a logic born of the individual. One man's fantasy is another's reality in a clash of advertisements, décor, wide screens, and architectural bravado which flickers preposterously along tree-lined avenues with all the gaudiness of screen gems.

Or do they? Isn't this capsule recreation of eras long gone, taken as a whole, a differentiated style unto itself? Isn't it a distinctly post-modern luxury to dwell in the midst of sham reality where the only consensus is in diversity? Are Trigger's hoof prints just another hieroglyphic? At the Chinese Theater?

Los Angeles is a city committed to images, but never to sources. An advertisement shows the bulk of the new Beverly Center as the chapeau on a dressed-to-kill model. A later ad shows it in steamboat drag, complete with stacks. A few miles away a landlocked 1930s Coca Cola bottling plant renders the steamboat in stucco. A saucer-shaped restaurant rotating atop a severely modern office slab bills itself as a crenellated antique. A serious downtown hotel takes "Things to come" too seriously, with comic results. A gigantic Man on Horseback lights a cigarette at the focus of a long axis while multi-million dollar homes look on.

Who's kidding whom? Are the inhabitants of this place simply gullible? Or are they able to row merrily through this shipwreck of icons as though it were a Sunday cruise? Every weekend abandoned corner lots in vacant corners of cities-within-the-city with names like Eagle Rock, Alhambra, and Arcadia are blasted by the giant lights and motor generators of mobile furniture showrooms. Without the benefit of so much as a tent, with NCR's safely in the truck, and while soft sculpture surrounds them on the crumbling asphalt, the omnipresent Valley housewives solemnly confer with their designer counterparts. They are afraid it won't go with their wall hanging. The color is wrong. The color is money. Surely the crew of the Discovery could not have felt more incongruous had they uncovered a grandfather clock rather than a black monolith in that pit on the moon.

If one avoids freeways, which promise reassurance in the form of a guaranteed destination, the surface of this planet LA is endlessly rewarding. It is an encyclopedia of mini-gardens and barely throttled power boats. It is like stepping off the Rue Montparnasse to explore the back alleys of Paris. No matter that Melrose Avenue is 120 feet wide, that it seems to carry more traffic than the autobahn, it is an alley nonetheless, and the pattern of freeways and street grids is topologically, emotionally, and urbanistically Beaux-Arts. No wonder Banham loved them.

Freeways focus traffic as if they were lenses, beaming the cars directly to the next interchange, blitzing the axis with a mega-dose of car-energy so intense it overwhelms. What would loom as opportunities in the landscape of lesser cities—sites charged with a view, perhaps a prominent bend, a vista—here are flung at the passing tide in a volley of words and images which ricochet from billboard to billboard, dazzling with a visual racket as violent as a Prohibition shoot-out.

I question the fact that nobody "exploits" those locations. Why do so few buildings address the shifts in axis which mark subdivisions long since annexed? And then I remember that there are cars in front and behind. There is a blonde in that one, the radio is on, and in the distance a string of cobra-like lamps stretches like a veil over a parade of billboards. And the car phone is in my ear.

In fact, unless there is some particular fixed asset out there—like oil—which must be consumed on the very spot, every backyard is exactly equal to every other backyard. And it is the producer sunning by the pool, surrounded by telephones and bikini'd cuties of either sex, who makes all the deals.

The magnificent images of cities designed to emulate, and even magnify, the manifold processes of industry and culture and crime and indulgence are not unlike Gainsborough's painting. They tranquilize, mystify, and romanticize the vitality of an as of yet uncongealed city which could be getting you off.

In this context, physical manipulation of the gross city fabric seems superfluous at best. Presumptuous and potentially damaging, cosmetic adventures like the Bunker Hill exercise seem destined to appear, like tidied-up office lobbies, wherever developers have a stake.

It might instead be more meaningful to address the way dislocations and distortions of the basic city fabric can accommodate eccentricities like the Blue Whale or the Brown Cow. Or one might consider how the message-beeper, phone banks, and express mail have already created a cybernetic city. One might ask how chain stores can be given significant roles which exploit their cumulative importance. Los Angeles has already evolved a unique texture in which these elements are the principal determinants. We are already the beneficiaries of a meta-urban state which offers proof-positive that scenography and urban function are no longer mutually exclusive. This condition suggests that uncoupling the diagram from the experience may be the catalyst which expands our definition of urban form to include explicitly scenographic intent: we can create "a good shot."

The dream each of us dreams is the locus of each individual, heating and cooling whole districts in a dynamic, sensory, always interactive experience linked to the fluid nature of the city itself. As designers, the architectural project which faces us is to disassociate ourselves from the fixation on buildings and to instead look in the rearview mirror.

Useful Ideas
for a Future LA

LOS ANGELES WEEKLY, MARCH 3–9, 1989

In two broadsheets produced on the occasion of the 1989
"Remaking LA" conference at UCLA, Hodgetts offers provocative
yet plausible proposals for reimagining life, work, and play in
LA. Featured ideas included micro-housing for the homeless, a
funicular connecting Chinatown with Dodger Stadium, "axial"
parking with housing above, and cable cars connecting the
Sunset Strip to Pico/La Brea.

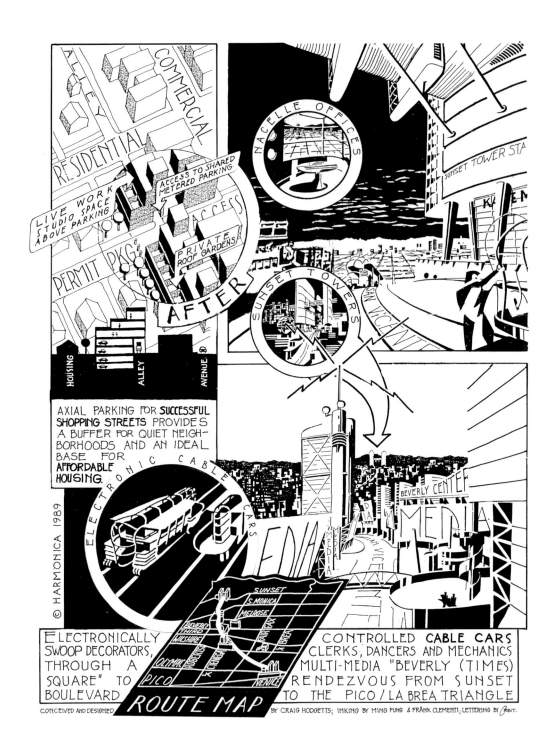

ALLEY

COMMERCIAL

RESIDENTIAL

LIVE WORK STUDIO SPACE ABOVE PARKING

ACCESS TO SHARED METERED PARKING

ACCESS

PRIVATE ROOF GARDENS

PERMIT PKG

AFTER

HOUSING   ALLEY   AVENUE

NACELLE OFFICES

SUNSET TOWER STA

SUNSET TOWERS

SAN VICAN

AXIAL PARKING FOR **SUCCESSFUL SHOPPING STREETS** PROVIDES A BUFFER FOR QUIET NEIGH-BORHOODS AND AN IDEAL BASE FOR **AFFORDABLE HOUSING.**

© HARMONICA 1989

ELECTRONIC CABLE CARS

BEVERLY CENTER

MEDIA

ROUTE MAP

SUNSET
S. MONICA
MELROSE
BEVERLY
THIRD
WILSHIRE
OLYMPIC
PICO
VENICE

ELECTRONICALLY SWOOP DECORATORS, THROUGH A SQUARE" TO BOULEVARD

CONTROLLED **CABLE CARS** CLERKS, DANCERS AND MECHANICS MULTI-MEDIA "BEVERLY (TIMES) RENDEZVOUS FROM SUNSET TO THE PICO / LA BREA TRIANGLE

CONCEIVED AND DESIGNED BY CRAIG HODGETTS; INKING BY MING FUNG & FRANK CLEMENTI; LETTERING BY ORBIT.

USEFUL IDEAS FOR A FUTURE L.A.

Craig Hodgetts

CITY EMPORIUM

DODGER STADIUM

MIDWAY SHOPS + EATERY

IMPORT SHOPPING BAZAAR

"SNUG" HOUSES* HARBORS FOR THE HOMELESS
ONLY ABOUT ONE HUNDRED SQUARE FT. PER HOUSE MEANS SIX UNITS IN ONE TRAILER SIZE FIBRE-FAB!

DOUBLE WALL FIBRE-GLASS SHELL WITH INTEGRAL INSULATION

WATER SUPPLY

SOLAR PANEL

WASTE

EXIST-ING PARK-ING LOT

WASH-OUT SPIGOT

*UNITS LIKE THESE ARE IN USE AS "BUSINESS" HOTELS IN TOKYO, JAPAN

FANS STOP FOR TACOS AT OLVERA STREET OR DIM SUM ON BROADWAY BEFORE THE GAME! THIS **FUNICULAR** PROVIDES THE LINK BETWEEN A RE-VITALIZED CHINA-TOWN AND DODGER STADIUM

ARRIVING AT THE TOP

DODGER STADIUM

CHINA TOWN

PASADENA FREEWAY

LOS ANGELES RIV.

HOLLYWOOD FREEWAY

NEW LAKE

COMMUNITY ACT. BRIDGE OVER R.R.

FORMER RAILYARD

COMMUNITIES

AT WATT'S TOWERS NATION'L PARK & REC. CNTR. THE TOWERS STILL PROJECT A ZANY ELEGY.*

* FOR SIMON RODIA, WHO BUILT THE TOWERS.

The Path to Recovery: Building an Ethnically Diverse "Shining City on the Hill"

LOS ANGELES TIMES (15 MAY 1992): T4

Writing in response to the 1992 Rodney King riots in Los Angeles, Hodgetts advocates a drastic reconsideration of the status quo of LA planning in an attempt to foster development that might bring street life and diversity back to central and south Los Angeles. He praises the older, denser fabric and vibrant street life of pre-1950s LA and denigrates the sanitized malls that have taken their place. Decentralized social services and a cityscape that encourages small business are major components of his thinking. Importantly, rather than (typically modernist) top-down planning and hierarchical centralization, Hodgetts advocates a nimble, case-by-case, flexibility that relies greatly on public involvement in the planning process.

This is the moment in the life of our city when we must transcend the limits of accepted planning and prove that what makes a city unique lies beyond efficient management, economic engineering and rapid transportation. The "mosaic city" was proposed as a powerful metaphor for a metropolis that had, at the time, only a fraction of the ethnic diversity found in Los Angeles today. Business and residential zones were systematically segregated according to strategies based on suburban ideals—and accelerated by white flight from the urban core. Topography, freeways, and lifestyle have now created a collection of urban "islands," which continue to maintain their individuality.

Not surprisingly, this has netted a bonanza for small businesses. The franchise was virtually born in Los Angeles—everything from banks to burger stands has been decentralized. Yet few cultural institutions or civic organizations have established the satellite presences that could bring them close to a majority of the public. In many places, even the most modest community entertainment and sports facilities have closed, with no plans to return. Among the problematic results of this strategy was the decision to reinvest in the Los Angeles Public Library's Central Branch instead of upgrading its network of community facilities.

Some seeds of the recent rage and destruction were planted in the 1950s, when Los Angeles "cleaned up" its streets, eliminating the outdoor vendors, cafes, and pushcarts that provide cultural diversity. Although malls offered some alternative for the upwardly mobile, street-oriented businesses were severely marginalized. With these sanitized public spaces, maintained through planning and zealous enforcement of trivial civil laws, is it any wonder that kids turned to their cars for a social experience?

We have created another city, one constantly on the move and grounded nowhere. Its citizens live scattered across a huge area. Most don't have the means to acquire the symbols for belonging to the "haves" of Los Angeles. They are largely African-American, Latino, and Asian, but also white and poor. They are disenfranchised and disintegrated. The infrastructure of the city doesn't work for them: buses are slow, services are few, and blocks are long, hot, and dangerous.

A good city plan not only allocates basic services but also encompasses the character and values of the individual community. Each community cultivates a sense of its connection to its neighbors through a hierarchy of symbols, places, and names. Rebuilding Los Angeles is more than replacing the tangled metal and melted plastic. We must try to redistribute the keys to identity.

This identity is more than signs. It flows out of preschools and storefronts, front yards and swap meets. It is inextricably woven from the occasions of life. It can't be synthesized on a planner's table.

Today we have the tools to sustain a dialogue between the people and the planners. The facts and images to inform urban decisions and test planning ideas are literally at our fingertips with computers. Neighborhood design workshops have shown how successful a dynamic interaction between professionals and the community they serve can be.

Hard choices need to be made. We have to decide what must be done first and what must be deferred—community by community. Decisions about everything, from human well-being to restoring the built and natural environment, must be made on a case-by-case basis.

From institutional structures to shopping malls to neighborhood shops, almost no part of Central Los Angeles went untouched by fire and looting. Unless we do something, the burned-out shops will be bulldozed and then gradually become vacant, garbage-strewn lots, cordoned off by chain link. We can't allow this to happen. Constant visual reminders of the conflagration make bad neighbors and dim prospects for the future.

Most of the devastation struck continuous shop fronts of a type no longer permitted in Los Angeles. Yet these are the very buildings that provided a base for significant retail expansion on Melrose Avenue, La Brea, and Third Street—especially in the last decade. Masonry construction, the absence of setbacks, and individual character are hallmarks of this classic urban type that has a remarkable ability to adapt to changing fashions.

But in South Los Angeles, where the building type is the same, the result is far from this ideal. There, businesses are often just barely surviving. Saving those blocks, and building on the character of the neighborhood in the process, calls for thoughtful re-examination and modification of building and zoning codes. In a market glutted with retail space, it will require stalwart tenants—old and new—and even changes of use, including decentralization of public services.

Where too little remains of the existing structures, higher density housing might be encouraged, with viable local shops, community markets, and day-care centers at the street level. This mix of social and commercial purpose—providing "eyes on the street," access to essential goods and services and community interaction—has been notably successful in many cities surrounding Los Angeles.

In these special places, storefront telecommuting centers adjacent to day care would allow parents the luxury of "one stop" as they walk to work. In addition, decentralization by major employers—the government, insurers, and banks—could reduce air pollution aggravated by mass commuting and workers could gain free hours to devote to other pursuits.

Our reaction to the losses suffered by Los Angeles could have far-reaching social, economic, and political implications, particularly if we seize this opportunity to explore models for the future. We can no longer afford to hark back to Eurocentric city planning, with its legacy of smokestack industries and a monolithic culture. An ethnically diverse population on the brink of the next century cries out for something else, something we haven't yet seen. Roles and relationships are changing and with them our ideas about the nature of cities and their architecture.

Let us forge a process of rebuilding Los Angeles, one that draws on a clear perception of human need and desire in all their dimensions, rather than withdrawing behind a façade that blinds us to one another. Our efforts to fill the gaps, bridge the voids, and restore order to our cityscape must bring color back to a place long devoid of it. We must transform burnt-out structures into the receptacles of our future.

018.1
Hodgetts + Fung, La città pulpa, Milan Triennale
XIX, 1996. Excerpt.

Notes for
La città pulpa

1995. WITH HSINMING FUNG. PREVIOUSLY UNPUBLISHED.

In this polemical preamble to *La città pulpa,* Hodgetts + Fung's contribution to the 1996 Milan Triennale, the architects advance, through the fictional narrator, I. N. Ternet, a radical set of principles to guide the design of cities. In their view, the forms of the city—from building types to urban textures—are conventionally devised in the name of utility and purpose and tend to suppress identity and difference in the name of "harmonious co-existence" of disparate cultures. Over time, they observe, city dwellers tend to devise alternative uses for the purpose-designed forms of the past, as when hay lofts and industrial districts are repurposed by artists. In Hodgetts and Fung's view, these repurposed zones are among the city's most vital, while newer areas, in which forms are more intentionally linked with function, suffer from their tedious predictability.

With *La città pulpa,* Hodgetts and Fung aim to demonstrate the possibility of city design that promotes identity and difference through improvisational appropriation of existing urban elements. The proposal took the form of a series of comic-book-style vignettes depicting a future Los Angeles reinvented by its inhabitants after a devastating earthquake. Seven new districts emerge in the city, each with distinctive characteristics (ad hoc survival in NuLax, technologically augmented individualism in Cyberville, health-crazed overachievement in Scoreston, etc.). Far from a fictional diversion, for Hodgetts and Fung, this balkanized city of differentiated villages "seems not only reasonable, but inevitable."

The script with which Hodgetts and Fung structured the narrative of *La città pulpa* is included on pp. 260-269 of this volume.

AUTHOR: I. N. TERNET

It must be remembered that the mature form of most cities is rarely achieved before the culture which brought them about has been consigned to the scrap heap. This is no less true of so-called "modern" cities like Los Angeles and Houston than of nineteenth-century industrial cities like Leeds or Pittsburgh or imperial cities such as Venice or Madrid. Each holds up a mirror to the culture from which it springs, embedding the percepts of hierarchy or lifestyle or belief systems deeply within the mass of stone and mortar which give it form, while all the time evolving new responses to the change which has come to seem inevitable in the growth of civilization.

These forms not only support and nurture the *activities* thought to be important in any given culture, but also suggest the behavior expected from those who reside within their boundaries. As such, the city is itself a powerful agent for the absorption and management of disparate cultures; the mechanism, one might say, for the *elimination* of "Identity and Difference" in the pursuit of a more immediate goal—that of harmonious co-existence in a competitive and often inhospitable environment.

Like today's pop catchword, cities are *immersive*. Cities offer a compelling and often self-serving version of reality. They dominate all of one's senses with the smell, sound, texture, and rhythm of their particular era. The manufacturing processes, social organization, and economic devices typical of an age conspire in the creation of a holistic and often unique environment. Cast iron, high voltage electricity, compact corridors, soot, and child labor suggest the ethos of a nineteenth-century Industrial City as eloquently as false fronts, mud, saloons, and gun fights suggest the frontier towns of the same era. The Elizabethan imagery of Shakespeare's *Hamlet*, superimposed on an Icelandic saga, specifies conducts as well as costume and context.

Since the devices necessary for the efficient operation of a new urban protocol generally have few, if any, local precedents, districts formed in support of a new technology—say light manufacturing—tend to locate on undeveloped land adjacent to already established centers, ring them with new growth, and drain them of entrepreneurial and intellectual vitality.

The resulting husks, shorn of utility, rich in memory and apparently devoid of opportunity, offer accommodation to society's extremities. Intellectual renegades, artists, and fashion daredevils compete with n'er-do-wells, addicts, and lost souls for territory in a no-man's land of no longer "useful" avenues and structures.

Why? How can a coherent set of norms, which everyone seemed to agree on

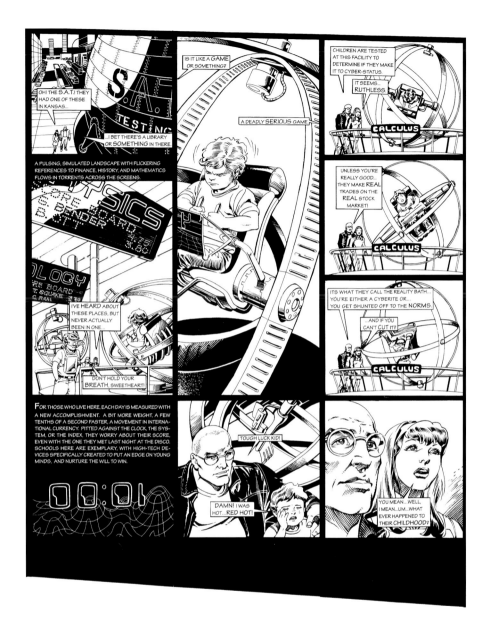

018.2
Hodgetts + Fung, *La città pulpa,* Milan Triennale XIX, 1996. Excerpt.

just "a few minutes ago" vanish, seemingly, into thin air? And do so, in the U.S., in a decade or less? Have the realities of urban life become so volatile that whole cities can, in the wink of an eye, abandon their hard-won network of shops and streets and homes?

The answer is yes. Look at Detroit. Mark its beginnings as the automobile capital of the world, its history of union confrontations, mob interference, grand boulevards, museums, corporate pride, and inventive genius. Detroit is the litmus for a sea change in the way labor and business do business. As the last American bastion of a Marxist division of class, Detroit crumbled before the inexorable growth of a working middle class determined to have a more fulfilling lifestyle, i.e., The American Dream.

To venture across nearly any city from edge to edge in such a way as to pierce its historical center, is to literally and figuratively wend one's way forward and backwards in time. Hollywood routinely uses downtown Los Angeles as a stand-in for nineteenth-century New York, and why not? Both were products of the first cycle of American urbanism—the product of a common belief in the value of capitalism, an expanding economy, and moral virtue.

So there is a kind of natural accommodation to change. The too small streets of the horse-drawn era are fringed first with the broad lanes of motorways, then surrounded by high-speed ring roads. The common-wall rows for living and commerce alike are replaced in waves by dedicated mid-rise buildings, free-standing suburban houses, malls, and office parks. Families that once filled a tidy townhouse now rattle around on quarter-acre suburban lots. Stables once dedicated to a single horse now accommodate a hundred horsepower or more, all dedicated to the motion of a single automobile, which, in turn, was once a carriage.

Such a constant improvisation, the use of "this" for "that," and the ensuing reverberation in the collective memory tends to imbue our physical surroundings with a vast scaffold of attributes, only some of which are useful in the here and now. There was a time when even the lowly streetlamp was considered such an important addition to the streetscape that its cast iron structure was wrought in the form of an ecstatic interplay of floral tendrils; a time when the proud logotypes of utility companies adorned every manhole; a time when highway intersections were seen as memorable occasions, to be celebrated by memorials to this or that armed conflict.

The hayloft is a good example. Originally a strictly rural storage space for animal feed above the working floor of a barn, and characterized by a high (lofty!) exposed structure, the hayloft found its way to cities by way of the stable. Located off the main thoroughfare for both aesthetic reasons (odor, flies) and practical reasons (import and export of large quantities of feed and excrement) the loft was typically unadorned, most likely because, as part of the city's "utility system," gentle persons were never required to see it.

With the introduction of the automobile and elimination of hay as "fuel," the term, and the "utility" function of the space it referred to, was given new meaning with the conversion of many of those spaces to low-caste business functions. The "loft" became an unassigned, conceptually "free" space in which a variety of tasks requiring relatively large rooms might be accomplished. As such uses multiplied, and the mercantile value of large, unassigned, spaces with little or no stylistic "signature" became clear. "Loft" spaces quickly transmogrified into entire "loft" districts where more mundane manufacturing tasks might be accomplished.

Still "off the thoroughfare," these districts were home to the garment manufacturing industry in New York City, small assembly operations in Detroit, packing and warehousing in Saint Louis, Los Angeles, and Chicago.

Recently, with the removal of manufacturing operations to areas more accessible by truck than rail (another story), and closer to the work force (which used its secure income base to purchase homes in the suburbs), lofts again became an unexpected spatial resource. But this time, the atomization of business energy, and the resourcefulness of a new generation, encouraged a new generation of individuals to seize the opportunity offered by what was, in effect, a windfall, and commandeer entire districts for a new style of urbanity. Soho, North Beach, Faneuil Hall, and dozens of lesser known districts in lesser known U.S. cities, became centers for a style of hip capitalism which mixed art, commerce, entertainment, and domesticity to create urban entities with new names like Tribecca, NoHo, and Bergamot Station.

That these last great swirls of relocation are simply the latest in the habitual turnover of urban centers, grants validity to the thesis that growth and definition are functions of accommodation to lifestyle, rather than the developer's hope to build generic space, then fill it with a vaguely defined constituency.

In fact, if one is unfortunate enough to live in the most contemporary section of most cities, it might seem as though nothing has yet taken root. And, although it is tempting to think of this alienation as a "modern" phenomenon, it must have been prevalent in each new section of cities that after a time we find charming, quaint, or even funky. After all, shopkeepers who are nervous with the risk that comes of being "first on the block" and landlords overly scrupulous in their choice of four-star tenants may ultimately guarantee repayment of the financing, but bring little to the district but a retread of an already threadbare franchise.

The risk which could bring vitality and excitement to urban life, the very *unpredictability* of use and custom, is therefore seen to be in short supply in newly constructed centers. Moreover, the need to obtain capital, reassure potential tenants as well as users, and placate civic authorities, conspires to eliminate *identity and difference* even if it were to be actively pursued.

That vitality, both in the past and the present, has come with changes which destabilize the patterns of use for which the environment was first created. The hip photographer in Michelangelo Antonioni's film *Blow Up* maintains a mod shooting studio over a former stable in '60s London for just the same reason the artists in La *Bohème* occupy a garret in nineteenth-century Paris, or the specialist in *arbitrage* occupies a loft in the film *9 ½ Weeks*. Because there is untapped potential.

These places resonate with different lives, creating nooks and crannies for spinsters, and skinheads, and scavengers. Within the continuum of change, it is possible to find aberrations, anomalies, and inconsistencies—the sutures of alleyways and industrial lots, like scar tissue drawn over the wounds of expansion. Here too are the immaculate estates of merchant builders, and the converted dwellings of "urban homesteaders," simmering in a stew of no man's land and dead-end streets.

It is these "cities," the ones neglected by planners and reviled by architects, that we find the most interesting. In these fragments of the "city beautiful" we find places of refuge, difference, and identity. These are the cities of Dostoevsky, of Victor Hugo, of Henry Miller. Cities in which life overflows the boundaries of streets, plazas, and rooms to become a runaway stream of intrigue and assignation. A city where things happen by chance, by design, by manipulation, by deceit, by coercion. But they happen.

If anything is true in the American city of the future, it's that the streetscape is on its way to a wild mix of Barnum and Bailey, roadside adventure, and treasure hunt. Some of it is already staked out. Shopping centers which mix Euro-kitsch with vague replicas of forgotten hilltowns emphasize the hunt, and toy with an urban landscape which merges the best features of an efficient mall with those of a hill town somewhere in Tuscany. People love it.

They love to get out of their cars, trek through the garage and *violà*, enter a realm apart from their everyday. Commodities one can obtain from the catalog. Sundries come all at once from a trip to the supermarket-cum-pharmacy-cum-auto parts store-cum-flowershop-cum-charcuterie.

We must talk about these things because it is critical if our society is to address the onslaught of population, energy requirement, and dwindling resources. We need to develop a holistic attitude towards the design and configuration of cities, the buildings which make them up, and the manner in which people use them. We need to develop a thoughtful awareness of what may be appropriate long-term resolution of the kinds of territorial conflicts which often occur between neighborhoods and users – some reasonable and hopefully non-politicized way to balance the equation and establish criteria to govern form and growth.

So this is not an argument about style *per se*. It is not an argument about power. It is, rather, a plea for knowledge. It is a plea for the wisdom to be able to participate in a meaningful way in discussions about development.

Are we, as architects, to become the guardians of an arcane tradition, and define our role in the evolution of the new city as necessary but limited providers of hardware? Is our role to be circumscribed by those few remaining stable building types with "architectural" meaning? Or are architects to redefine their role to give definition to an intangible urban vision?

A new fabric of visible social priorities has imposed a complex, often obstinate network of "clients" in a system structured only to deliver well-crafted buildings for well-defined goals. What are architects to do in an industrialized society in which "making" is a largely autonomous function of manufacturing processes far removed from the building process?

Surely there is a calling higher than that of artful configuration, higher still than that of skillful assembly, (although Buckminster Fuller observed that the architect of the future would function as a purchasing agent). What we as architects "make" is increasingly a network of decisions which attempt to optimize highly defined constraints. Very often, in fact, architects expend the majority of conceptual effort on the "solution" to the puzzling, mostly fractal outlines of the project in all its aspects, then skate through the "technical" problems of specification and construction. In short, the potential exists for a redefinition of the craft of making architecture to the craft of making experience itself.

In *La città pulpa*, we have suggested that coming revolutions in lifestyle, communications, education, and construction technology will create a need for specific enclaves defined by the affinities of their inhabitants, rather than the practicalities of adjacency, or the logistics of supply and demand.

Such a city will have an unprecedented variety in building type, street pattern, behavior, and expectation. It will have the idiosyncrasies of texture and event associated with cinema and literature, rather than the predictability of classical urban structures. Synthesized from a palette of unrealized expectations and the rise of new business models, *La città pulpa* is a city in which specialized enclaves encourage inhabitants who share values and goals to live close together regardless of income and maturity.

The new city. A city of *identity and difference*. A city where the vagaries of consumption and production no longer define the neighborhood. A city in which people and their differences carve out a unique place for one another.

Look at where we live now. It's as though an ironic game had been played by a master manipulator. We do not know our neighbors, and if we do its only to nod and complain. They don't know where we work, what we do, how we do it. It's enough to them that we keep the grass neatly trimmed, that our children are polite, our auto well kept.

But the computer has changed all that forever. Just cruise the internet.

They say it's no longer necessary to trudge back and forth to a job in a "business" quarter of the city. No longer necessary to manufacture endless rolls of paper for the morning newspaper, no longer necessary to create huge buildings for the clerks and managers who answer the phones and keep the books. No longer necessary to build the desks and files and elevators. No longer necessary to build the subways and superhighways. Except from habit. Or for pleasure.

Technically, the city was constructed for a pragmatic purpose. It was for defense, or trade, or some other function, yet we found pleasure in it. Likewise, the office building was brought about by the corporate need for record keeping, but we found pleasure in it, and created our cities around it. And of course the highway is necessary for the transportation of goods, but piloting an open car with the wind blowing in our hair is full of pleasure. And although the worker next to us on the assembly line may live a life we cannot understand, we may yet find pleasure in his company.

In all of these things it is the users who have brought life and joy to the functional structures that make up our cities.

The modern city, purpose built, a nearly pure diagram of efficiency, has little in common with its medieval antecedents. The arc of freeway interchanges and the endless grids of access are as rational as any industrial product. Our address books can pin point a location in an instant. We can graph it and document it. It is, given its millions of inhabitants, surprisingly knowable.

And yet, compared with its medieval counterpart, this modern city is a divider of people. It is a device better suited to the transactions of business than those of individuals. In its single-minded devotion to purpose, it has come to fulfill expectations of plenty, but few of quality.

La città pulpa suggests a new structure for the modern city. One that supports identity and difference in place of *role and counterpart*. Such a city, in its street patterns, its mix of typology, and its communications, will provide the *mise-en-scène* for the evolution of culture since the Internet.

There are already examples of tendencies which suggest that such a city may already be evolving within the form of a modern city like Los Angeles. Cities within the city are, unlike the ghettos of the past, centers of culture which attract those from other, different centers, in a continuous exchange of energy. These districts—West Hollywood, Sunset Strip, and Venice Beach—often have a vivid lifestyle that sets them apart, even alienates them, from the city proper, yet encourages the realization of individual fantasies, creativity, and goals. SOHO, NOHO, SOMA, King's Row, the Haight, the French Quarter, Silicon Valley, Taos, Space City, Montmartre, Roppongi, and Madison Avenue were staked out by a generation hungry for identity in cities which had no place for them. Harlem was such a place in the '30s; Venice in the '20s; and The Montmartre in the gay '90s.

The list is endless, and mostly made up of bohemian quarters, artist's enclaves, and entertainment districts; but let us image a city in which everyone (not just artists and social outcasts) "travels light." Let us imagine a city in which the present factors dictating *location*, the telephone wires leading to one's desk, the presence of water and power, the presence of services and information, and *even the ability to get there at all*, were to be replaced with factors such as proximity to those with similar lifestyles, or great food, or lots of sun, or great night-life! What if the factors that defined a district were not housing, offices, factories, and shops, but something far more complex and subtle, which could only exist now, with the help of our new technologies?

What if the conventions of modernism were replaced with the transcendent linkages of improvisations and communication? What if the unmoving mass of architectural form were to shape *identity and difference* rather than utility and purpose?

Part III
Predecessors, peers, and protégés

019.1
James Stirling on site at the construction of the Cambridge University, c. 1967.

Inside James Stirling

DESIGN QUARTERLY 100 (1976)

Originally written as part of a full issue of *Design Quarterly* edited
by Hodgetts and devoted to the work of James Stirling, this
essay chronicles the triumph of the personal over the routine in
Stirling's work. In it, Hodgetts adopts a personal tone and focuses
on the sensual, even erotic aspects of Stirling's architecture.
Throughout, Hodgetts draws significant distinctions between
Stirling and his contemporaries, as in the distance he establishes
between the (romantic) Brutalists, who in his view repeated
the mistakes of the interwar masters, and Stirling, who found
in mechanical pragmatism and vulgar efficiency a way forward.
Mechanical metaphors abound, as does a general celebration
of straightforward mechanical elements assembled to achieve
a unity not through compositional control but rather via a
coherence that emerges in their functional interaction.
In addition to this text, Hodgetts produced a series of photo-
collages and a cut-out model kit which ran in the magazine.
These are included here on pp. 162–169.

James Stirling's work—inventive, prolific, and controversial—is judged by most critics to be instrumental in extending the interpretation of the principles variously known as form follows function and International Style; yet, to the general public, his buildings are disorderly examples of an arrogant idiosyncrasy which ought to be checked. Some critics are so impressed by his audacity that they evaluate each project not on its merits, but on its value as a polemic device in the continual jockeying for position characteristic of modern architectural criticism. A close look at the buildings themselves suggests still another evaluation.

The meticulous care Stirling brings to the making of architecture may not be necessary in theory, but the results are clearly worth the painstaking effort. Like a film director, Stirling refuses to relinquish control over the often tedious aspects of building in order to indulge an intellectual priority. His buildings rarely if ever need a defensive explanation about the nature of industry or the impossibility of union labor.

In spite of the technical virtuosity of each project, Stirling's sensibility remains uniquely personal in a context made increasingly systematic and routine. One of his early projects, a cluster of apartment units in a suburb of London, still has a powerful impact which is obviously respected by the tenants, who use the premises as though it were a classic automobile, given them for safekeeping. Like an automobile, the building is clearly an object which exists to be used and would suffer greatly from an over-protective stewardship that might throttle the vigorous life the building now contains.

Stirling achieved his characteristic work in the execution, with James Gowan, of an engineering laboratory for Leicester University, in 1959 [019.2]. Here, with the almost simultaneous appearance of Louis Kahn's Richards Laboratories at the University of Pennsylvania, and Paul Rudolph's Art and Architecture Building at Yale, the confrontation of classic functional architecture and romantic formal architecture became a central issue. Unlike past masters of the modern movement, Stirling and Gowan made no attempt to rationalize the intentionally harsh functional arrangement of their design with easily digestible images of ocean liners or rational geometries of squares and cubes. Neither did they create spectacular spatial effects, as did Rudolph, or quasi-metaphysical geometric patterns, as did Kahn. Instead, they clung stubbornly to the roots of traditional English building technology to design a structure reminiscent of the anonymous nineteenth-century engineer-inventors.

I first became aware of Leicester in 1964, while the shock waves of Kennedy's death were mingling with the growing anger of students and new tunes from the British Isles. It had the impact of a high-speed auto collision, the seductive

019.2
Stirling and Gowan, Leicester University Engineering Building, 1959. View of the entry.

raunchiness of one of Fellini's sirens, the glow of moonlight on the Mississippi, the revolutionary glint of *Borstal Boy*, the semantic craziness of *Alice in Wonderland*. It was an assault, a caress, a loony grin, a puckish swagger, a hot rod. It yawed up through the trees against the pea-gray sky above that English campus like a mechanical hobgoblin: gritty, not clean; dockside, not nautical; sincere, not cerebral.

One could almost hear it clank.

Like English motorcycles and automobiles, the building is organized as a visible collection of discrete functional parts assembled to a chassis and linked together with weatherproof fairings. Auditorium, lecture hall, offices, and laboratories assume the correct position without compromising either shape or function. Instead of an ad hoc arrangement of rooms and utilities concealed in a standard building form, the shape and arrangement of the rooms themselves, with the joinery and structural support occasioned by their position in space, creates the architecture. Thus, while approaching the building one can appreciate the individual components of the structure much as one might enjoy identifying the parts of a steam locomotive.

A vast, serrated glass roof, cranked forty-five degrees off the rectangular walls below, admits light to the testing laboratory.

A chambered, glazed tower, reminiscent of Wright's tower at Johnson Wax, effectively isolates faculty offices from noise and traffic generated by the laboratory and affords views to the surrounding campus.

Two wedge-shaped auditoria are positioned at the base of the office tower to provide immediate access from both campus and laboratory wing while curtailing through traffic.

A tower with special no-draft windows, immediately accessible from each floor of the office tower, houses small teaching labs. Unlike Kahn's similar arrangement at the University of Pennsylvania, however, Stirling and Gowan make a powerful distinction between "office" fenestration and "laboratory" fenestration. The graphic unity of the building is destroyed in order to answer a utilitarian bias.

*

James Stirling grew up and studied architecture in Liverpool, a city much like Detroit. It is a manufacturing, not an intellectual, center. Pragmatic, no nonsense, getting the job done, industrial centers like Liverpool sported concentrations of military designers during World War II, whose designs for radar huts and cockpits were controlled by human factors, such as angle of view, reach and accessibility. Henry Dreyfuss pioneered that methodology in the USA, but the architects who were his contemporaries—Eero Saarinen, Kevin Roche, et al.—were apparently unable to visualize an architecture in those terms.

It remained for Stirling to return from service as a paratrooper and discover that the design of buildings, like the design of war machinery, might be generated exclusively by urgent organizational priorities. That point of view—always blunt, and infuriatingly alienated—has allowed his work to develop in a framework uncluttered by architectural precedents. That is, unlike the majority of architects who share "cultivated" backgrounds that tend to reinforce "normal" design decisions, Stirling does not need a stylistic or intellectual justification for the "complexity and contradiction" implicit in each of his designs. He is simply unwilling to court the support of historians and critics at the expense of the built form.

*

We had just watched the long tambour wall at Stirling's Olivetti Training Center coil tightly around the spindle on which it is stored. Everything worked without a hitch. "I suppose you've got to have people like Stirling and Le Corbusier," said Brian Bagnall, now president of Concrete Limited and formerly student at Liverpool with Stirling, "but you've got to be careful what you let them do."

*

In the early '60s, painters like Richard Hamilton and Allen Jones showed work filled with industrial artifacts posing as sensual, threatening, or erotic companions. Nudes and housewives were surrounded by toasters, white porcelain refrigerators, and black-tipped bumper guards which were all accorded equal pictorial focus. The objects, in fact, ceased to be "backgrounds" in the classical sense. Instead, fully autonomous, they competed fiercely for space with their suddenly static human companions.

The ascendency of the object was a natural follow up to the "Kitchen Sink" of the '50s, when angry young Teddys and Rockers were portrayed by writers like Osborne as operators in the generally mean and deteriorating environment left over from World War II. When the burgeoning clockwork finally brings forth the streamlined Jaguars, chromed toasters, and Hoovers which had such an impact on English life, Harold Pinter devotes nearly an act of *The Caretaker* to a malevolent vacuum cleaner:

> (Suddenly the electrolux starts to hum. A figure moves with it, guiding it. The nozzle moves along the floor after Davies, who skips, dives away from it and falls, breathlessly.) Ah, ah, ah, ah, ah, ah! Get away-y-y-y-y! (The electrolux stops.)

In a similar way, one has the feeling that Stirling's best buildings are somehow sentient. That they are able to feel footsteps, hands on rails, the throw of switches. There is an exhilarating series of revelations about the buildings them-selves within a strict vocabulary that is voluptuous, yet pragmatic—finished, yet raw and revealing.

Many of these conventions had their origins in Pop Art. Just as Lichtenstein or Hamilton might appropriate a frame from Krazy Komix, tune it up and slot it into an arts context, Stirling, with insight worthy of Duchamp, has substituted off-the-shelf blowers, vents and maintenance equipment for painting and sculpture. The substitutions are not those of a teacher, who is anxious that we understand what makes the building work, or of a neo-Calvinist, who is persuaded that we must learn to admit contradictory elements into an otherwise homogeneous context. Rather, Stirling's dramatic instinct employs these objects as a rhythmic punctua-tion of otherwise ordinary architectural events.

Stirling's work, like that of Charles Moore, camouflages outrageous formal and cultural configurations by bracketing all of these issues in a simple, often conservative building vocabulary. At Leicester, Cambridge, and Oxford, the visitor encounters glass and red tile surfaces supported by exposed concrete; at Runcorn and St. Andrews a robust precast concrete; at Olivetti Training Center, glass and fiberglass. In theory, this is like a newspaper that manipulates a single system with a few simple rules, similar to those that govern tile, to spell out messages ranging from routine to urgent. Moreover, the "content" of the newspaper does not infect either the integrity of the type or the quality of the object any more than the config-uration of Stirling's buildings affects our fascination with the pattern of tiles or the quality of the surface they provide. Like erogenous zones, these surfaces invite admiring glances, sustained contact, manipulation.

The turbines at the apex of the reading room at Cambridge, seen sugges-tively through a chenille-like layer of frosted glass from the reading room below, are privately bared through a small clear light on the balcony above. A tumescent vent at Oxford rises from a stepped mound swinging a green tassel from its tip. The central column descends from its sheath at Haslemere as the window washer spreads cyclically along the length of the link.

Stirling did have some models around. Butterfield, from nineteenth-century England; Le Corbusier, especially in work like the Philips Pavilion and later Brut work, like Maison Jaoul; and John Soane, the English eccentric who was finally knighted by William III. But the profane in architecture was essentially uncharted territory. Eric Mendelsohn had taken a whack at it with the Einstein Tower in Potsdam, and a few Russians had proposed things about the time of Potemkin, but a really profane architecture had only been a vague suggestion by the time Stirling took to the boards with partner Gowan to outline the labs at Leicester.

It's possible even they didn't know where it was going to end, but there was a stir in the consciousness of pop-fad London when Stirling and Gowan stuck a cast iron plumbing joint on the wall of a building. The joint was a WC mounting elbow, which, in England, was not only indiscreet, it was baffling. Even conservative critics were intrigued by the boldness of the gesture, however, and linked Stirling and Gowan to the Brutalists which, of course, missed the whole point.

I prefer to think that quite early in his career Stirling placed his confidence, not in the codified world of architectural theory—a reference even for the Brutalists—but in the vulgar authority of objects functioning well in their place that we call the real world. Recognizing that the source of that authority was not in the form itself, but in the total dedication of a singular form to a singular function (not in itself a revolutionary attitude), Stirling saw the strenuous complexity of even a simple function as a generator of form. The standard designer's injunction, "form follows function," which has generated nearly three-fourths of a century of our architecture, has been operating on the premise that the only measurable requirements are quantitative and static. These Teutonic qualities discriminate, to be sure, but only between acceptable modes: one does not make love in the living room, therefore, one need provide privacy only in the bedroom.

Stirling's work allows more complex realities to exist. Thus, what came to characterize his work was not the intolerant nineteenth-century "honesty" that governed the work of others—in itself a still unchallenged legacy of the Bauhaus—but a tolerant formal consciousness which, coupled with a healthy regard for utility, produced genuine inventions.

The Brutalists would cast some concrete against some rough boards and explain, in a scene right out of *Catch 22*, that they despised romance, but it was the only honest thing to do, and still believe they had preserved their functionalist credentials. But Stirling and Gowan went the other way. They made their buildings more refined, more complex, more accommodating, until the organization and detail had the quality, not of a Braque, for God's sake, but of Picabia, of Bugatti, of Wernher von Braun.

*

Katrin had a new watch [019.3]. It sat on a perforated plastic band that nearly matched her vinyl Courrèges boots. It was 1967, the USA had not yet gone to the moon, the students at Yale had not yet set fire to the Art and Architecture Building, and pocket calculators were five years away. But Katrin, who worked with Warren

019.3
Bulova Accutron Spaceview wristwatch. 1967.

Platner over at Saarinen's, and hung out with Jim's friend Keith, had discovered an electronic watch, run by batteries, tiny copper coils, and a tuning fork, that sang if you held it up to an ear. Jim tried it on right away, remarking on the anodized green framework which you could see behind the hands. "Too bad buildings aren't like that," he muttered, and drove out to get a watch like it. But since it was Sunday, the best he could do was locate one with a flashlight in a shop window sometime after midnight, after an odyssey of A & W's, Safeways, police lieutenants, shopping malls, and icy telephone booths.

The next morning he was there when the door opened.

*

Accuracy has engineering value. It is measurable. It is ruthless and objective. It tracks down requirements like a computer, and follows measurements like a micrometer. Concepts like unity, composition, and tradition are inherently *inaccurate* except as sophisticated symbols of good breeding. From that point of view, the object-icons that Richard Hamilton and the Independent Group were painting and writing about had no pedigree at all, so why did a building need one?

After all, those great ships that haunted the eye of Le Corbusier, and still haunt the Eastern seaboard, for instance, were unified because their design had to be capable of resisting wind and sea. But fragmented, styled up, and installed on the beach on Long Island, those dreadnaughts are simply reminders, bookmarks, really. Looked at this way, the Brutalists were trapped in an intellectual *cul-de-sac*. They would not refute the principles that underlay their work—Stirling had not even done that—but they made the mistake of assuming that the founding fathers had *correctly translated those principles to architecture*. Their own work, extruded along the guidelines laid down by Gropius, Mies, and Corbu, inevitably repeated all the errors inherent in the original die block.

What became clear at Leicester and later at Cambridge was that the resources available to modern building were diverse enough to make polymorphous accommodation practical in engineering terms. That the engineering limitations which may in the past have dictated a purebred solution with heavy dependence on a single material or a single means of fabrication were in fact only strategic limitations.

The best way to understand the History Faculty Building at Cambridge is to climb one of the stairs at either end of the V formed by the office block. After giving the Day-Glo orange handrail one last, affectionate pat, the cascading surface of the skylight dominates the view. One could inch along this corridor as though it were a plank bridge above a waterfall if it were not for the feel of the pipe rail clamped to the mullions, and the birch partitions opposite, which seem as secure as compartments on an excursion vessel. A few doors down the corridor, the windows narrow as the rake of the skylight cuts diagonally along the outer wall, then opens dramatically to frame glimpses of the mechanisms and structure within. It is like leafing through the illustrations in Andreas Vesalius's sixteenth-century treatise on anatomy, as first the skin, then the vessels, and finally the muscular tissue itself are magically peeled away to expose the viscera. In a gesture more cinematic than architectural, the roof completes its transit and a gallery of windows bulges outward into the void of the reading room as into an aquarium, enabling the visitor, now encased in a protective capsule, to observe the strange life of the scholars below [019.4].

There are five layers of these gallery/corridors, each different from the one below, owing to the diminishing space below the skylight. They terminate at grade in a circumferential arrangement of library stacks, and at the top in a cluster of three air extraction devices, each as large as a Corvette, painted red, yellow, and blue. Thus, the roof itself is the organizing device for a near miraculous transition

019.4
Stirling and Wilford, Cambridge History Faculty Library, 1968. View of reading room.

from the domain of machines to the domain of knowledge with a commensurate discipline and insight devoted to each.

The building vocabulary employed so successfully at Leicester is extended at Cambridge, leading the visitor over and around the building, into otherwise prohibited areas, on tiles defined by close diagonal ribs and a gently depressed gutter. The subtle reinforcement of the plasticity of the surface, much as it had at Leicester, enables Stirling to treat walls, glazing, and accessories as separate elements. A vocabulary, consisting of specifically unrelated parts until, placed within operating range of one another, like a critical mass, they cohere. Seen through a scrim of surrounding trees the building has a surprisingly modest scale. Reddish brick planes tug gently at memories of Victorian buttresses, the glassy enclosures are reminiscent of railroad sheds, the assembly of tubular steel is indeed something like rocket scaffolds. All these evocations flicker persuasively over the surface of the building. Yet the overall effect is that of simple technologic authority, finally domesticated and comprehensible, placed as comfortably as a Hoover on a shag rug.

*

After a show at The Museum of Modern Art, a large color transparency of the building at Cambridge had been installed gloriously, if incongruously, on the ground floor of the Stirling office. When important visitors were expected, Jim would darken the hallway, plug the thing in, and wait for the gasps of appreciation as they rounded the last landing of the stairs.

One such morning a new American member of the staff, whom Jim had found at the the American Academy in Rome, was standing before the transparency as I came down the stairs.

"What do you suppose governed the arrangement of the overlooks?" he asked me.

"He probably just put them wherever he could," I replied.

"What, you mean there was no system? I don't believe it. Look how carefully it is detailed!"

I agreed that it was a marvelously crafted space, and was attempting to convince him that there was no causal connection between craft and geometry when Stirling appeared on the landing.

The young man looked at him seriously and asked what governed the arrangement of the overlooks.

"Nothing," said Jim.

*

So Stirling, amused by the scramble to identify the precedent of this or that, stead-fastly refuses to burp up the secret. Yet, on occasion, there are clues—a note in his "big book" scribbled over the exhausts on the dormitory at St. Andrews says: "These are not guns, Charlie," to Charles Jencks, whose long semiotic analysis, to the bemused Stirling, had missed the point completely. The old infantry song is closer:

This is my rifle
This is my gun,
This one's for fightin'
This one's for fun.

For Stirling, dune buggies, hot pants, and low riders are themselves symbols of a largely scatological reality. It is not his intention to sublimate the erotic energy of his work in a "hot" passage of chromium and plastic as Hans Hollein might, or to invoke the fetish quality made popular by highly finished work characteristic of California artists like McCracken and Kauffman. The intentional vulgarities of the buildings at Leicester and Cambridge celebrate a Rabelaisian consciousness. Like Oldenburg in his Ray Gun days, Stirling searches out the crude, the offensive, the profane as alternatives to the International Style. His direct use of materials is a metaphor for a consciousness impatient with the constraints of modern architecture.

Digging through the archives at the Stirling office, I came upon the original copy of his 1950 student thesis—a community center [019.5]. Stylistically, it falls somewhere between Leslie Martin's Royal Festival Hall and Le Corbusier's Marseilles block. Both had set powerful directions for European architecture at that time. But, he doesn't let it go at that. There are peculiar, pointed exceptions to the prototypes.

Like Marseilles, Stirling's thesis includes a roof garden with mechanical equipment designed to function as roof furniture. But he rips off the sculptural disguise adopted by Le Corbusier, and fantasizes about the dynamic qualities of the exhaust stack, positioning his by now characteristic wind vane atop the building and strutting out the whole affair with guy wires like the equipment it is, rather than treating it as an abstract sculptural form.

The building is also on *pilotis*, like Marseilles, but the planning reasserts connections to the ground in a manner Le Corbusier strenuously avoided, by the creation of a lounge-coffee shop at the interface.

Why the *pilotis*? In an elaborate analysis, Stirling demonstrates the economic

EAST ELEVATION

019.5
James Stirling, Community Center for Newton Aycliffe, Thesis project
at the University of Liverpool School of Architecture, 1950. Elevation.

advantage of *pilotis* over columns and, in a sublime political gesture, concludes that he must suffer their effect upon the design, which in turn forces heroic measures to rescue the continuity of the plaza.

Finally, like the Festival Hall, there is a sense of veneer, of the building as a thin container. But where Festival Hall's formal composition is gratuitous and ingratiating, the community center becomes airplane-like with cross-braced wires and modular panels emphasizing the structural rigor of the design. No concessions whatever are made to the paunchy conventions of "civilized" postwar Britain. It is, over all, an abrupt, rhetorical reply to the signal prototypes after the war. It says, "I'm not having any," without so much as a thank you.

The effect of the project on other students at Liverpool was scandalous. They felt his work was disruptive, even immoral. He struck them as having a working method with a remarkable tendency to create untenable, even unworkable premises which threatened the whole profession.

*

In a conversation with Nikolaus Pevsner (Sir Nik, as I came to think of him, champion of English architectural criticism) I approached the subject of Stirling with caution. Frail, gaunt, tall as a tree, Pevsner became increasingly stern as I edged the topic into Brutalism, then popped a question about Stirling. His opinion was on record, he assured me, in countless articles and critiques. Why bother about him? I explained the dialectic as I saw it, that Stirling's architecture was nearly alone in a wasteland of English dilettantes.

"But Stirling is a rude man," he told me, "and the buildings he designs are rude as well."

*

We are standing in the kitchen, Jim and I. I am leaning against a stack of three-legged Aalto stools, which Jim has decided are good for commodity seating—like elegant orange crates.

Mary, his wife, isn't home, but their family friend who edits an English yachting magazine has offered to make some sausages. Jim doesn't cook.

Sir Nikolaus, I told him, had been reluctant to talk at all. Jim nodded. He knew from the batting around he'd gotten in the press that Pevsner would be difficult, even haughty. It had been a curious meeting: Sir Nik had carried the contest triumphantly until he tried to recall a particular comment he'd made about Leicester Labs. "That was the building you said was blue," I said, and he looked at me. His eyes twinkled—they had been lance-like before—and he said, "Oh yes, Jim caught me up on that one, didn't he?" and I allowed that he had. Jim chuckled. "He'd never even seen the building, you know." "Right," I said. "He knew he'd have to come clean with me then. He's a very chivalrous man—almost a real knight. Like Don Quixote." By now Jim was thoroughly engrossed with this distant contact with the mythical Sir Nik. "I wonder if I'm in it?" he said, and opened up Pevsner's *Dictionary of Modern Architecture*.

> They [Stirling's buildings] have a ruthlessness which militates against their achieving a more than passing success.

> "So he thinks I'm ruthless, does he? It says here that Charles Rennie Mackintosh was erratic, not an easy man. Do you think that's superior to ruthless?"

*

It is drizzling lightly on the temporary causeway that links Runcorn Southgate to the shopping city and, in the drizzle, the umbrellas of a single file of house wives weave uneasily. Eventually, the corpi[1] say, this gap will be filled in by an expansion of the city. But for now, one negotiates the quarter mile on a fifty-foot-high steel scaffold, shut in by plywood hoardings to just below eye-level.

Behind us, the closed, jar-colored banality of the shopping city retreats. Ahead, there is only Southgate itself.

Returning from lunch the day before, Stirling had walked me around the nineteenth-century London block in which he maintains his office. He described its organization like that of a machine, eagerly pointing out the service yard a full story below the street level. Here there are doors which give access to storage areas below the street itself to exploit the otherwise dead zone under the public right-of-way. We continued, his conversation dotted with observations about the light, the texture, and the lifestyle accommodated in his neighborhood and I realized that I, like one of those shipwrecked Adventurers rammed by the Nautilus, kidnapped and taken to a utopian undersea world, was in the presence of Captain Nemo himself.

Around the back of the block, the planners had contrived to provide a court behind each house closed in by a smaller carriage house which gave onto a mews for the stables and garbage.

"That's where they filmed *Alfie*," he said, pointing out that the carriage houses have become perfect studios and lofts for artists and designers in these days of the motorcar.

He might have been showing me scenes from *Things to Come*.

The next day we had our first glance at Stirling's version, out the window of a passenger train. From there, the long buildings lay low and parallel like louvers in a valley of grass and trees. Looking ahead to the steaming atmosphere of Liverpool, we could already imagine the formula—one of the constants in England's program of new towns—separated functions, isolated energies, specialized activities. Stirling's response lies ahead now: band on band of concrete, bright-colored plastic, circular openings, ribs, promenades, crossings [019.6].

The girl at the first intersection, chewing gum, listening to Barry White on her wrist radio, puts a hand on her hip. "You're not from around here, are you?"

A Mercedes long-distance bus glides by below. Its windows look up at us. We continue on the wide walkway, past lace curtains and driftwood plaques, past orange and yellow dish towels, mementoes of Covent Garden, soccer trophies, and nodding dachshunds each pressed furtively against the sliding glass windows.

---

1   Corpi is residents' slang for a representative of Runcorn's housing corporation.

An engineer would have liked those windows with their aluminum frames and neoprene gaskets and curved, efficient corners.

"The man who designed it used to design boats," says the girl in the lavender apartment.

Occasionally a door is ajar. A big one for a dwelling, or a small one for the astonishingly efficient waste collection. We stop to watch the crew drop the black polymer bags into a waiting truck. They wave and shout like sailors on the fantail of a liner, and it occurs to me that the nautical atmosphere has less to do with style than with control and efficiency; that our ground economy rarely requires the taut discipline that is normal to life at sea.

We step over the portal into a bright green room right out of Pinter:
I'd have afromosia teak veneer. *The Caretaker*

A younger Malcolm McDowell flashes into the room. There are two stereo speakers; one sits atop a pile of pillows, the other shares the cushion of a Danish modern chair with a pictorial arrangement of brass wire, beads, and velvet.

"I made that," says the lady of the house. "D'you like it?"

We allow that we do, and ask if she painted the place herself. "Naw, that was the corpi did that. They was all painted different when we came. D'you want some tea?"

Exactly what did Stirling have in mind? It's clear from the drawings that there was an intention to create a lifestyle of extraordinary grace and generosity within the constraints of low-income housing. Its repetition is clearly a device adopted from Georgian town houses, rather than the canons of industrialization à la Bauhaus. Its scale refers to the crescents at Bath, or Stirling's own block in London, the terraces and orientation to Atelier 5's terrace housing in Switzerland.

Yet it is sometimes awesome where it should be grand, rigorous where it could be adventurous.

*

"Mr. Stirling polishes these himself—he's very particular you know," and I excuse myself to wander back upstairs, past the little fuzzy birds wedged behind the mirror, past the teddy bear bank on the marble pedestal, past the Lichtenstein and the lithograph of someone removing his braces, to touch that toggle switch and have another look at what Mr. Stirling spends his time polishing.

I had heard about the collection back in the States. It seemed peculiar for an architect of Stirling's character to have a collection of antiques. But then, this is

019.6
Stirling and Wilford, Southgate Estate, Runcorn New Town Housing, 1972–77. Street view.

019.7
The living-dining room of Stirling's home in London, with many examples
of antique furniture he and his wife collected.

019.8
Stirling's desk at his office in London.

England, where the BBC broadcasts daily exhortations on the identification and proper pedigree of domestic items. I begin to understand that as Jim and Mary wedge themselves into matching Corbusier chairs and balance TV dinners on little Aalto stools to watch a parade of experts ho-hum the date on a six-piece sterling service. Even so, it did nothing to prepare me for the audacity of the objects he has chosen [019.7].

There is a brass-bound round table which stands on a fly-cut pedestal in such a way that the profile of the top fits explicitly into the arc of the supports.

There is a pair of wooden chairs so perfectly carved that their smooth shells might have been molded by matched steel dies.

There is a small transparent plastic stool, like a saddle, fitted with a rotating yellow probe.

There is a pair of steel and leather chairs in which the primary function of the elements seems to be to engage the air which surrounds them.

There is a delicate rosewood shell mounted on a rectangular table surprisingly supported by a cross-legged stool, flanked by a pair of gilded sphinxes.

There is an enormous diamond-tufted sofa which dominates one end of the room and was used only once during my three-week visit, to contain Jim as guru in blue shorts during a tense meeting with our publisher.

There is an angry white record player, with holes the size of shotgun shells to indicate the location of speakers.

There is a strong slate-topped desk with absolutely nothing on it.

*

At his office drafting board, Stirling clamps the last inch of a soft pencil. His other hand cups the area he is marking, as it must have in grammar school. His concentration on that fragment of paper is awesome. There is nothing pretty about the emerging drawing; smudged, ragged, it is already an antique to be deciphered. The notes here and there direct attention to a system of construction, or a difference in inflection. The shapes are particular: a column capital, a handrail, the arrangement of glazing.

All fragments [019.8].

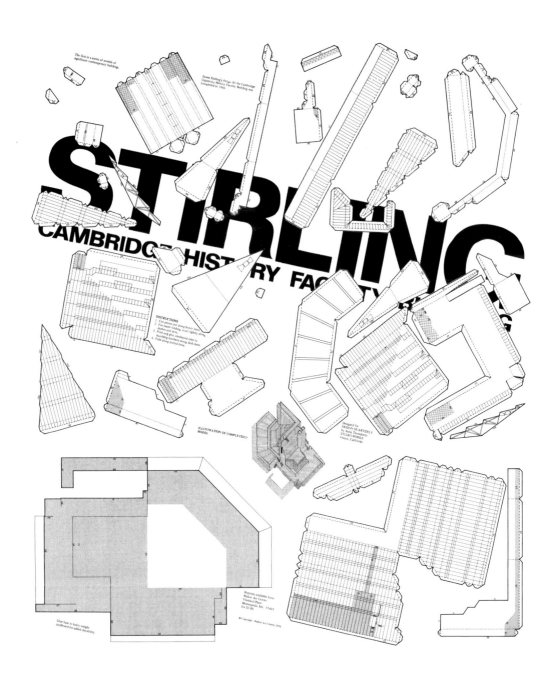

The first in a series of models of significant contemporary buildings.

James Stirling's design for the Cambridge University History Faculty Building was completed in 1968.

STIRLING
CAMBRIDGE HISTORY FACULTY

INSTRUCTIONS
1. Cut pieces out along heavy lines.
2. For easier folding, "score" lightly along dashed and dotted lines.
3. Fold and glue numbered tabs to matching numbers along dash lines.
4. Fold along dotted lines.

ILLUSTRATION OF COMPLETED
MODEL

Designed for
DESIGN QUARTERLY
by Anna Thorsdottir
STUDER WORKS
Venice, California

Reprints available from
Walker Art Center
Vineland Place
Minneapolis, Mn. 55403
for $1.00

© Copyright Walker Art Center 1974

Glue base to heavy-weight
cardboard for added durability

Collages for "Inside James Stirling"

DESIGN QUARTERLY 100 (1976)

In addition to his text, Hodgetts produced an Archigram-esque cut-out model kit of the Cambridge History Faculty Building (opposite), and a series of photo-collages based on Stirling's work (pp. 164–69) which are published here for the first time in color.

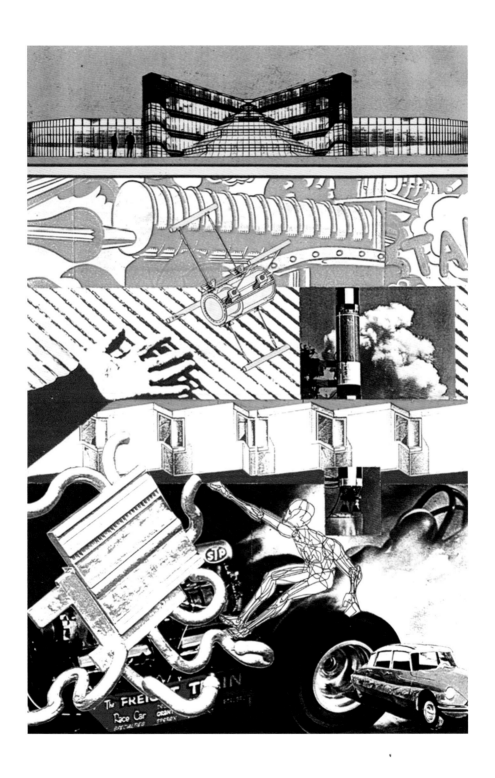

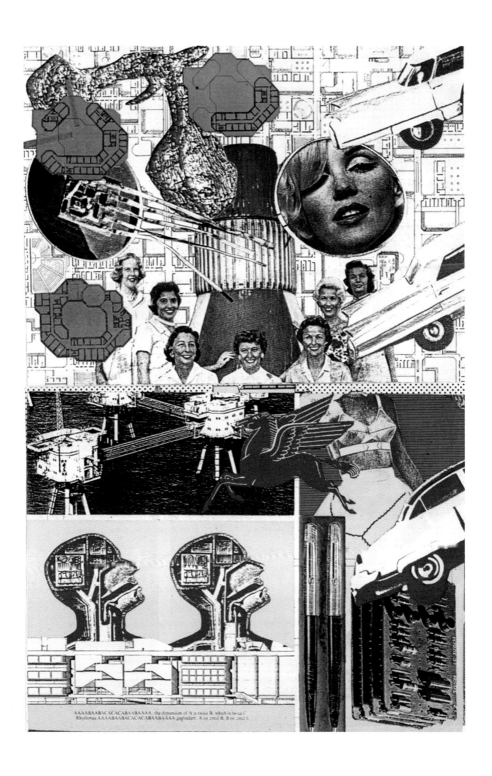

AAAABAABACACACABAABAAAA; the dimension of A is twice B, which is twice C
Rhythmus AAAABAABACACACABAABAAAA gegliedert: A ist 2mal B, B ist 2mal C

020.1
Frank Gehry, Gehry House, Santa Monica, 1977. View of living room.

Hot Stuff*: The House that Frank Gehry Built

C. 1978. PREVIOUSLY UNPUBLISHED.

Hodgetts describes the "pleasant cacophony" of Frank Gehry's house in Santa Monica. The house, in his view, provides carefully crafted echoes of "American life style"—cooking on the driveway, lounging in the attic, etc. He focuses on the familiar freedoms that Gehry has assembled in the house, and how Gehry assembled them out of fragments, in the manner of Robert Rauschenberg. The descriptions echo Hodgetts's earlier assessment of James Stirling (see "Inside James Stirling," pp. 143–161), who also worked productively with fragments.

* a.k.a. ZAP, Krazy Glue, Eastman 910

One suspects that the art of assemblage didn't really begin to gather momentum until the late '50s because until then all of us, mechanics, upholsterers, accountants, and, yes, architects, were struggling with brads and rivets and clips and something called rabbit skin glue, no doubt for good luck, because it was damn near impossible to stick two things together, even in grade school, where that stuff called mucilage was supposed to paste paper together and never did.

But now it's been twenty years since Rauschenberg glued a goat to an automobile tire, and architects still talk about modules and structure and hierarchy just as they did before silicon and epoxy and Elsie the Cow; and even the technically adventurous are just now getting around to pasting glass together.

Nobody knows how long it will take to get around to the goats.

So houses like the one Frank Gehry has built for himself in Santa Monica are usually the work of retired seamen, or widows with endless ruminations, or acid-generation carpenters who just get off on it, man.

Almost never architects.

John Soane might have been the last architect who cultivated such an overtly mnemonic style, or allowed his work to become so obsessively nostalgic. The rest have been throttled by an abstraction so rarified that the stylized grunts and titters of Post Modernism are welcomed as a return to Content.

Even Charles Moore, at first glance the preeminent eclectigarian of our time, has little of the curatorial finesse, or the wry appreciation that might characterize the way Gehry has preserved a tattered shag in one room, or a scrap of particularly evocative wall paper in another.

His house echoes with memorials to the American lifestyle: if one cooks in the driveway it's what used to happen on Saturdays in the summer; if the living room feels like an attic it's probably more fun to be there anyway; if the terraces end in backstops you can at least play catch. And on and on in a seemingly endless recital of refrains and ditties, all carefully preserved within a rather forbidding fortress of glass and corrugated metal which itself is a snapshot of some dynamited auto graveyard between here and there.

Here, being where Frank Gehry lives, and There, being maybe as far East as Kansas City.

A quick turn through the collection of spaces within, then, isn't a great deal different than a drive across the back lot at, say, Paramount Studios, where one finds fragments from every era jostling together in a kind of pleasant cacophony which allows each player to shift moods as easily as we shift locations or, more importantly, to shift locations to suit even transitional moods.

There is the main entrance, which has a certain back stage ennui to disarm you for your main entrance ... a living room dominated by a dialectical wall that seems to propose that plywood, now, equals exposed lath, then ... a teasing passage into the old (new?) part of the new (old?) house and its new (new?) old (old?) fixtures ... iridescent bits of galvanized metal ... a kitchen and dining area inside on the driveway overlooked by what was a bay window ... a cascade of shingles intercepted by slowly repeated square and a few big blue bins ... Alejandro invoking the alphabet from the papal opening ... Alejandro readjusting the cakes at tea ... ground up Wheaties in the blacktop ... Alejandro walking on air ... And outside, splayed two by fours propping up a cactus and a wall.

One can then return, through a greenhouse, up a short stair past a rustic lounging area to the living room, thence upstairs to more wonders like wire glass gutters, inexplicable chain link gargoyles, and a galvanized duct in the shape of a crucifix, touching faded wallpaper and hardened plaster with equal ... tenderness.

021.1
Robert Mangurian and James Turrell, Domaine Clos Pegase winery, 1984. View of model.

All the Ideas

JULIA BROWN, ED., **OCCLUDED FRONT: JAMES TURRELL**
(LOS ANGELES: LAPIS PRESS, 1985): 95–99

Hodgetts assesses Robert Mangurian and James Turrell's
1984 competition entry for the Domaine Clos Pegase
winery competition He carefully describes the then-vogue
"Mediterranean" forms of the scheme but stresses the distance
between Mangurian and Turrell's proposal and contemporary
historicist works by focusing on "the drama of perception" at
the heart of the project. Rather than trade in phony symbolic
associations with historical precedents, the scheme conjures
associations with more ambiguous, archetypal mysteries. Careful
solar alignments highlight the seasonal process of wine-making
and further deepen the experiential quality of the space.

Artist	We've used up all the ideas either one of us will ever have.
Architect	We'll have to find another architect and artist.

With that, Robert Mangurian and James Turrell, architect and artist, playing out their roles, clearly enjoying the moment, completed work on the *Domaine Clos Pegase* competition project.

It had been an exemplary effort from the beginning, when vintner Jan Schrem and his wife were drawn to the singular geometry of a tiny knoll in Napa Valley and decided to establish within its precinct the winery they had envisioned. It was to produce a modest quantity of good wine, drawn partly from their own vineyards and bottled on the estate. The label would be derived from a fine little painting by Redon depicting a flying horse. Thus *Domaine*. Thus *Clos Pegase*, the red blood of Pegasus.

And it was to be more than that. The knoll spoke to Mitzko Schrem of its volcanic origins. Its worn shape suggested eons of rain and heat. They would need a symbolic structure as well as a factory—a residence, some fusion of function and art that would sustain life as well as industry.

When Curator Helene Fried suggested that a collaboration of artist and architect might produce a feasible design, it was against the lackluster history of such liaisons, which never seemed to match the brilliance of that achieved by Rauschenberg and Cunningham, or Stravinsky and Cocteau.

But the time was right. Crossover artists had migrated far from the constraints of their media to invade companion arts. Architects had already begun to plunder the vision of artists engaged in environmental work. The opportunity was ripe to provide a venue capable of spanning the void.[1]

In the proposal offered by Mangurian and Turrell, two main buildings, one a vast hollow factory surrounding a square at the base of the knoll, the other containing a smaller, but still square, residential courtyard surmounting the hill, are united by a jangle of platforms and grottos strewn along their common axis. To the north and south are two other, more conceptual axes, which cross the first at right angles. One, marked by huge portals fronting east and west in the factory square, will accommodate trucks laden with the harvest. The other, a tunnel piercing the hill beneath the residence, is designed to mark the vernal and autumnal equinoxes.

---

1 Thus, in principle at least, the collaborative project by Mangurian and Turrell, shown for the first time at San Francisco's Museum of Modern Art, is a significant prototype. Other projects invited for the competition, by Solomon/Bofill/Dillon/Stauffacher, Solomon/Carpenter, Saitowitz/O'Brian/Levey/Zimmerman, Batey/Mack/Saari, and the winning scheme by Graves/Schmidt covered the spectrum of professional collaboration without the exhilaration of a true duet, while that of Mangurian and Turrell offered a tantalizing glimpse of truly harmonic sensibilities.

There are echoes of Turrell's earlier installations, especially those dealing with architectural space, and flashes of the cryptic geometry typical of Mangurian. But the studies suggest more than the application of geometry and illusion: *Domaine Clos Pegase* sets the stage for collaborating artists to search beyond compatible motifs and decorative flourishes. Had it been built, it would have substantiated an even higher form of collaboration: the quest for shared meaning.

A mutual understanding of the uses of phenomena and gesture informs their work, providing a rare link between context and audience. Within a simple vocabulary of formal alignment and apertures, these devices can focus attention on, in *fact give meaning* to, the surroundings chosen by Mangurian and Turrell. Thus they are able to communicate by understatement, preferring passive, static markers to the formal invention favored by their more bombastic contemporaries—the drama of perception, as in the controlled oscillation of solar rays in the warehouse, to that of architectural gesture.

At the winery, this strategy of invisible instructions is manifest throughout the design, affecting the alignment of the entry road, the orientation of the paving, even the arrangement of ponds for settling out waste. Each element is, moreover, housed in a building of such ordinary (one is tempted to say *primitive*) description that one cannot doubt the functional rigor of the whole. Yet the buildings and their surroundings defy easy definition, seeming to cloak ever more intriguing mysteries within an apparently undistinguished Mediterranean form.

The perfectly square courtyards of the residence and winery have numerous precedents in farms throughout France and Italy. Robust construction and regular lines are evident in both. But Mangurian and Turrell want to unite the sky and the building, and so pare off the cornice to a pure, optically invisible edge rather than duplicating the embellishment normally employed to return our gaze to the building surface. Because of the precise calibration of sight lines between the courtyards, it is then possible to superimpose the cinnabar red wall of the residence on the blue sky plane seemingly stretched between those edges.

Such entertainments, couched in a language simultaneously architectural and sculptural, defy questions of authorship. Where the proposal is most intensely architectural (for instance, in the arcades surrounding the nearly twin courtyards), it is also most subtly artful (as in the choice of a color to enhance the effect of the *Ganzfeld*).[2] Or conversely, where it is most persuasive as a work of art (as in the placement of a horizontal tunnel beneath the house), it is also most memorable

---

2   The *Ganzfeld* is a space in which there is no perception of form due to a homogeneous color field.

as an architectural device, summoning up images of blast tunnels, Jeffersonian bunkers, and the strange, inclined tunnels of pyramids.

Mangurian and Turrell give no practical explanation of its purpose, leaving it to the visitor to discover what is going on. But it does have a purpose, which becomes more evident each day, as the earth keeps ticking on its orbit like the hand on a clock until, incredibly, light from the rising sun rushes up the inclined floor of the tunnel, contacts a prism stationed at the crossing, deflects skyward, then scatters through exotic metal halide filters to project a fleeting corona on the floor of a small, intensely geometric space positioned directly above, within the house. This room is known, without a trace of irony, as the Sun Room—which it immediately ceases to be until the earth comes around once more, and the instrument again registers an impulse.

Heron of Alexandria conjured up similar spectacles for the temple-goers of his own time, devising trumpets that sounded at the opening of a ceremonial door and a mechanism which opened the temple doors in "spiritual" response to a sacrificial fire on the altar.[3] His motive power, described in *Pneumatica*, was that of air, the "earth's breath," and like Mangurian and Turrell, his aim was less the productive use of his various inventions than their remarkable effect upon his audience.

Resonance, not regulation, is the ticket. Mangurian and Turrell have perfected the aesthetics of the tweak, funneling the forces of cosmic order through minimal devices to maximum effect. Gravity, light, space, and time have been assembled as though they were themselves architectural elements, and it is their composition, not that of stone and glass and steel, which we perceive as art.

The various axes which terminate in a sister volcano across the valley, the equatorial position of the sun, and the *Nebula Pegase*—each primeval fix indicates that Mangurian and Turrell were trying to fine-tune the buildings, the vineyards, and the harvest to the spiritual and mechanical resonance of the seasons; trying to use that congruence to leap into the metaphysics of viticulture and create a winery dedicated not to the cliché-ridden "Good Life" to be imagined every time we pull a cork, but to the poetic realities of time, nature, and enterprise exemplified by the process itself. So, the image will not, indeed *cannot*, decorate a label or be captured in the most intricate TV spot.

---

3   Heron describes his inventions in remarkable detail, as the following text will reveal: "Let the temple stand on a pedestal, on which lies a small altar. Through the altar insert a tube with its mouth inside the altar and the mouth contained in a globe below, reaching nearly to its center. The tube must be soldered into the globe, in which a bent siphon is placed. Let the door-hinges be extended downwards and turn freely on pivots: and from the hinges let two chains, running into one, be attached by means of a pulley to a hollow vessel, which is suspended—while other chains ... are attached by means of a pulley to a leaden weight, on the descent of which the door will be shut." From Jack Lindsay, *Blast-power and Ballistics* (New York: Harper & Row, 1974): 332.

It must be experienced.

However, wine-making is a business. It is a good business, with a lengthy pedigree and near-institutional status. It is even possible, given a good year or superb craftsmanship, to bottle a wine of exceptional quality. But the *mythos* of the wine-maker neither requires nor deserves the pious tone implicit in much of Mangurian and Turrell's design. One can understand their need to invest the complex with enduring values, and they have; but aren't there other values, equally persuasive, in the American imagery of farms and warehouses? After all, Northern California is a long way from Europe; and stainless steel, refrigeration, and spectral analysis have transformed beyond recognition the processes housed in traditional buildings.

So what motivated Mangurian and Turrell's choice of imagery? The answer is in their work, in the obsession with abstract qualities of light and space which formed the basis for their collaboration.

Like Malevich, who sought to transcend the bonds of referential imagery, Mangurian and Turrell have attempted to create an architecture of pure geometric simplification. By banishing symbolic elements and concentrating on technical means to achieve geometric purity, they have divested their buildings of associative imagery and achieved a vocabulary of self-contained, harmonic experiences.

"An ineffable sensation," says Melinda Wortz, "much like that sought in transcendental philosophy ... the dissolution of opposites like figure and ground can be seen as a precise correlate for mystical states."[4] This weaving in, eliminating the edge between wall and universe, function and art, has much to do with Islamic tradition, wherein the space demands to be seen as a whole. Explicit devices like cornices, moldings, or capitals are replaced by contextual, visually ambiguous motifs which function to eradicate, rather than elaborate, the syntax of construction.

As architectural substance is removed, to be replaced by invisible sutures, the alchemical translations of enclosure, from stone to water to air, form spatial vessels unlike any we've experienced. Its totality delivers the message (rather than an emblem which denotes it) so that, like the music of Terry Riley and Philip Glass, melody is abandoned leaving the undefined rhythmic chant: the rhythm of the arcade or, as Louis Kahn has said, the rhythm of "Light, no light, light, no light ..."[5]

In the system of architecture currently in vogue, the message is represented in the work. If the architect wishes to express elegance, let her show something

4   Melinda Wortz, "Architects of Emptiness," in *Architectural Sculpture* 30 (Los Angeles: Los Angeles Institute of Contemporary Art, 1980): 37.
5   Louis I. Kahn, "Space and the Inspirations." *L'architecture d'aujourd'hui* (February–March, 1969): 15.

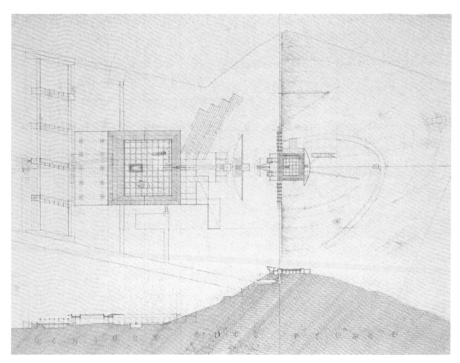

021.2
Robert Mangurian and James Turrell, Domaine Clos Pegase winery, 1984. Plan and section.

reminiscent of aristocracy; if vulgarity, let her display a billboard. But these messages can only be deciphered by the conscious, *analytical* part of ourselves, rather than the unconscious. Historicism insists that we isolate a corner of the whole, react to its message, proceed to the next, and so on, until we have digested its entirety. Moreover, in its insistence on the literal embodiment of cultural precedent, it presupposes a world of finite dimensions, excluding the realm of the spirit and limiting access to those who share the code.

Thankfully, for Mangurian and Turrell there are no codes, no hidden messages. Yet, far from the foreign abstraction we might expect to encounter, their design provokes a surprisingly visceral response, accessible only by participation. Those stairs, that tangle of platforms and grottos, placed to lead visitors through what might otherwise be a labyrinth of close encounters, have much in common with French landscape architecture, particularly that at Vaux-le-Vicomte and Pontchartrain. There, the unparalleled elegance of Cartesian geometry, organized by André Le Nôtre and his architect-collaborators Louis Le Vau and Jules Hardouin-Mansart, knits a family of fences, statuary, fountains, and moats into a compositional unity much as Turrell and Mangurian unify their assortment of illuminated rain birds, black-pool settling basins, and obsidian stairs.

Both embrace the spaces between objects and people, peppering the terrain with a witty interplay of near and far objects. Both animate reality with virtuoso illusions. Both create harmony between various individual components in order to ensure the perception of the whole.

This could not succeed if Mangurian and Turrell had not interwoven perception on so many levels, with such obvious authority, so as to create a panoply of art experiences within the working principles of the whole. Art is infused throughout the site to create a place where the sky and the stars and the seasons will suffice.

022.1
Charles and Ray Eames, Case Study #9, Pacific Palisades, California, 1949.

Review: *Eames Design: The Work of the Office of Charles and Ray Eames*

AA FILES: ANNALS OF THE ARCHITECTURAL ASSOCIATION 20 (AUTUMN 1990): 108–109

Hodgetts reviews a monograph on Charles and Ray Eames by James Neuhart, Marilyn Neuhart, and Ray Eames, published by Thames and Hudson in 1989. Like Stirling, the Eameses were important influences on Hodgetts, and their multi-disciplinary and distinctly American version of postwar modernism in many ways is more akin to Hodgetts's own architecture than Stirling's work. In them, Hodgetts saw the pursuit not of conceptual purity but rather of creative opportunity. Despite his positive assessment, Hodgetts notices a tension, particularly in the Eameses's late work, between a desire for "intellectual clarity and production quality" and "need for emotional truth" that could descend into folkloristic vernacularism.

Try to capture the magic and it vanishes. Yet that's what we were attempting to do that fine, brave Sunday morning. The fog and the eucalyptus had blurred the regular black grid of the house that Charles and Ray built. The reflections seemed to have reflections—to merge and mirror not only the little group and the whirring Arriflex, but toy train with blade of grass, Turkish pipe with railroad tie, photograph with distant surf. We peered at it as one might assess the configuration of a strange, miracle-laden vessel barely visible on the horizon—laden, we were sure, with treasure.

Ray's voice broke in. She was sorry to interrupt, but thought we might like some coffee. There it was, presented on the tiniest, lightest, wire-framed table, with a perfectly formed strawberry for each person, and cream that poured like it does in the commercials. As we ate, she smiled that radiant smile, and told us about all the great things the younger designers in our town were up to. Then she fretted over the brittle Scotch tape that had been waiting so long for Jack Lenore Larsen, who was supposed to be supplying new curtains.

The house, a major icon of a philosophy of design which attended to human needs with unswerving intelligence and concern, was just turning forty. In Eames's own words, the design would "make no insistent demands for itself, but rather aid as a background for life in work." It seemed almost incidental that, along the way, they were to attempt to apply the technological achievements of the twentieth century to aspects of life as incalculably ancient as seating, storage, and shelter.

There was something in the air as well. Not the pervasive stench of consumerism that pollutes today's design world, but a genuine belief that simplification of the basic artifacts of living—those banal things which hold our socks, our trinkets, our memories, and our families—would allow us to get on with it. Charles and Ray were, after all, humanists who, with Eero Saarinen, Alexander Girard, and the Case Study gang, saw the end of the Second World War as the beginning of an era in which "naïve" American values might finally prevail. They were arguably the first of a species of designer who was capable of achieving the objectives of low cost, long life, and universality, with no sacrifice of intellectual elegance. Yet, until now, there has been a notable absence of discourse on the Eames legacy.

The evolution of their work, from the early kitchen-table experiments with molded plywood, to the final dense overlays of media, text, and chronology that were characteristic of their historical exhibitions, is the subject of this long-awaited volume by John and Marilyn Neuhart. Within its 456 pages can be found a precise accounting of processes and procedures amply documented by the Eameses' own photographs and detailed descriptions by the authors. Humor abounds. A photo of Charles and Ray, spread-eagle and pinned to the ground by the suddenly feral wire frames of a

022.2
Charles and Ray Eames, DCM, molded plywood dining chair
with metal base, 1946. View of the underside.

dozen chairs, or the outline of a very contented cat drawn on the fiberglass shell of a
Plastic Armchair by their friend Saul Steinberg, or the office staff decked out in Froggy
masks which recall nothing so much as the later antics of Big Bird and the Muppets.

There are great behind-the-scenes portraits of strange machines like the
"Kazam! Machine" which electronically bonded the laminations for a Second-
World-War splint, or the mock up for a mechanism to repeatedly demonstrate
the Fibonacci series. And there are ravishing photos lifted straight from the sales
brochures and exhibit ephemera which promoted their work. Accompanying
each, in a format which religiously avoids cross-fertilization, is a short explanation
detailing who, where, and when, only occasionally digressing into anecdote.

There is a strong impression that an exceedingly judicious mind has sorted
out all the material, arranged it into neat piles, and given one a magnifying glass
for good measure. Little apologies for the quality of reproduction, for instance
those quite wonderfully grainy frames blown up from a 16-mm film on toy trains,
suggest not only a rare quest for quality on the part of the authors, but another,
darker, aspect of the Eames persona. In the mature design work of the office,
intellectual clarity and production quality often conflicted with an admittedly
'post-modern' need for emotional truth, forcing the unfortunate surrender of the
'accidental' to folk arts and nature.

With even a superficial survey of the evolution of their work, a puzzling division
emerges between the concise articulation of fiberglass, wire, and rubber which

characterizes their furniture designs, and the data-crunching of sprawling, unwieldy exhibitions like *Franklin and Jefferson*. The chairs, which radically separate structure and anatomical support, permanently redefined the concept of seating. Their use of experimental materials and configurations laid the groundwork for value-engineering, by solving problems of fastening and fabrication on an individual basis. Yet the exhibitions *normalized* events and personalities without so much as the now-famous "rubber shock mount" to articulate their relationship, leaving the spectator to sort out the meaning as best he or she could. In fact, they seemed to adopt a positive resistance to the manipulation of space and scale, which might have enticed a more ordinary designer, and there was such an over-reliance on written text that they were criticized even in their day for being "textbooks on a wall."

Charles himself was a subtle and persuasive photographer, capable of transcending context and scale in the search to discover a truthful—one is tempted to say neutral—appraisal of reality. He was at his best one-on-one. The short films *Toccata for Toy Trains, Tops*, and *Clown Face*, and especially *Powers of Ten*, reveal an uncanny ability to make the exotic familiar and immediate. Each teaches without imposing formal structures or demanding allegiance to fixed values. Each presents a singularity. Each neglects the distractions of reality, in order to neglect nothing about the subject. And each required the invention of dozens of devices, like a halved toy-train parlor car to allow the camera access to the interior, or the "instrument panel" so important to the continuous zoom in *Powers of Ten* (and so like the "window" on my own Mac II, some twenty years later).

It wasn't until the office made the leap to multi-screen slide presentations that the full force of his vision became clear. Liberated from static arrangements, and the economics which forced him to reproduce only the "hero" image, the office startled the world in the IBM pavilion at the New York World's Fair. Images danced from screen to screen, jostled one another, and multiplied. In one glorious leap the language of multimedia design was given the vocabulary which still resonates down Sesame Street and fuels the videos on MTV.

Curiously, one comes away from the Nueharts's book convinced that film, furniture, exhibitions, and multimedia installations were all creative extensions of the Eameses' idealistic version of democracy. Communication, even about process, was inseparable from the work itself. Drawings, photographs, and design motifs were as clearly conscious of the popular mind as a Chevy. Their mystique, if there was one, seemed to emanate from a studio housed comfortably among the warehouses and auto-repair shops of Washington Boulevard, identified only by the number 901. Charles was fond of complaining that the office was not part of the

Los Angeles "design community," yet the alumni of the office—Deborah Sussman, Don Chadwick, Glenn Fleck, Annette Del Zoppo, and the authors themselves—are at the core of it today. Thus it seems fitting that the book itself, like the grid of the Eames house, communicates everything accurately, even handsomely, with a restraint that echoes that of its subjects.

To a cynic, the gridded structure of the house, with its red, white, and blue panels, may bear a troubling resemblance to Old Glory, or even worse, a kind of homespun Mondrian, but I believe the Eameses had a different agenda. From the Tibetan bell positioned over the door, to the moveable rigid fiberglass shades and their teak runners, to exterior panels decorated with photo imagery, the grid is clearly governed by creative opportunity rather than conceptual purity. The Eameses, as Richard Rogers likes to point out, looked awfully "open-ended" from his perch as a student at the AA in the early 1950s, even as their fellow travelers in *Arts and Architecture* magazine came under fire for their left-wing political views.

Charles and Ray, with John Entenza, had helped to found the magazine in the early 1940s. Crammed with urgent editorials on prefabrication and low-cost housing, splendid graphics by Herbert Matter and Ray, and obscure articles on music and the arts, it was a curiously lyrical, polemical, large-format, native California version of the avant-garde, as different from the rituals of its European counterparts as it is from the Neuharts's classicizing format. Yet one can't help thinking that the scrappier graphics, in particular, have gained significantly from the book's excellent paper and printing.

It was a heroic moment, charged with political and social optimism, imbued with a confidence in technology, and helped along by the galloping enthusiasm of a nation comparatively unscathed by the brutal war that had just ended. Hot rods and surfboards made their appearance, along with drive-ins and LPs. Venice, California, became home to the Beats. Kerouac and James Dean parked their hogs within blocks of the office. The same plastics being laid up by hand in the Eameses's shop were touring suburbia at Tupperware parties. Out in the world, Mies was building Seagram, Le Corbusier was building Chandigarh, and Wright was finally getting the Guggenheim off hold.

Back at the Eames house, the cinematographer motions us to inspect the shot he has just composed. We nod. The angle is based upon a 1948 black-and-white print we picked from the archives: there is the stack of decorative pillows, the hide thrown casually over the back of a lounge chair, a scattering of candlesticks, the bowl with foreign coins, the fragment of embroidery, an Eskimo doll, an ivory pipe, a heap of magazines and books. Time hasn't touched a thing.

023.1
John Lautner, Sheets-Goldstein Residence, Los Angeles, 1963–94. View of master bedroom.

Larger than Life: The Architecture of John Lautner

1995. PREVIOUSLY UNPUBLISHED.

Hodgetts penned this admiring portrait of the "cowboy" architect, John Lautner, for an unrealized monograph planned by Wayne N. T. von Fugi. After outlining his early affiliation (and eventual falling out) with Frank Lloyd Wright, Hodgetts goes on to praise the dynamism of Lautner's spaces, the daring of his structures, and above all, his comfortable (if occasionally begrudged) occupation of the peripheral fringe—both professional and social—of Los Angeles. In these, Lautner exceeded the achievements of his master. Wright was a mere "urban cowboy." Lautner, in Hodgetts's eyes, was a true maverick.

The pieces of a Lautner house *KA-CHUNK!* together with the inevitable force of a fallen tree. These are not houses for the faint of heart. Vast, fissured floors give way to ponds, cascade past branching beams, brace themselves against mountains of earth, and catapult over dizzying chasms that would challenge a motocross champion. Jagged areas for dining, reading, and relaxing poke from an interior landscape only a bit more civilized than that to be found outside, and kept apart by an almost invisible plane of glass. A tumult of materials defies the containment of a mere building, and pulls the occupant mercilessly towards distant landscapes— towards the setting sun—towards formations of clouds, stars, and the lonely cry of a circling bird.

Now these are virtues, but not necessarily those most likely to enshrine an architect in the Hall of Fame. The gusto Lautner brings to a job, the relaxed rhythm of plugged railroad ties, exposed welds, and rough concrete reminds one mostly of mine-works and industrial yards; the floating, extra-terrestrial planes suggest a desert mirage, not the Pantheon; the exaggerated geometry and hip-hop gestures infer recklessness, not historical calculation.

In fact, Lautner's language simply defies the niceties of architectural expression in favor of a raw, adventurous reality that redefines itself with every discovery. There is a clear line of development, a quick-draw resolution of monumental contradictions, and a commitment to expressive materiality, but, Venturi look out! this is not an architect who plays the game of complexity and contradiction unless it is on his own terms. Nor one that particularly values the accrued lore of the culture of architecture. It is not at all clear that he was looking at the Russians, or the French, or the Finns, or indeed at any of the "heroes" who shaped the twentieth century's icons of contemporary architecture.

As a young man, he sought out the studio of Frank Lloyd Wright, becoming an apprentice at Taliesin in 1936. There he learned Wright's philosophy by cooking, cleaning, and drafting along with the other apprentices, developing an appreciation for what he later came to call "real architecture," by observing the role of architecture in the daily life of the studio. Wright was fond of him, assigned him work on the "Broadacre City" project, and then Wingspread, a sprawling house for H. F. Johnson, Jr. in Racine.

It was while supervising still another Wright house in Los Angeles, the Sturgis Residence, that the young apprentice and his master first disagreed. Lautner innocently allowed an Aalto chair to be positioned in the sacred precinct of Wright's design and was chastised for its "unnatural use of wood to simulate steel springs"

023.2
John Lautner, Sheets-Goldstein Residence, Los Angeles, 1963–94. View of living room.

which was "totally unsuited to (Wright's) buildings—a farce in fact."[1]

It was a defining moment. Lautner's bold and inclusive visual instincts were artistic miles apart from the razor-sharp indictments of the older man. He never returned to Taliesin.

Once in Los Angeles Lautner became adroit at manipulating the brew of shamanism, ego, and idiosyncrasy that Wright had spurned in a letter to his then-apprentice as the "Hollywood Experience." In what seemed like no time, his spacy, futuristic roofs were sheltering the restaurants that defined the '50s. Exuberant, colorful, and anarchic, brandishing names like Googies with graphics to match, they exemplified the culture of hot rods, surf boards, and the Sunset Strip. His freewheeling structures, called decadent and exhibitionistic by East Coast purists, set off a fire-storm of imitators, and quickly became stigmatized as coffee shops, banks, and car washes with quirky geometry sprouted up across the USA.

But Lautner's world reached far beyond the creation of an architecture seemingly "made" for exploitation. Those forms—aeronautical, cave-like, rustic, mechanistic, even hedonistic—were born of a virtuosity that reinvented structure

---

1   Frank Lloyd Wright, *Frank Lloyd Wright: Letters to Apprentices* (Berkeley: University of California Press, 1982): 143.

and enclosure on a project-by-project basis. In his hands, at the Mauer Residence, a series of common plywood bents, prefabricated and projecting from a stone floor, assumed the elegance and excitement of a line of aircraft ready for take-off. In his hands, the cantilevered structure of the driveway at Silvertop became a spiraling halo, ramping hard up into the sky.

Necessity and a willingness to experiment with unconventional solutions fueled designs that went far beyond the merely cosmetic. Moreover, given his unique blend of pragmatism and exuberance, such exotic forms were most often found to be the most cost effective way to get the job done. So what is one to make of Lautner? As an apprentice to Frank Lloyd Wright he was unabashedly enthusiastic about Mr. Wright's philosophy, crediting it as the foundation of his life's work. Yet, while Wright was a world class polemicist and formidable master of design, his architecture never approached the explosive technical and formal ingenuity of Lautner's signature buildings. Taliesin West and Falling Water may have provided the inspiration for Lautner's approach to his subject, but Wright was just another urban cowboy compared to Lautner's maverick spirit.

Look at the hallway in the Stevens Residence—the effortless transit of that impossibly thin concrete parabola across cabinetry and herringbone pavers—its vault over the louvered staircase and final encounter with a frisson of mullions so randomly deposited they might have washed up on the beach. Or consider the Sheets Residence, with its "the Martian's have landed" bedroom hovering surrealistically over the vast circuit-board of the Los Angeles basin. Or try to understand the "desert flower" roof of the Elrod Residence, itself a film star many times over, which allows an apparently impossible sliver of landscape to completely surround the house.

In Lautner's best work, it is not only the eye of the designer and the mind of the engineer, but the imagination of a storyteller at play. He seems to be fascinated by the animation of man's encounter with nature—not simply the portrayal of their separate states of being. For Lautner, each minute in the life of a cantilever is the opportunity for another event. It is, for him, profoundly never the same, as it continues an unending dialogue with the rocks, the horizon, and the solar pendulum. Lautner's houses do not sit passively by the ringside, they get in there and wrestle with the landscape.

Viewed in this way, one can attribute the interaction of the elements of Lautner's design to his sense of drama. A huge concrete tension ring teeters from the top of a natural stone at the Elrod Residence, only to be balanced, precariously, on a Calderesque footing, then embraced by a curving utility space. Effortless, yes.

Pragmatic, yes. Simple, yes. But by that Noguchi-like transposition of material and substance, Lautner achieves an illusion of levitation that would not be out of place in the stage magic of Houdini, and performs an exercise in structural dynamics that, were it a circus act, would rate as death-defying.

At the Carling Residence, an even more daring proposition was realized; an entire wall of the house, with intricate sloped glass and an integral day bed, can be pivoted onto the surrounding deck, outdoors. The resulting transformation allows one to enjoy the climate—of course—but also redefines the nature of space and time in a manner consistent with architectural theory of the late twentieth century, when "the only constant is change" became the mantra of avant-garde architects around the globe.

And at the Arongo Residence we understand that the curvilinear path of a surrounding pool is a practical alternative to a railing, but what are we to make of the snake-trail of reflections as it spirals out to the horizon, punctuating the night sky as gently as a nebula?

It's not clear that Lautner wants us to know, or even that he's very interested. His published statements on architecture emphasize a kind of primitive idealism. Utopian, spiritual, and passionate, he stood outside the mainstream, creating a formal language which rejected the commonalities of the marketplace for what he perceived to be far more important values. That he was able to induce like-minded clients to seek him out, often for projects as "ordinary" as low-cost housing or auto showrooms, upon which he lavished the same inventive genius as on more "important" projects, suggests that he flourished in the egalitarian ethos of postwar Los Angeles.

No master builder in the Ayn Rand manner, though his style would belie it, Lautner seemed genuinely perplexed by the lack of celebrity that weighed down his career—turning bitter, and becoming belligerent towards a profession, which seemed to systematically exclude him from its ranks. Certainly he was denied the commissions which normally accrue to great talent. There are no important civic or institutional buildings in his portfolio. Not even a library. But one could argue that his vision, coupled with his refusal to compromise, presented an insurmountable hurdle in the artistic climate of Southern California.

Truly great talent—one thinks of Stravinsky, Berthold Brecht, Thomas Mann, the great Russian film director Sergei Eisenstein, the list goes on—have never secured anything but a slippery instant in the motion picture business, and the region's appreciation for the arts goes downhill from there. Architecture as civic identity can be dismissed from any discussion of Los Angeles, as can conventional ideas of civic beauty. (Lautner himself says Los Angeles was "the ugliest thing I'd ever seen."[2])

Yet he was able to rally another significant attribute of the Los Angeles scene to his side. Those were the loners. The entrepreneurs with an independent spirit and the kind of optimism that spelled success in the cut-throat milieu of the '50s. Crazy inventors! Millionaire showmen! Legendary hucksters! These people were to form his client base, and if they were only a pale shadow of the Hapsburgs and Medici, and assorted royalty that gave architecture an aristocratic luster in ages past, that seemed to be alright with Lautner. They granted him the freedom to follow his passion, rather than the prescriptions of an always timid Society. They danced with him through the bullying whims of government agencies, small-minded bureaucrats, and uncomprehending building inspectors. They stuck with projects, more often than not, until patience and pocketbook were worn to the point of failure.

It is possible to speculate, from the evidence of the larger projects, on the results should Lautner have had the opportunity to build at large scale? There are glimmers in the Bob Hope Residence of what might be in store for an architecture of defiance when it must come face to face with the bourgeois requirements of an institution. And the bloated details of some later projects make it abundantly clear that the encroachment of regulations had become an overwhelming artistic challenge in his later years.

After all, the era of the cowboy is over. The urban condition more often demands the *Blade Runner* instinct than that of the guy in the white hat who rides slowly into the sunset. Lautner gave it his all, and we should be grateful to him for paving the way for a new generation of outlaws.

2   "Responsibility, Infinity, Nature," John Lautner interviewed by Marlene L. Laskey (Los Angeles: University of California, Los Angeles, Oral History Program: 1986): 61.

023.3
John Lautner, Silvertop (Reiner-Burchill Residence), Los Angeles, 1956–63.
Renovated by Bestor Architecture, 2015–18.

Requiem for a Heavyweight

BLUEPRINT (DEC/JAN 1995): 59–63

Hodgetts provides a lucid description and candid assessment of Stirling and Wilford's science library at UC Irvine. His descriptions are typically insightful and lyrical, but his assessment, while maintaining a positive spin, betrays his preference for seeing the library "to be the core of a dynamic information exchange" as opposed to seeing it, as Stirling and Wilford apparently did, as a "spiritual center for the intellectual development of the vested, scholarly class." Nonetheless, Hodgetts has much respect for this important late work by Stirling and Wilford, defending its material shortcomings by indicting the short-sighted cost-cutting of the client and comparing the building favorably to Louis Kahn's late project for Jonas Salk in La Jolla.

Say Irvine to a Los Angelino and you curdle the blood of anyone with left-of-center credentials. Irvine is the stomping ground of Ronald Reagan; Nixon's Western White House is just round the corner in San Clemente; and you can feel the numbing conformity of hundreds of land grant institutions strung out along the freeway. Irvine is more company town than city, with no apparent governmental bodies. Down here, the petrol stations look like Paleolithic museums, the greens of golf estates border the streets, and the tributary developments hang on the carcass of the university like so many leeches.

Worse, the campus street grid of this branch of the University of California is made up of a litany of perhaps more favored university towns: Berkeley, Harvard, Yale, Cornell. This one is at once bucolic, pedestrian, and inseparable from the shopping malls which surround it. Everyone wears a smile. You wonder if their tutors are working them hard enough.

Like an amphitheater-come-lately, James Stirling Michael Wilford and Associates' only work in Southern California (completed in association with IBI Group/L. Paul Zajfen) manages simultaneously to dominate the campus skyline as though it has been here since the beginning of time and to suggest that it has only just arrived from the sky. It has the presence of an architectural object so dense you think it must be milled from a solid chunk of kryptonite; it sits so heavily on the surface of the earth that there must be a vast "other" beneath the surface or it would surely over-stress the crust and plunge straight to the center.

As you get nearer the building, the premise becomes clear. There is a base—heavy, circular, with few details, and impenetrable save for axial terminations at the east and west. Above this, a light-colored matched piece seems held on by gravity. Tiny, even vestigial, windows emphasize the severity of the mass. And above that there is a fragile, burnished metal ring. You can see light and air between it and the rim of the mass below.

Stretching to the east, a pedestrian axis—or street, even—flanked by a mosh of other buildings, bustles up to the portal, swagging ever so slightly downward, to extend the diameter of the circle. The street falls away below the mass in the manner of Le Corbusier's Centrosoyus, bringing your vision directly in line with the ideal horizon of the building; directly in line, in fact, with the protruding balconies above, so that entering is like disappearing into a great maw as the zig-zagging balconies pass overhead.

It's here that you get it. The building is a machine! A vast, *Forbidden Planet* kind of a machine organized with impeccable, even alien logic. The ground floor—that base—is all but inaccessible. Two doors lead to an abbreviated lobby, an

024.1
Stirling, Wilford, and Partners, Ayala Science Library, University of California, Irvine, 1994. Entry façade.

elevator bank, and an improbably triangular stair wedged viciously into an otherwise unbroken floor plane. It's as though you've stumbled across an abandoned silo on your way to somewhere else.

Above the circular plate of the floor, three planes containing the library stacks describe a concise triangle of sky. They are part of a different reality: a mass of reflections and an impressive change of scale creates a hovering effect, amplified by the chromatic cadence of a colonnade. It's extra-terrestrial with a Euclidean bent. The triangle of sky is like a paean to all things ex-Irvine, and as shocking to the vaguely Hispanic orthodoxy of the place as the Masonic order must have been to Papal Rome. There are no triangles in Southern California, at least not native ones. (Michael Graves's library at San Juan Capistrano introduced pyramids across the street from a writhing Spanish Colonial cathedral a few years back, but that's another story.) It's fair to say that there are few, if any, "pure" forms to be found in the California tradition at all. So, with Stirling and Wilford having abandoned their characteristic contextualism for a surreal imperial order, the building simply sits its huge mass at the center of this most Arcadian campus and doesn't even try to look comfortable.

This is Stirling and Wilford's fourth project in the United States. If the truth be told, two of the other three are severely compromised by what can only be called (delicately, please) the *American Situation*. I can remember Stirling's incredulity at being unable to incorporate a window configuration of his choice at the Rice School of Architecture; his puzzled amazement when he realized that in the United States you have to beg for those things which are considered to be the architect's responsibility around the rest of the world.

You get the feeling that, at Irvine, Stirling and Wilford girded their loins and adopted a posture calculated to allow them to triumph over the fits and starts of the American system. The result is a building where carefully metered ratios of peripheral wall to volume skirt the hair-trigger constraints of the university's guidelines. Perhaps by cloaking the structure in the language of bureaucracy it was up against, they hoped to gain a great degree of freedom on another front.

From the outset, this building took no prisoners. It was meant to be inscribed into the campus hierarchy like the missing keystone of a long-lost geometry which establishes an axis with the effect of instant recall. It was, or so it feels, already described and anticipated by the campus master plan. Yet there is also an unnerving sense that its arrival has forced the restructuring of the university life around it.

Irvine has enjoyed a brief architectural celebrity under the auspices of campus architect David Newman. He had already enlisted Frank Gehry and Eric Moss among others to help propel the campus into a frenzy of architectural excitement, before approaching Stirling and Wilford. As often as not, the new commissions veered towards disdain for the earnest but undistinguished buildings which form the bulk of the campus inventory. Imagine his surprise, if not dismay, when Big Bad Jumbo Jim and the boys pulled into town and set up a revisionist shop. Imagine his amazement when this outrageous bunch from *over there* began to knit their work so dutifully into the despised fabric of the existing campus that the others had railed against.

Context has always played a significant role in Stirling's theoretical, and built, projects. But you need to look into the recent chronicles of his work to find the true, if hypothetical, origin of such an idea. Go back to the recent dark ages, circa 1980, and you find a time when architecture's fit of self-flagellation had invaded every sanctum and a suffocating mist of orthodoxy seemed to cover all. Two unbuilt projects, both for museums, both by James Stirling, proposed a way out. A third, the Staatsgalerie in Stuttgart, was met with widespread acclaim for its brilliant superimposition of modernist devices on the carcass of an Imperial Artifact. Ingratiating and dramatic, with a sweeping scale that prompted comparisons to heroic antiquities, the Staatsgalerie appealed to the pluralism in every man without compromising principle.

The arrogance of the work or the man is in no doubt. It's enough to recall a delicious afternoon when a prestigious—but, sad to say, American—editor visited the Stirling home. Sir Jim lolled about in shorts, with those great hairy legs draped over the edge of a cavernous sofa, while she sat primly conducting an interview and he, wickedly, one guesses, thoroughly enjoyed her discomfort. In the United States, a foil for such naughty exuberance is rarely a reality, particularly in the dead and altogether uninspired badlands of Irvine, where a numbing sense of senseless propriety prevails. To work up a froth here would seem a waste of energy.

Stirling's other, earlier library—the petite, seductive, and climb-all-over-me-I'm-a-slut-and-I-love-it History Faculty Library in Cambridge—is, to say the least, a contrast to the one at Irvine. They both share a certain geometric obsession with Stirling's best work, but at Irvine the great, circular form is dominant. It subsumes all else, and strategically positions the library's vast bulk in a desultory array with its surrounding buildings.

Cambridge, poised at the brink of the information age, challenged formal conventions, both academic and architectural, but carefully sustained the routines of library life. At Irvine, on a site deep in the heart of the cybervillage, Stirling and Wilford either didn't ask what was going to happen now we've started down the information superhighway, or they just didn't think it was relevant.

Nonetheless, there is more at stake here than form. The very concept of the library is bloodied by the battle between the telecommuting electrotecture bunch and the urban campfire; look at the new central library in Chicago, which suggests nothing so much as a reincarnation of all that was ever wrong with the library-as-warehouse in the first place, or the *bibliothèque* in Paris, where OMA's provocative submission of a cyberspace funhouse of information activity was passed over. The question is whether you consider the library to be the core of a dynamic information interchange, or see it as the spiritual center for the intellectual development of a vested, scholarly class. At Irvine, it would seem that Stirling and Wilford have taken refuge in the latter view. Over-reacting, perhaps, to the surfboards and bikinis lurking in every boot, the footprint of the building, its axial nature, even its introverted bow to Asplund, all suggest residency in a village of forms modeled on classical European universities.

There is a suggestion here that the real subject of the library is student life. This is particularly striking in the attempt to frame individual students going about the activities they are meant to go about—sitting at their desks, studying, flirting, sleeping, and eating—against the mass of the building itself. Tiny glass study carrels are thrust out on to the main axis of the campus, hovering above it like observation blisters; they offer a glimpse of students hard at work, apparently blind to the constant parade of hunks and beauties passing below. There is no effort, as there was in Cambridge, to frame the faculty and administration. Both are relegated to the block which forms the building's western flank, and elaborately protected from incursion by students.

The stacks are carpeted, accessible, part of the daily contest for student hours, mingling with group study rooms and quiet enclaves. The light which suffuses these areas is clearly appropriate to the use, but the drama of the gesture to lift that mass of information high above the periodical and service floors is somehow lost in the internalized circulation of the building. You desperately wish for something other than the rainbow-colored columns to link those areas to the concept behind the building.

Compositionally, the library wants to be a great column base, grounding the structure, creating a heraldic emblem for the campus and cloaking the secret within. With the housing of the stacks, and particularly the expression of their presence as a crisp intervention within the cylinder of the inner court, there is no doubt that the scheme is inspired, if flagrantly out of context.

But the articulation of this premise depends on something rather deeper than the appliqué materiality which passes for substance in Southern California. The execution of the project does not match the concept. The first hint that something is awry comes from the uncharacteristic transition from the red rock to the stucco flanks lining the axis as you pass under the building above. You can almost feel the red pencil of the *budgetmeister* peeling back the very skin of the building with no sympathy for the architectural premises. You can sense the dismay and distaste with which Stirling and Wilford must have confronted the endless meetings, budget contests, and bidding wars which eroded the reality of the building. Or maybe they said: "Why not do what the natives do, but really do it?" Thus achieving, in a blinding moment of inspiration, both the mocking insight of a job well done and the power that only a truly contextual building can exert.

It's worth remembering that the Richards Memorial Laboratory and the Leicester Laboratory—the signature buildings of Louis I. Kahn and James Stirling—were completed at the same time. Now, Kahn's Salk Center down the coast at La Jolla and Stirling's library at Irvine—mature buildings each—stand only fifty miles apart, both in strong contrast to the abiding metaphor of Southern California architecture. It's too bad Jonas Salk wasn't the client for both.

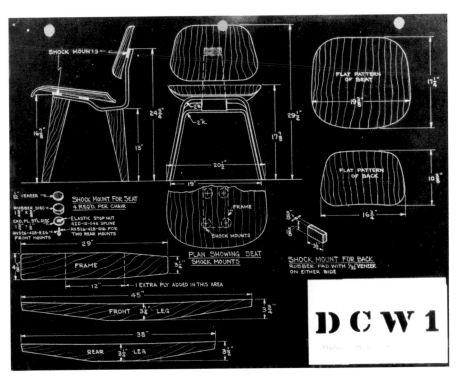

025.1
Charles Eames, DCW, molded plywood dining chair with wood base, blue print, 1945.

Kazam! in the Bedroom: Some Notes on the Design Process of Charles and Ray Eames

1995. PREVIOUSLY UNPUBLISHED.

Hodgetts lays out a meticulous history of the development of the DCW-1 plywood dining chair by Charles and Ray Eames. The text was meant for the catalog to the exhibition, *Eames Design: A Legacy of Invention* (for which Hodgetts + Fung designed the exhibition), but ultimately was not included.

In it, Hodgetts traces the Eameses's furniture experiments from Charles's early collaboration with Eero Saarinen at Cranbrook in the late 1930s to the launch of the DCW-1 chair after the second world war. Ray Eames's development of the Kazam! machine, a homemade device for bending plywood, becomes a touchstone for the Eameses's attitude, made all the more poignant by its initial location in the spare bedroom of their Richard Neutra-designed apartment in Los Angeles. For Hodgetts, the Kazam! machine stands as a device not only for reinventing the chair, but also, alongside the revolutionary plywood chair it made possible, for reinventing modernism in an optimistic, elegant, and distinctly American mold.

DCW1. The initials were stenciled like military code on a set of drawings that, patent-office-wise, sought to convey nothing but the facts about the design of what was to be the first production chair from Charles and Ray Eames [Fig. 25.1]. It showed a muscular, vaguely anthropomorphic silhouette patterned with a penciled representation of coarse grain, meticulously positioned fasteners, and an uncommonly broad, sloped, seating surface. To the untutored eye, it must have had all the pubescent grace of those dream cars penned on the backs of English class notebooks.

It slouched. It pranced. It was a laconic retort to all those prim, sit-up-straight-at-the-table dining chairs that came before it. A penchant for accuracy informs the notations. Technical details are in evidence. Much later, Charles Eames, pressed for scientific evidence to back up the successful ergonomics of the chair demurred, saying that it was simply, "designed for how people really sit," to which he might have added that the revolution he and his wife Ray had started was simply a reflection of a distinctly populist, above all *American* way of life.

Arlene Francis, first in a line of sophisticated television hostesses for CBS, deemed the chair and its author, Charles Eames, worthy of an in-depth interview, but insisted that such an ingenious new product must be the work of a singular, preferably male, author, and certainly not of the woman who stood "behind" him; thus mistaking the very ideals which had driven the creation of the chair in the first place.

In a single stroke, the structured relationship of furnishings to architectural volume in the European tradition was deconstructed. Thonet, Louis XIV, Aalto, Gropius, and even Stickley chairs *lined up*. They huddled against walls, felt uncomfortable in the center of the room, and if consigned to that unlikely place, were certain to be arranged at right angles to everything in sight. It wasn't that they *had* to be that way, just that their owners were somehow made to feel more secure if they were. And, since they were heavy, and not a little awkward to handle, they tended to stay where they were put. Yet here was not only a chair, but eventually a *genus* of furnishings which would give a kind of constant read-out of the activity in a household. Pulled up tight in a circle for a game of charades, helter-skelter after a football game on T.V., even out in the patio looking good. You could almost hear the formal living room beginning to tip-toe out.

So this particular breed of chair began its commercial adventure as the advance guard for a different style. Not far behind were the inside-outside landscapes of the California style, the clean, ozone-sharp Malibu convertibles from General Motors, and the swoopy roofscapes of restaurants and libraries from Palisade to Palisade.

From the covers of catalogs, in shop windows and on sales floors, Charles and Ray portrayed the chairs as, well ... animate, as though they had just leapt in through an open window or perhaps were about to land, light as a gymnast, from some aerialist rig hanging from the ceiling. This was furniture inviting admiring glances not simply from the standard 5'- 4" vantage point of the average American, but close up, from nether angles, of the construction details usually hidden from view.

In photograph after photograph Charles portrayed DCW1, as he did all their projects, in beautifully composed states of disassembly, with such evident passion for his subject that, were it not simply a chair, we might be embarrassed by such an intimate portrayal. Here are the parts of the chair, arranged as though floating in space, and lit as through Scavullo or Avedon have set the lights for a screen test. Here is the magnified silhouette of the chair, big enough to stop traffic, dwarfing the actual, three-dimensional object, but making us look twice at the elegance of its profile. And here is the chair again, this time in parts, abstract as a Calder, the sole occupant of a magazine cover. And here is the chair again, the parts splayed out like choice cuts of beef, with a candid description of the processes used in its production. And here are the fastenings, the rubber grommets, larger than life, as if the chair itself were a leviathan.

Such an extraordinary continuity of vision, from an initial technical/visual/functional concept through production engineering and on to packaging, user instructions, advertising graphics, and marketing displays, with no perceivable flagging of interest or energy, became an Eames hallmark. In brochures and magazine prints, Charles's photos were combined with playful, sophisticated graphic patterns that immediately conveyed an aesthetic realm far removed from that of conventional American furnishings, and farther still from the boundaries of "good taste" in the years immediately after World War II.

Perceiving that, to a large degree, their own sweat equity had produced viable prototypes and captured the interest of the international design establishment, they quite rightly seized the opportunity to be their creation's marketing gurus—promoting, persuading, and demonstrating the superior quality of their product with the enthusiasm of carnival barkers. Indeed, Charles's admiration for the seamless activities of the circus, "the concept of appropriateness, this how-it-should-be-ness has equal value in the circus, in the making of a work of art, and in science,"[1] parallels the top-to-bottom integration of the output of the Eames Office.

---

1 John and Marilyn Neuhart, *Eames Design: The Work of the Office of Charles and Ray Eames* (New York: Harry N. Abrams, 1989): 90.

Once the boundaries of a project had been defined, the Eameses, like Edison and the Wright brothers before them, explored every conceivable creative avenue until either the solution was self-evident or a pragmatic choice could be made between viable options. It wasn't enough to have the generalized concept, *plywood chair*, then search for a compelling form. There were to be unvarying criteria, "constraints" in Charles's design philosophy, which would define a design concept much as a "hook" defines a popular song. Some were drawn from an enthusiastic endorsement of mass production. As Charles said in a 1972 declaration of faith, "It would be a chair on which mass production would not have anything but a positive influence."[2]

That meant, in the argot of the Eames Office, that icons of production, rather than those of status, would govern the appearance of the chair. Thus the nearly universal concept of *edging* furniture made of plywood, in order to conceal its "lowly" origins, was abandoned by the Eameses in favor of exploiting the pattern formed by the plies themselves. And the legs and spine were to be unceremoniously sliced like sausage from long, gutter-shaped moldings.

But it was also to extend and exploit certain *idées fixes* which Charles had determined to be prerequisites: the use of electronically bonded rubber shock mounts for points of attachment, the use of a single molded plywood component for the seat and back, and separate molded plywood parts for legs and support structures. More subtly, there was an implicit visual discipline, echoing the style established by Ray Eames in her earlier paintings and her covers for *Arts and Architecture* magazine.

Prototypes meeting those constraints littered first their apartment, and then the workshop where they began production of a military splint derived from their experiments with forming plywood. Here, a remarkable (and characteristic) ability to avoid categorical thinking encouraged them to pursue a venture which, on the face of it, could not be farther from their goal—the splint was a disposable, aesthetically neutral device with little or no connection to people's daily lives! And yet, those splints, and the experimental litters and aircraft parts which followed them into production at the Molded Plywood Division laid the groundwork for the production technology which made DCW1 feasible.

Well enough, but that the experiments that led to the production of hundreds of thousands of splints and then DCW1 chairs took place in the spare room of a significant work of avant-garde European architecture, and that they were

---

2   Digby Diehl, "Charles Eames: Q & A," *Los Angeles Times West Magazine* (8 October 1972): 14.

conducted on a Rube Goldberg-like device invented by the Eameses themselves and dubbed the Kazam! machine, and that the name derived from the magic utterance of a popular comic book hero known as the Phantom, and that an automobile inner tube was the primary component of the Kazam! machine, all point to an innocent confidence in the exuberance of just "doing their thing."

Charles and Ray had moved to Los Angles in 1941 from Cranbrook, where they had met during Charles's tenure on the faculty. At Cranbrook, Charles had replenished his career as a Midwestern architect with an injection of modernist principles heretofore absent in his work, while Ray had focused on the making of things in order to extend her already sophisticated artistic vision. The catalyst for their partnership was the competition, "Organic Design in Home Furnishings," organized by the Museum of Modern Art in New York (MoMA), in which their design philosophy seems to have emerged fully formed.[3]

In their proposal, Charles Eames and Eero Saarinen (who was to become a famous architect in his own right) suggested a range of furniture supported on wire-thin legs, with body-hugging shells formed of an unnamed material (it was 1939) that looked, more than vaguely, like a bunch of sandpipers cruising on the beach [Fig. 25.2]. Ray provided a compelling visual format for their proposal, Charles contributed a characteristically lucid, unadorned text, and the "Eames Style" was born.

Radically different, yet simple in appearance, their winning proposal had all the overtones of a manifesto, receiving wide acclaim from the Museum of Modern Art and bringing them to the attention of John Entenza, the young publisher of *California Arts and Architecture* magazine. Entenza's offer of an editorial role in the magazine promised to be a perfect outlet for the Eameses' creative energies and an ideal sounding board for their ideas. Already known for his enthusiastic support of modern art and design, Entenza directed them to a dramatic apartment block which had just been built by Richard Neutra, and Charles and Ray found themselves surrounded by the pristine white rooms of a minor architectural masterpiece.

Right from the start, they focused their attention on solving the puzzle of molding plywood into three-dimensional curves, even though it meant smuggling tools, resins, and materials into a spare room of what was to be their first residence-*cum*-manufactory. Soon, with Charles working a day job as a set decorator,

---

3   See the catalog Eliot Noyes, *Organic Design in Home Furnishing* (New York: Museum of Modern Art, 1941).

025.2
Charles Eames and Eero Saarinen, Presentation panel for
MoMA "Organic Design in Home Furnishing" competition, 1940.

with what came to be known as the Kazam! machine occupying the bedroom, and with the French farce of "being discovered" an ever-present danger, Ray set about trying to unlock the process that would allow plywood to be curved in two directions, and thus gain not only a sculptural presence, but a soft, "organic" form suitable for seating. That Kazam! machine, ensconced exactly where Neutra would have been apoplectic (He once had vilified a client who had the temerity to change the interior color of a closet.), typified a commitment to living and working that culminated in the Eames house and studio, and is finally, fifty years on, becoming an accepted pattern for the cybernetic society [Fig. 25.3].

Just a few years later, it must have been with a sense of profound *déjà vu* that Charles described the program for Case Study House #9 (their own house) as being for "a married couple, both occupied professionally with mechanical experiment and graphic presentation. Work and recreation are involved in general activities: Day and night, work and play, concentration, relaxation with friend and foe, all intermingled personally and professionally with mutual interest."[4] For all its terse phrasing, this describes the relation between home and office which sustained the Eameses for more than forty years.

Entenza was also to provide Ray with a highly visible forum for her graphic art, and Charles with a rostrum for the polemics of design principles which were to remain a life-long passion. Ray's cover designs for *Arts and Architecture* expand and refine what will later come to be seen as the Eames Style [Fig. 25.4]. Rife with humor, ingenious juxtapositions, and an eager eclecticism, the covers are to the world of proper graphic design what the Eames house is to Mies van der Rohe's Farnsworth house—MTV to IBM! Often structured by Charles's photographs, but just as often incorporating strikingly original combinations of collage and graphic design, the covers were one-of-a-kind attractors which virtually guaranteed *Arts and Architecture* a following among students and connoisseurs of modern design. Curvilinear silhouettes create powerful negative spaces, linear elements dart play-fully "in front of" and "behind" the picture plane, and the functional role usually played by typography is joyfully subverted. Stencil lettering gets pride of place while uptight Swiss faces are banished to datelines. How like the DCW1!

The stencils, of course, had more to do with art than the military. Like stigmata for the cognoscenti, their use was initiated by avant-garde French architect Le Corbusier (himself following the lead of Picasso and Braque) to signify

---

4   Charles Eames, "Case Study Houses #8 and #9," *Arts and Architecture* 62, no. 12 (Dec 1945): 43.

his rejection of the complacent values of the bourgeoisie. Curiously, although Charles had seen and admired Le Corbusier's buildings on a trip to Europe, it was not until his arrival at Cranbrook that he wholeheartedly signified his allegiance to modernism, and adopted the style that was all the rage with Rapson, Bertoia, and the younger Saarinen.

The anomaly was that Charles and Ray, with their cohorts first at Cranbrook and later at *Arts and Architecture*, confronted the wide-open spaces of Los Angeles with much the same reformist zeal with which the Europeans sought to "modernize" congested medieval cities. The yearning for "clean," clearly ordered spaces "occupied" by animalistic furnishings was a formula created by Le Corbusier and later adhered to by émigrés from his studio as diverse as Jean Prouvé, Charles Correa, and Juan Kurchan. Moreover, a great many of the modern architects thought important to the International Style had a presence in LA—Richard Neutra and Rudolph Schindler had built dozens of spare, clean-lined homes by the early '40s, and the Wright clan had established a sizeable stake in the hills of Hollywood.

But where the Europeans seemed stuck in a net of elitist conventions (despite their radical social[ist?] intentions), the Eameses seemed actually to *believe* in the efficacy of mass production, utility for the masses, collaborative endeavor, and the rest of the left-of-center, red-tinged political philosophy. Their elaborate diagram of prefabricated housing production/distribution, published in *Arts and Architecture* in 1944, maps out the activity which would engage them throughout the postwar years in amazing detail. In it, they declare the role of the designer to be that of "provider," eschewing the commonly held view of design as an aesthetic luxury, offering instead the view of the designer

That the design submitted by Charles and Eero Saarinen was to be made of a yet-to-be-invented material, with a process not yet proved practical, echoed a vision shared by "modern" architects throughout the world. Wasn't there, they speculated, a way to conceive of that most basic item of furnishing as a totality? Shouldn't it be possible to unite the elements of a chair, for instance, in a single, modern material that simultaneously and seamlessly accomplished its purpose without resorting to a hopelessly antiquated vocabulary of spindles and shanks which up until that time defined the idea of a chair? In fact, the title of the competition for "Organic Design in Home Furnishings" made an agenda of such a search, and turned up proposals ranging from James Prestini's suggestion to literally *grow* a chair as a dense shrub within a transparent mold, to a submission by Bernard Rudofsky incorporating raw materials such as jute, caroa, and hemp.

025.3
Charles and Ray Eames, Kazam! machine, shown the bedroom of their Richard Neutra-designed apartment in Los Angeles, 1941.

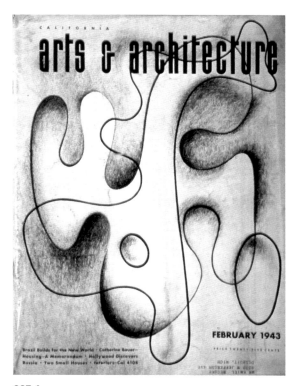

025.4
Ray Eames, cover of Arts and Architecture, February 1943.

It was 1944. The country was at war. What we now call the military-industrial complex had spent millions developing materials we now take for granted, and applying them to the war effort. Metals were scarce and expensive, especially aluminum, and Southern California's aircraft industry spearheaded a fast-track effort to develop alternatives such as plywood and plastic for airframe components.

Among the garage culture of small suppliers that took root near Douglas Aircraft was the Molded Plywood Company, brainchild of Charles and Ray, with financial and strategic aid from Entenza. Together with the Evans Plywood Company, they began the experimental production of small batches of aircraft components and a hands-on exposure to the basics of manufacturing.

I believe it must have been this experience which connected Charles and Ray to a spectrum of concerns both more demanding and gave them a unique vantage point from the "paper designs" of their peers in the design world. After that experience, one can imagine the impatience with which they viewed conventional methods of manufacture: the sheer waste of carving shapes from solid blocks of material; the erratic grain structure; the unpredictability of structural strength. After all, it was 1945. The dawn of a new era. There had to be a better way!

The better way was plywood. Laid up paper-thin sheet upon paper-thin sheet and glued together over a mold, it could be shaped into strong, beautiful, functional forms for almost any use. The Kazam! machine, for all its prowess, didn't look like much—a few two by fours hinged together so that they could close like a vise, a bicycle pump, and a loop-the-loop of wires from an electric heater—but it could press those thin sheets into complicated, curving shapes that were miles ahead of anything produced until then, into a perfect image of the vision taking place in Ray's imagination.

A look at Ray's sculpture reveals a vocabulary of abstract forms heavily influenced by the paintings of Miró. And yes, there are hints of Noguchi and Hepworth and Moore, but they hacked their work by hand from great blocks of material, while Ray developed her forms in concert with a thoroughly new manufacturing process. These were forms that required study before production. Molds had to be prepared. Time-consuming decisions governed the layout of parting lines and the lay-up of materials.

Ray's work, in contrast to her Abstract Expressionist friends Lee Krasner and Jackson Pollack, put the emphasis on *abstract*, as in intellectual, conceptual, and non-representational, rather than *expression*, as in action painting. There are flickers of Gabo as well in those sculptures, and Gabo was clearly fascinated by the

025.5
Charles and Ray Eames, DCW chair, 1948.

allure of modern materials, but even he failed to employ a process so fundamentally different from those employed by artists before him.

Ray's vision was unique. Whether in the smooth radii of a plywood splint devised for the military (over 150,000 manufactured!) or in the guise of the playful animals she and daughter Lucia cut from rejected blanks for the splints, she paid extraordinary attention to the continuity of each form and the line she devised to describe it.

But one problem was to confound them, and wasn't to be solved until Charles redefined the goal. The original concept, the one the Kazam! machine was designed to deliver and that the Museum of Modern Art had honored, was a chair in which the back and the seat were formed of a single sheet of material. And in fact, Ray's Möbius-strip-like sculptures show that it could be done. But the goal of the chair design, like that expressed in *Art and Architecture's* philosophy, was good design at low cost. And the one-piece solutions, beautiful as they were, were prone to defects and failure. Three-legged designs were also rejected, as were innumerable variations of flat metal bars, rods, twisted plywood, and sometimes ungainly attempts to joint two otherwise perfect components. Like all the Eames designs, DCW1 benefitted from both the right and left sides of their collective consciousness.

With production first by the Evans Plywood Company, and later Herman Miller, the first chapter of the Eames design saga came to a close. A product which had taken some seven years to evolve from an initial idea created for the MoMA Organic Design competition had finally reached fruition [Fig. 25.5].

Acceptance was instantaneous. An avalanche of publicity in *Life, Look,* and the shelter magazines heralded the chair as *the* symbol of postwar progress. And indeed, the shoe fit. The DCW1 was among the first wave of products introduced to a nation hungry for evidence of its premier status as leader of the free world. Old habits were seen as the residue of a discredited regime, and people were eager to proclaim their optimism for the future. It was an era in which the ballpoint pen earned kudos for "writing underwater," a humble plastic container with a seal-tight lid found a place in every home, and frozen-food lockers sprouted in every neighborhood.

That the DCW1 exploited state-of-the-art technology at a time when mass-market furniture was neither technologically advanced nor particularly artful, established an unprecedented niche which the Herman Miller Company was to exploit dramatically in the ensuing years. It also helped that features of the finished product, particularly the process of forming the plywood and the use of shock mounts, enjoyed the protection of patents, and thus warded off competition.

But the Eameses were also quick to take an integrated approach to packaging and marketing the chair, through a series of exhibitions featuring it in environments which typified "good design," and by the creation of a graphic identity for the Herman Miller Company which, though loosely based on the *Arts and Architecture* covers Ray had designed, nevertheless served to establish Herman Miller as a company with just the right mix of design integrity, good taste, and reticence.

Like Charles's documentation of the prototypes, these advertisements were notable for unabashed viewpoints and surprising transpositions of scale. Unadorned with the usual commercial messages, they were among the first advertisements for any products to feature the multiple views, graphic devices, and almost clinical photographs which have long since become standard repertoire for everything from automobiles to toothbrushes.

And indeed it was the very persuasiveness of the identity created for DCW1 and its descendants that makes appreciation of its contribution to American culture so difficult to identify. One might postulate that the identity programs of IBM in its heyday, or the famous advertisements which brought VW to market, are the progeny of DCW1. But what of the countless museum catalogs and posters which isolate their subject in a space which has neither floor nor ceiling nor wall? What of the photographs of Avedon and the installations of Baldassari?

Even a cursory look at the prodigious output of the office, in the realm of furniture, at least, will confirm that there was an unflagging idealism in their designs which, even today, affirms a perfectly plausible (and in fact never better realized) unity of means, convenience, and functionality. The origin of each design to emanate from the office was equally rooted in an ingenious manufacturing process, a strong functional solution, and a powerful sculptural resolution. The search for balance, then, was to be the all-consuming work of the office.

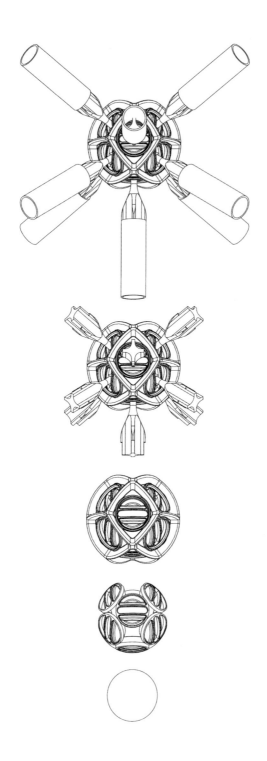

026.1
Alexis Rochas, OCTA.BOT®. Diagram of component assembly.

A Provisional Genealogy for OCTA.BOT®

LOG 19 (SPRING/SUMMER 2010): 45–52

On the way to endorsing Alexis Rochas's OCTA.BOT® node, Hodgetts lays out a sweeping historical treatment of the showdown between flexibility and pre-fabricated uniformity in architectural assemblies. On one hand, he notes a familiar desire for flexible, DIY, accommodation, on the other, the obvious benefits of mass-produced standard parts—that is, the two-by-four vs. the Eameses' kit of parts. Each has obvious advantages and blind spots, and Rochas's OCTA.BOT®, conceived by a single author/tinkerer and digitally fabricated to incredibly precise specifications, seems to offer a way to achieve the best of both worlds, as evidenced by Rochas's SCI-Arc exhibition and the graduation pavilion he constructed for the school. In the OCTA.BOT®, Hodgetts sees the realization of dreams at least as old as Fuller's and Wachsmann's.

Whether swaddled in vacuformed jackets or sandwiched within a metal-studded suit, the joinery of twenty-first-century buildings is mostly out of sight, out of mind. Not since the nineteenth century has the prudish Victorian habit of "covering up" been quite so pervasive as it is today, with building surfaces super-streamlined to envelop all annoying evidence of gravity, effort, or human effect in a seamless Pixar-like skin. It wasn't always like this. Exposing the art of joinery—from laces and stitches to threads and patent fasteners—traditionally signaled an aesthetic derived from the act of making things, and self-consciously celebrated the obscure, the erotic, and the sometimes-magical work of simply holding things together.

Before R. Buckminster Fuller famously dangled three loose sticks and then transformed them with a flick of the wrist into a structural mandala, there seemed to be a tacit understanding that Real Architecture required mass, while for less important structures—pavilions, sheds, aircraft, boats, and vehicles—designers were free to exploit the tension side of the tension/compression spectrum. There were exceptions, to be sure. Gustave Eiffel's lacy structures in Porto and Paris assembled a mind-boggling number of dissimilar components to achieve rigid, truss-like structures, and Joseph Paxton's cast-iron filigree was in fact an elaborately camouflaged truss. But such examples are few and far between. For the most part, structures like that of Le Corbusier's chapel at Ronchamp, with its aerodynamic ribs sandwiched between concrete skins, or Frank Furness's Pennsylvania Academy of the Fine Arts, in which artful masonry conceals a technologically advanced cast-iron skeleton, stood out more for their envelopes than for the stuff that made them stand up.

There was, of course, good reason for caution. In the beginning, the simple act of joining two similar materials was hampered by primitive tools that lacked the precision required to make fastidious, and thus long-lasting and strong, connections. The forged chains girding Brunelleschi's dome, the massive links of the London Bridge, or occasional swaged tension bars supporting floors were ancillary elements, for the most part subservient to the greater "architectural" agenda and almost never the main act. There were too many exigencies for such elements to find their way into the mainstream. Gravity remained the force that held most structures aloft.

Asia, however, was another world. Owing to a unique convergence of craft and technology, a highly disciplined, precise, and aesthetically pleasing system of joinery began to evolve as early as the Neolithic period in China. Remarkably straightforward yet durable and reliable, it eventually put to shame the crude technology of the Spanish fleet in the era when shipbuilding was the focus of Europe's most advanced designers, and routed the clumsy (if admittedly charming) half-timber construction typical throughout Europe in the sixteenth and seventeenth centuries. Certainly much credit goes to the advanced tools that were developed and employed. An almost mystical devotion to the design and maintenance of the craftsman's repertoire of planes, chisels, and assorted mallets pervaded Asian culture. Books about tools were carefully illustrated, and their elaborate cases testify to the status of the craftsman, whose skills were reciprocated by such fine instruments. One can only speculate that Leonardo da Vinci's stillborn ideas might have reached fruition if such a culture had existed in Italy during the fifteenth century. In fact, it did not, and thus innumerable advances were shunted aside by a European material culture focused primarily on surface effect. I would argue that, as a consequence, genuine advances in construction technology were put on hold from the thirteenth well into the nineteenth century.

Meanwhile, in Asia, intricate, multidirectional structural systems were devised, first for palaces and temples, and eventually for homes and commercial buildings. A remarkable conjunction of symbolic icon, graphic character sets, and structural motifs emerged and seems to have engendered a discipline that bridged various fields of activity. There can be no doubt that such a harmonious aesthetic has had profound impact. Today, evidence of this coincidence of objectives resides, for example, in the Yamaha logo, which depicts crossed tuning forks in the embrace of a perfect circle. Contrast this with the American equivalent, which trumpets breeding and provenance over quality and technology, and one of the underlying reasons why your father's Oldsmobile has finally bitten the dust becomes clear.

Not until the 1950s, when Fuller's mesmerizing triangles began to take hold with the proliferation of the radar domes and agricultural sheds that led to his triumphant American Pavilion for Expo '67 in Montreal, did the art of joinery become fashionable in the Western world of design and architecture. Charles Eames showcased furniture employing rubber shock mounts bonded to formed plywood, Jean Prouvé articulated the connections of wood to stamped metal, and for what now seems like an instant, nuts and bolts were all the rage. On the other hand, an incipient taste for prefabrication (led by Carl Strandlund's visionary Lustron Corporation, which manufactured around 2,500 homes in a retrofitted aircraft plant in Columbus, Ohio) generated few (if any) sales, and the exquisite joinery devised by Konrad Wachsmann with Walter Gropius for their Packaged House (patented in 1942) never really got beyond its prototype installation, despite ecstatic critical reception at the time.

In retrospect, most if not all of these efforts had a fatal flaw that could not be blamed on the market, or building codes, or labor, or even popular taste. It may

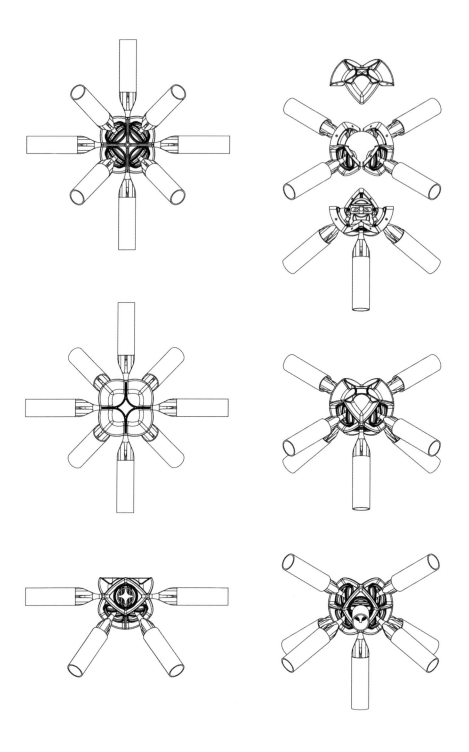

026.2
OCTA.BOT®. Various assemblies and views of eight-arm flexible joint.

026.3
OCTA.BOT® in an assembled space-frame system.

have been, as I have come to believe, that each demanded subservience to a total-izing system whose inherent modularity, insistent rectilinearity, and rigid material palette simply failed to offer the consumer what other products of industrialization suggested was possible: *Pastels! Automation! Velocity! Ease! Mobility! Sex appeal! Lots of chrome!* The design community responded with: *Limits! Orthodoxy! Monotonality! Shackles! Chastity! Lots of chrome!* Today, it could be argued that this reflected not only a certain cultural elitism, but also the limited resources and reach of the niche markets targeted by avant-garde designers of the time—or even a progressive, populist designer like Raymond Loewy. In any case, the whole affair stalled out in the late 1970s with the resurgence of styles laced with historicism, academic postur-ing, and, worst of all, cynicism.

Well, it's finally here! The great mash-up that connects all the dots: products that jump from the desk to the shelf. The stretchy, anti-sclerotic, spidery electron-ic plumbing that funnels just about anything but *real stuff* has arrived. Hooray!

Promised for years by William J. Mitchell and Isaac Asimov (not to mention yours truly), implemented and actualized by FedEx (having swallowed up Kinko's), the seamless translation of ideas into finished products on offer is a done deal. "Think, Print, Ship" is now officially "Think, Print, Make, Market, Ship." Participants in the production process, at one time clustered around guilds, which in turn were clustered around local markets, local resources, local talent, and local brawn, are now linked by 0s and 1s, and can volley transcontinental missives, thus accomplishing in days tasks that once took months or years.

Time-saving is, of course, not the only result. The least obvious, if by far the most revolutionary, consequences have been the reduction of authorship from a bouillabaisse to a single *auteur*, and the reduction of a process that typically engaged successive waves of experts, consultants, draftspersons, and machine operators to a simple matter of pointing and clicking—from your own space. So what has been lost? For starters, the social network that binds career and fellow travelers. The anonymous, screen-name-only-thank-you environment of the Internet sacrifices face-to-face dialogue in favor of results-based transactions: I send, you receive. In addition, the high precision of computer-aided design coupled with equally precise desktop-to-fabrication machinery all but eliminates the oil-stained machinist standing by with a caliper in one hand and a wrench in the other. The resulting exchange of pure information, unadulterated by gossip or personal habit, allows a design to be dispatched from an inventor's kitchen table with a certain degree of confidence that a finished product will arrive via ground or air transport in a matter of days.

Also gone, though perhaps without regret, is the parade of intermediaries, gatekeepers, and facilitators with their machinations and their mantras. Thus, instead of jockeying through a field of bureaucrats, a would-be inventor-entrepreneur can be the only (if lonely) guy on the playing field, with a straight shot at a midnight infomercial, or even a guest appearance on the Discovery Channel. And, of course, ultimately lost in the great, centuries-old battle of industrialization is the tradition of hand craftsmanship, which gave us Empire furniture, Bugatti, and Fabergé—although here it may be remarked that the extraordinary achievements embodied in those works could only be appreciated by the elite who could afford to underwrite the painstaking effort required, while anyone looking at the guts of a crushed iPhone must experience the same sense of awe that accompanied the opening of a Fabergé Easter egg. It was ever thus.

Until recently, such an uncompromised, streamlined pathway (invoking sci-fi notions of matter transmission) was still a matter of disparate and isolated parts.

But just as photographic film was sidelined by digital photography, not only the craft, but the tool itself, has been replaced by three-, then four-, and now five-axis automated milling machines capable of fabricating the most complex surfaces imaginable from solid billets of steel, aluminum, or any other material. The high-strength plastics injected into the resulting molds have largely displaced metals, resulting in a game-changing intersection of chemistry, digital design, and mass production technology.

Is this a good thing? Certainly the proliferation of consumer products can be cited as a symptom of a throwaway culture based on capitalism spun out of control, but that pertains to the *application* of such techniques, rather than their inherent *value*. While the good old American image of the inventor as tinkerer has a certain folksy charm, the geeky, bespectacled, pajama-clad digital maverick who has replaced him or her is rapidly becoming the prototype for a new genre—the hyphen-ate conceptor who answers to no one but his or her own instincts. Turning around the business plans of large corporate enterprises can take decades, as the sad decline of General Motors and Chrysler has demonstrated, but the profound impact of enabling individual entrepreneur-inventors and harnessing them to vast produc-tion and distribution networks cannot be overestimated. Bringing green products to market, for instance, is now only a matter of inspiration and commitment, as nimble multinational production facilities coordinate via videoconferencing to execute the most adventurous concepts. Hodgetts + Fung's own Tokyo project benefitted from an on-site camera that we were able to manipulate from our Los Angeles office, and Neil Denari's HL23 condominium project in New York City, like many consumer products, is in the process of being assembled from components prefabricated around the world. In fact, the project that inspired this essay is one of the first adopters of this state of affairs.

The new breed of designers looks on modularity with disdain. Surrounded by flat screens and handcuffed to their laptops, able to morph tall buildings in a single keystroke, they seem oblivious to the limits of construction technology. In their world, if a form can be described, it can be made manifest, and if it can be made manifest, then it can be inhabited by some entity that will appreciate and flourish within its voluptuous environment. Barbarella's "Orgasmatron"—what Doctor Durand-Durand called his "Excessive Machine"—would be right at home in this milieu. Here, at last, is architecture's answer to the Harley Earl years at GM, when tail fins rode high above buttocks-like bumpers, and multihued paint was perfectly matched with the pastel sheen of faintly metallic leatherette. People seem to like it. And why not? And why not plough that black-on-black Beemer through a rhapsodic environment? Why not park it in front of your very own curvy castle? There's only one hitch: building it. And, oh yes, paying for it.

As an increasing number of aspiring designers have discovered, the technology of the two-by-four is ill-suited to the task, and there are precious few materials out there which would really "make manifest" their designs. It would seem that no one had applied him or herself to the proposition from the construction side of the equation. Wachsmann, Eames, and others envisioned a world in which regularity provided a critical element in the formula for industrialization. For them, it was essential to maintain a rigorous, self-defining system of elements, which by their very nature would enable a consistent, repeated, and predictable system of joinery. The system prevailed, and thus the faint aroma of fascism, which even the generous, affable, and certifiably liberal Eames could not fully eradicate. Fuller's geodesic structure is indeed curvy, but not parametrically so, since the equilateral triangles at the heart of the system employ "hubs" that rigidly position each strut in order to produce (again) a regular, geometrically consistent array. Not too long ago, Peter Pearce, an ardent follower of Fuller's principles, invented a multi-axis hub that was famously used to construct the ill-fated biosphere, but it, too, lacked the single most elusive quality that we take for granted with the two-by-four: flexibility.

That is about to change. In a pioneering demonstration of the linked-up ability of the Internet to supercharge startup efforts, a recent installation at the Southern California Institute of Architecture (SCI-Arc) featured a prototypical structure that combines the inherent rigidity of Fuller's triangles with the flexible, adaptive geometry of the two-by-four. The project took shape in the hands of Alexis Rochas, a young Argentine architect on the faculty at SCI-Arc frustrated by the limits of his handcrafted but exuberant structures. Rochas began, project by project, to reimagine the constraints of available, off-the-shelf connections, and to improvise, joint by joint, a new, systematic approach that would enable the construction of the fluid, parametric forms he was imagining.

A hastily built pavilion to shelter an outdoor graduation ceremony on the unrelieved asphalt parking lot at SCI-Arc provided the final impetus. With a diameter of eighty feet and a height of ten, Rochas's canopy successfully departed from the geodesic formula by means of a unique hub assembled from two-dimensional, laser-cut hardware, which accepted struts of any length and at any angle. This was revolutionary.

If one imagines a spherical surface—say, that of a pin cushion—into which it is possible to stick a pin at any point, a clear picture of the purely geometric consequences of this idea emerges. But to imagine the structural consequences—drilling, inserting, threading, welding, and so on—is to confront a really stubborn problem: how to accommodate one position without sacrificing the ability to accommodate another, perhaps only slightly different, position. Or how to accommodate a multitude of positions without some kind of custom "tailoring." Indeed, how to create a "one-size-fits-all" structural hub that can be modified "on the fly."

This is where the internet truly comes into its own, because once the design Rochas improvised from readily available components had matured in his mind to a universally adaptable construction methodology, it had taken on a form that could be tested, replicated ad infinitum, retested, and rendered available for general use. It had become a refined, complex joint, not unlike those employed by Japanese craftsmen in aesthetic terms, but radically different geometrically, and dependent on absolutely critical dimensions. He could draw it, and did, creating a three-dimensional digital model in his studio, but there was simply no way to make it without a five-axis mill. And no way to even test it without generating a fully functioning prototype.

That prototype arrived in the mail soon after Rochas emailed his digital model to a production facility in Minnesota. A week later, an initial production run arrived, ready to be incorporated into a series of demonstration projects installed in the SCI-Arc Gallery (January 22 through March 7, 2010). On inspection, the Rochas hub, which he calls OCTA.BOT®, is more toy than game-changer. Rather than a perfectly machined Teutonic sphere, it is animalistic—bristling with stubby threaded nubs that flail about like the arms of a hungry spider. Arcing cavities bridged by sliding chocks create a Piranesian inner space, which when joined to corresponding struts resists both tension and compression forces. The resulting array then acts in concert with adjacent hubs to create a continuous, triangulated fabric. Accessories, still to be developed will enable various surfaces to be supported in order to develop x-y-z curvilinear envelopes easily and efficiently, leading to applications in architecture, aerospace, and industrial design.

While architects are increasingly drawn to exploit the vast formal potential of digital design, the complementary craft of realizing those designs has languished for decades. (Finnish architect Kivi Sotamaa recently remarked that boat builders capable of constructing complex, three-dimensional forms are no longer active in Finland, for example.) There is a clear need for ingenious systems like the OCTA. BOT®. Freed from the constraints of both custom fabrication and fixed geometry, a formal universe beckons. What may very well become an everyday "thingamabob" in a bin at Home Depot took exactly eight weeks from concept to reality, and has the potential to jump-start the transformation of an industry.

Big Jim

ARCHITECT (DECEMBER 2010): 49–53

Hodgetts offers another personal reflection on James Stirling to coincide with the 2010 CCA exhibition, "Notes from the Archive." In it, he focuses on Stirling's humorous functionalism, deadpan presentation style, and unwillingness to theorize his work (in contrast to many whom he influenced, including Peter Eisenman, Richard Meier, and Robert Venturi). Despite his seeming fade from the spotlight after his death, Hodgetts sees Stirling's work as brilliant and unequalled.

Here's the rub. Big Jim, a.k.a. James Stirling, went at architecture the way a heavyweight on the way up goes after a doll.

No. Scrub that.

Here's the incongruity: Sir James Frazer Stirling addressed the profession of architecture in a manner that reflected his humble origins, but along the way ...

No, no. Way off. He was no social climber.

Okay. This is the real deal: Stirling's blunt, intensely personal, confrontational, even hyperfunctional style was something he wore as naturally as his fluorescent-green stockings and cadmium-blue dress shirts.

Too many words.

Sir Jim said very little about his work, sticking to very disciplined (never flowery) descriptions that were absolutely devoid of jargon. In fact, one might infer that he was dismissive of the "elevated" discourse some think is appropriate when talking about architecture.

It's one of the conundrums of his legacy, because there is so much to chew on. A review of his built and unbuilt projects over a mere forty years is startling, not only for its sheer quantity, but for the consistently challenging concepts which he regularly launched from his crowded atelier. In the beginning, one waited in line for a fresh cut from the Beatles, wore the latest thing from Mary Quant—and watched for a salvo from Big Jim.

Ham Common was Aalto redux. Preston was more of the same, but better. Leicester was Aalto *delicto*, and from there on, it was time to call in the bomb squad, or the morals police, or the guardians of British culture—whoever could get there first. Remarkably, at least for a while, the commissions kept rolling in, from prestigious universities and planning councils and industrial titans who (one must assume) were advised to catch him quick, while he was on the way up.

Sir Jim's delight was to join the puzzle pieces of a program into an assemblage that was barely reined in by structure and weatherproofing. This teetered on the edge of a critical precipice, which, of course, is what engendered such a babble of commentary. With his champions—the critics Reyner Banham and Colin Rowe—leading the incursion, architects around the world were alerted to an aesthetic so fundamentally removed from their own that only a brave few would sign up for it. After all, who among them had ever imagined that brightly colored air extractors might stand in for the "plop art" with which they adorned their windswept plazas; or that one might manage airflow with cleverly placed inverted vents, rather than a ducted system? The forthright, often scatological functions which Stirling celebrated sometimes made an assault on the senses. At his Leicester University

Engineering Building, the infamous vent at the prow of the terrace wafted the olfactory delights of the restroom below.

At that time, in the late '50s and early '60s, artists such as Charles Mingus, Allen Ginsberg, and Francis Bacon were producing work that drew on the same strain of radical reconception that provided the DNA for Stirling's early buildings. In marked contrast to his contemporaries, Stirling seems to have been less preoccupied with the (narrowly defined) "culture of architecture" and far more engaged with broad cultural tremors which he could not ignore. An *ack-ack* of unprecedented built and unbuilt projects underscored his willingness to risk all in the search for a matching paradigm: raw concrete and brightly colored molded fiberglass at Runcorn; more extremely molded fiberglass for Olivetti; a ribbed, precast concrete system for university housing at St. Andrews; an unbuilt proposal featuring gigantic rotating sunscreens for Siemens.

With each jab of his famous stub of a pencil, he pushed both aesthetic and technological boundaries further into an unknowable future. And yet, later, the punctuation often took the form of veiled historical references, such as the concave cornices on the Siemens design, and the depressed Piranesian footprint that gave his competition entry for the Wallraf-Richartz Museum an epic, even elegiac, quality.

This tendency—to oscillate between a functional, programmatically driven parti and a visual narrative blending episodes old and new—endowed his projects with something like the "nose" extolled by wine connoisseurs. It was a melding of influences, overtones, and subtle references that never approached the banal cynicism of Philip Johnson's Chippendale pediment.

In the States, Peter Eisenman, Richard Meier, and Jaquelin Robertson circled his camp, as each was carving his own place in architectural history; House X and the High Museum were in vitro experiments during the period of Stirling's greatest influence among the avant-garde, as was Paul Rudolph's nearly simultaneous Yale School of Art and Architecture and Robert Venturi's Guild House. Wildly divergent styles marked the break with classical modernism, mirroring challenges to the social and political order of the culture as a whole. Yet only Meier and Venturi found acolytes to carry on their principles: Eisenman's celebrated match-up with Jacques Derrida led to a wider breach between theory and practice, while Sir Jim's forthright diagrams caught flak from an establishment committed to the status quo, and above all, in thrall to its conservative, corporate clientele. Stirling's complex design rhetoric, difficult for critics and architects alike, seemed to sow only confusion among even his most ardent followers.

A less adventurous Stirling emerged in the late '70s, "curated" by Léon Krier. He left behind agitprop to create a series of projects which, while still idiosyncratic, cloaked functional flourishes—such as the monumental exhaust stacks framing the entrance to the Fogg Museum—with thin, often disingenuous disguises. This work, embraced by many of his students at Yale, extended the premise of the Staatsgalerie by relying on a material gravitas (mostly absent earlier) that was supplemented by an assemblage of primary geometries in order to convey a sense of civic authority.

This turn of events mortified many of his admirers, while inspiring a kind of hybridized postmodern affectation that quickly became the hallmark of innumerable schools, libraries, and courthouses. Possibly the most-often quoted project of this period is the theater arts project at Cornell University, which features a slender bell tower, an Italianate arcade, and a hilltop village layout. Devoid of the somewhat pompous air which found its way into many of Sir Jim's later projects (the No.1 Poultry building in London comes to mind), Cornell pulls off a kind of pleasant, synthetic vernacular. But it is difficult to reconcile its placid countenance with the ferocious originality which brought him to the attention of the architectural world. American disciples are thin on the ground, but echoes of the first (the "good") Stirling can be found in Frank Gehry's early projects, and one thinks of Marion Weiss and Eric Owen Moss. Then there's our own studio, a throttled-down, road-going version of the ATV screamer that Jim was piloting.

Retrospectively, his influence seems as fleeting as that of Ledoux and Boullée, even though, within twentieth-century architectural history, the sheer brilliance of his work has no equal. While such a quick fade from memory may be due in large part to his reluctance to theorize, it's meant that just "getting the job done"—as Sir Jim liked to say—has given way to the unbridled rush to get to the head of the line?

028.1
Le Corbusier, Voiture Minimum, 1936. Digital model by Antonio Amado.

Corb's Car

THE ARCHITECT'S NEWSPAPER (11 AUG 2011)

In this brief review of Antonio Amado's *Voiture Minimum: Le Corbusier and the Automobile* (Cambridge: MIT Press, 2011), Hodgetts praises Le Corbusier's attempt, with his Voiture Minimum, to fashion a car suited to both mass production and the masses. The crux boils down to a set of familiar concerns in Hodgetts's writing: the connection between architecture and bespoke objects for the upper class, a similar connection between mass-produced goodies and a broad, popular audience, and the difficulty of making architecture available and meaningful to the masses. As Hodgetts puts it: "architecture was fine for the estate, but not for the road." Nonetheless, Le Corbusier tried. Amado does not attempt to dig too deeply into the conflicted relationship between elite culture and industrialization, nor does Hodgetts fault him for not doing so. Rather, he uses the review to sketch in some of the uncomfortable (and still unresolved) details.

To be honest, my budget hasn't included any of the twenty-six or so books devoted to Le Corbusier that have arrived in the last decade. More than two books a year would make anyone proud. But *Voiture Minimum: Le Corbusier and the Automobile* is something different. A few pages in, I realized that I'd been gulled. Corb is in there, but only as a walk-on. Built around a few scrappy sketches from the '30s, Antonio Amado manages to lasso an entire era in which the automobile, not architecture, represented the ultimate design challenge. Think about it. While we take the suburban zeitgeist of SUVs, ATVs, minivans, and Rovers for granted, in the 1930s it looked as though it would be the automobile that would transform cities. It would be the automobile that led material culture away from wood and rabbit glue, and it is the automobile that refined and popularized the formal language that today's Young Turks aspire to apply to their buildings. The tale of Le Corbusier trying to duke it out with the auto industry is a bit like a varsity wrestler trying to make it in the Ultimate Fight Cage. He simply lacked the chops.

But he loved cars! Gatsby had nothing on Le Corbusier, at least when it came to fast machines. Voisin, the high-end automaker, was a friend and patron—witness the Voisin Plan—and then take a good look at the images of Corb's stable of sultry Voisins, with their long noses and dinner-plate wheels, as they idle in front of Villa Stein, or lounge in the shadow of Villa Savoye. That car was the Bentley coupe of its day. It was enormous, stylish, extraordinarily well crafted, with rectilinear lines that conferred the status and breeding its well-heeled owners wished to declare. And it was about as far from a people's car as it could be. This is the image of Corb that the paparazzi would have devoured, the one with the bespoke car in place of the manifesto, the one with Josephine Baker perched on a running board, and product placement high on his agenda.

Streamlining was in the air when Le Corbusier visited America, where he toured Ford's assembly plant in Detroit and came back besotted with mass production. At that time automobiles were either hand-crafted and ponderous or down-market and basic. Designers and some brave architects around the world were jousting to introduce aerodynamic silhouettes that challenged the upright architectural profiles then in vogue. Ferdinand Porsche's People's Car, the Czech Tatra, and Gordon Buehrig's Cord Speedster were beginning production, and Chrysler's Airflow was on the drawing boards. A competition for a low-cost automobile had just been launched by a consortium of producers, and even though it omitted architects from the roster of invitees, Le Corbusier wanted in. After all, Gropius had done it, and so had Loos, and it's clear from the tone of this letter that Le Corbusier had an itch he simply had to scratch: "I would be very pleased

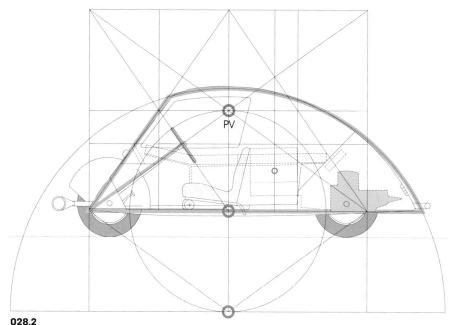

028.2
Voiture minimum. Proportional study by Antonio Amado.

to design the body of such an automobile," he wrote. "I have been familiar with the question for many years and I am convinced that cooperation with automobile engineers would make it possible to develop an elegant model with class. If you are able to make this disclosure known to whoever is interested, I would appreciate it." But the letter was late, as the industry had already become established, and he found himself up against some very stiff competition. Amado beautifully reproduces plates of seventy-eight entries by rivals, many featuring rear engines, earnest attempts at streamlining, a surprisingly agile juggling of features, and, *quel scandale*, a progressive industrial rather than architectural language. Viewing them as an ensemble, as a snapshot of the struggle to represent fluid (read sexy) forms with an engineer's kit, I'm once again made aware of the hair-raising digital revolution we are witnessing today, and reminded of the incredible breakthrough embodied in pioneering designs like the Cisitalia. Le Corbusier, focused on the Modulor and the harmony of intersecting lines with no Xenakis in sight, was caught off-guard. Lacking béziers and splines, locked into antediluvian T's and angles, he found himself far from the shells and airfoils he lauded in *Towards a New Architecture*. Nevertheless, he soldiered on, eventually producing drawings for a strange, pug-nosed vehicle which would be right at home in Trey Parker's garage.

Slab-sided, and aggressively Euclidian, with arcs and planes where his peers imagined aircraft-like swoops and ogee curves, it has all the charm of a self-propelled, home-built travel trailer. Interior room presses to the margins, barely acknowledging the running gear, popping the wheels half the way into the passenger compartment. As soberly utilitarian (it fairly shouts "Home Depot!") as the Voisin is proud and majestic, the design is a tart reminder of the disconnect between Le Corbusier's rhetoric and his bid to personally enter the world of the industrialist.

That world, at least on the surface, seemed willing to entertain his entreaties. Amado has unearthed fascinating letters politely shunting Corb to those the authors deem likely to collaborate, which, like a spurned lover, he pursues with increasing ardor. Between the lines, however, the message was blunt: architecture was fine for the estate, but not for the road.

Conflicted? Indeed. This was an era in which the contesting forces of industrialization and elite culture were uneasy companions. Architects, noses in the air, were awash with grand illusions. Gropius shed his austere identity to build his very own bling-mobile, and Frank Lloyd Wright tooled around in a grand but off-putting Continental with portholes (the automotive equivalent of Johnson's Chippendale tower!). Fuller and Molino threw their hat in the ring, but, ultimately, there was no there there. It was up to a new breed of industrial designer—Norman Bel Geddes, under-the-radar William Stout, and of course Raymond Loewy—to crack the code that separated elite patronage from the all-powerful consumer. Matter of fact, there is still no way to connect the dots. The Citrohan House, the Lustron House, and the Wachsman/Gropius Panel House all failed to work out the simple fact that the public eyeballs buildings but craves consumer goodies.

Amado doesn't try, which is to his credit. Discussing the Citrohan House along with the Stein house, Amado avoids a mash-up by confessing that his passion for automobiles drove him to cross conceptual and academic boundaries, finally giving birth to a thesis that favors fervor for the subject over academic limits, and leaving us with the tantalizing thought that the automobile was the secret force behind Le Corbusier's urban vision.

He gives us the goods, packaged in a generously designed format, which fills page after page with foolscap sketches (in color), and a remarkably astute collection of period photographs. Corbusian lore peppers the pages, sparked by the occasional well-chosen bon mot and, above all, untainted by a whiff of undeserved authority. This book is clear and innocent, and the author is passionately devoted to his subject. Leafing through the reproductions of the competitor's drawings, I thought as Le Corbusier must have thought, perhaps for the first time, "*Merde*—all the good ideas are taken!"

029.1
Syd Mead, *LA Skyline West*, 1988.

The Future
According to Mead

THE ARCHITECT'S NEWSPAPER (11 AUGUST 2011)

Hodgetts provides a glowing portrayal of production designer and illustrator Syd Mead, on the occasion of a 2012 exhibition of Mead's work at the Forest Lawn Museum in Los Angeles. In it, Hodgetts laments architectural culture's seeming disregard of Mead, whose work has so clearly (if subconsciously) invaded the field's collective subconscious. For Hodgetts, Mead is the real deal —analog techniques and all. Architects need to get on board, even if it means getting out of their (cliquish) comfort zones.

In the beginning there was pulp sci-fi. Lurid cartoons of future cities riddled with aerial tramways and flying cars, and throbbing with atomic power. For the most part they populated the covers of newsstand offerings like *Popular Science* and *Amazing Tales*. But all that was before Syd. He changed all that. He was a futurist. He invented the term. He created a new genre.

One can forgive the nearly one thousand visitors at the opening exhibition of *Syd Mead: Progressions* if they missed the irony: there was the acclaimed futurist himself, dressed all in white, receiving friends in the faux-medieval courtyard of the Forest Lawn Mortuary and Museum. Joining the throngs of the faithful as they jostled for a better view of his paintings, and searching in vain for even one fellow architect, one could not help wondering why the place was not swarmed by young designers. And one was reminded once again of just how insular the architects of the "Me Generation" had become.

On display were images depicting cityscapes and buildings that might have been snatched from the most recent international competitions. Lustrous metallic surfaces, twisting towers, parametric volumes, all hauntingly beautiful, and all bearing dates—wait for it—from the early *1970s and '80s*! That's right! Before most of the maestros of Rhino and Maya had been potty-trained. Yet from the depths of the postmodern era, like a latter-day Jules Verne, or a reincarnated Piranesi, Mead had anticipated the seamless, gestural designs that are multiplying on screens around the world.

Mead is perhaps best known among architects as the visionary designer whose work on 1982's *Blade Runner* set the stage for the edgy, post-apocalyptic style that shoved postmodernism into oblivion. Originally hired as an Art Center alum car "thug" to visualize Rick Deckard's hovering cop car, he couldn't resist plunging the auto, in true Mead fashion, into imaginary street scenes cluttered with a goulash of cryptic signs and symbols and draped with a spaghetti of cables and pipes, as though the whole of Los Angeles was on life support. Those images, now part of our collective subconscious, propelled Mead into a stratosphere of designers whose vision embraced consumer goods, transportation, and everything else the eye could see, down to the typography on a food cart.

The surprise is that the images in Mead's luminous gouache paintings from the 1970s and '80s, while not by any means photo-realistic, create such a powerful sense of *being right there*, that even the most sophisticated digital renderings seem pallid by comparison. These are images composed with such flair, such lyrical attention to the combined effect of reflections, surfaces, and primary form, that the mind is lost in a space that is simultaneously ecstatic and revelatory.

029.2
Syd Mead, *Pebble Beach Panel Two,* 2000.

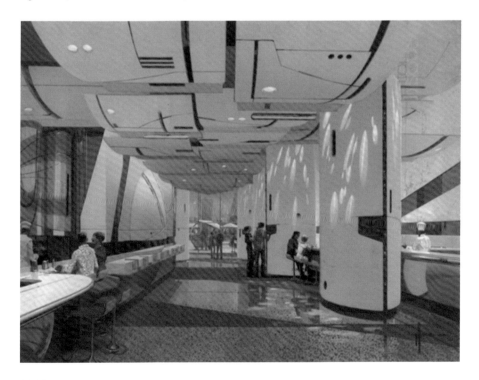

029.3
Syd Mead, *Foodparc,* 2010.

029.4
Syd Mead, Artwork for US Steel, 1961.

There is no doubt that Mead's genre, heavy on willow-thin, armed vixens, shoulder pads, and upturned collars, has sadly consigned his best work to the science-fiction catalog, especially among those whose aesthetic appreciation is dictated by political correctness. But Mead seems unfazed. True, the products of his imaginings are often situated in star fields and endless interplanetary space, or in the purple haze of an otherworldly sunset reflected from the spit-polished canopy of an idling coupe. But what's important is the existence of, indeed the fact of, those reflections, the *fact* of the sunset, the *fact* of the coupe in the foreground, framing a distant view of a many-spired city, and the *fact* of the deeply textured fabric of the driver's jacket that conjures references to Velázquez and Tintoretto. Yes, the paintings do exalt a now-banished monarchy, and yes, the bejeweled courtiers do embody the appalling, self-indulgent posture of the aristocracy, but those issues should not displace the astonishing artistry compressed into a few millimeters of paint.

Like the great classical artists, Mead's primary palette is light. Limpid, hard-edged, violent even, it splashes, spurts, and eddies in mercurial pools, restlessly articulating his subjects. One cannot detect Mead's hand in this. The brushstrokes (yes, he used brushes, young Turks) melt into the subject matter, revealing first the glint of a visor, then the almost imperceptible texture of a darkly shadowed overhang. The overhang, the shadow, and the barely visible activity within might be framed by a highly reflective pool, leading the eye to an off-camera transaction scorched into a jagged rockscape. There is intrigue, a mesmerizing stillness, and a fully realized yet improbable culture framed as carefully as a tourist poster. The geometry, rendered in great, sweeping gestures that bind the composition, would have provided a feeding frenzy for art scholars like Rudolph Arnheim, but for poor mortals, it is the proto-erotic, fetishized imagery itself that lingers in the memory.

Surprisingly, Mead has only occasionally stepped out of the world of fantasy—whether cinematic or graphic—into the world of steel and concrete. His concepts should blend seamlessly into our near-seamless global economy. One thinks of Neil Denari, and Zaha Hadid, and Tom Wiscombe, whose gestures and surfaces have more than a whiff of Syd, or of Marc Newson, whose products, but for their jocular nature, might have a place at the table. But that's another story. Right now, I'm planning to dine at Bar Basque, Syd's first venture into the "real" world. I'm told the food is delicious, but I'm going there for the design.

030.1
Frankenboyz (Frederick Fisher, Robert Mangurian, Eric Owen Moss, Coy Howard, Craig Hodgetts, Thom Mayne, and Frank Gehry at Venice Beach), 1980.

Architects' Statement

TODD GANNON AND EWAN BRANDA, EDS., **A CONFEDERACY OF HERETICS** (LOS ANGELES: SCI-ARC PRESS AND GETTY RESEARCH INSTITUTE, 2013), WITH ROBERT MANGURIAN.

Hodgetts, in a piece co-written with Robert Mangurian, reminisces about the formation of what would come to be known as the "LA School" of architects in 1970s Venice. Written for the 2013 exhibition *A Confederacy of Heretics* at SCI-Arc, Hodgetts and Mangurian provide a succinct first-person account of the burgeoning scene of artists and architects and, in particular, their 1979 show at Thom Mayne's Architecture Gallery.

Whatever brought this bunch of guys to the desolate Pacific fringe, Los Angeles, in the late '70s and early '80s is not clear—nor does it matter very much. What matters is that they were all recent graduates from architecture schools spread all across the country, and that they shared a discomfort—disdain even—for the trappings of the then-dominant architectural culture. Maybe they liked being on the actual edge of the country as well. What is clear is that they felt profoundly disenfranchised. What is unclear is how they found each other.

Venice, in those days, was a haunt of mostly vagrants, itinerant trailer people, Hells Angels, and the remains of the hippie culture. The beach was littered with battle-scarred motorhomes, careering seagulls, and bordered by a few scab-by coffee joints. Artists were the first to arrive—Eric Orr, Ron Cooper, Ron Davis, the Dill brothers, and others. The cheap rent, left-over storefronts, and desolate ambiance had a considerable appeal to them and, never far behind, architects.

It was not a pre-ordained, structured, manifesto *à la* the New York Five. Far from it! There was no sheltering institution, no MoMA, no Philip Johnson. The players were all playing out their own hands, together in their ennui, their search for a sympathetic audience, but ultimately, acutely on their own. Consensus, such as it was, was always implicit, apparent in the work itself. The nearest approach to a codified, unified front was the "Silvers" conference initiated by Tim Vreeland at UCLA, which proposed a West Coast retort to the "Whites and Grays" on the East Coast.

There were some collaborative arrangements: Coy Howard and Hodgetts worked together briefly on designs for a then forward-thinking computer firm (1980) and Michael Rotondi helped to refine the Hodgetts-designed Punchout line of furniture before joining Thom Mayne to form Morphosis. But overall, the orbits of the Venice studios were principally tethered to two institutions: UCLA, which, under the stewardship of Vreeland, looked eastward for succor, and SCI-Arc, which had gathered together most of the talented and vocal young architects under the leadership of Ray Kappe. It was Kappe who led a revolt at Cal Poly Pomona, commandeered a decaying West Los Angeles metal shop, and began the school from scratch with a group of students which included Rotondi.

Between them, the schools were able to lend a modicum of support to the growing body of younger architects—partly financial—but much more important-ly by offering them a platform from which to promote a unique vision. A vision which in retrospect was intransigent, iconoclastic, and—shudder—doomed to be regional, but which was, in fact, solidly grounded in a fresh appraisal of the unexplored material potential unfettered by European antecedents.

030.2
Thane Roberts, Robert Mangurian, and Craig Hodgetts at Studio Works, Venice, California, 1974.

Where there are artists, of course, there will be galleries, and in the late '70s two galleries that were to assume major roles set up shop on Main Street in Venice rather than join the flourishing, established scene on La Cienega. Ace led off with a Robert Irwin installation which removed the entire facade of the building and replaced it with a transparent fabric skin. The other, commissioned by Larry Gagosian, resulted in the first Los Angeles project by Studio Works, then a bicoastal operation with Mangurian in New York, one floor above Warhol's Factory, and Hodgetts, who had come to Los Angeles from NYC to head the design department at CalArts, in a studio at the foot of Rose Avenue, which he shared with artist Eric Orr.

Others in the constellation of young architects had found similar spaces pretty much within walking distance of one another. Roland Coate, Eric Moss, Howard, and Mayne occupied storefronts strung out between Speedway and Electric, and entrepreneurs like David Greenberg, who founded Environmental Communications, and artists-turned-developers Tom Sewell and Guy Webster had a presence on nearby Pacific Avenue. Soon thereafter, Tony Bill, the producer and director of Shampoo, LA's first boutique grocery, and Leonard Koren's *Wet* Magazine fleshed out what was fast becoming an enclave of young, energetic, shoestring endeavors which were defiant misfits in the prevailing culture.

When Frank Gehry, then conducting a largely commercial practice from a spacious industrial loft, decided to join the club and relocate into a cramped, messy storefront a few yards from the beach, it was clear that what had begun as a coagulation of misfits was emerging from the shadows.

Los Angeles Times reporter John Dreyfuss and *Examiner* critic Sam Kaplan noticed. A flurry of articles documented the scrappy architecture then emerging in Venice, which contrasted vividly with the polished, corporate architecture then favored by both papers. The controversy expanded as Dreyfuss dug in, highlighting design events like Hodgetts's Venice biennale proposal and offering intelligent commentary on the scene. At times, Dreyfuss seemed to channel the DNA of the emerging architects, championing those who designed it as well as the work itself. It felt like Hollywood.

By the time Mayne captured that energy—self-sponsoring a series of exhibitions at the storefront where he practiced and lived—the 'gang' had a modicum of success. Projects, exhibitions, installations, rhetoric, and manifestoes were multiplying rapidly, while opportunities for lectures and teaching—mostly at SCI-Arc and UCLA—were lending both visibility and credibility to what had been a far-out fringe.

Each exhibit was self-curated by the participants. Often assembled at the last minute, without a budget, and with only minimal promotion, the series played out like an off-off-Broadway production, attended by a motley crew of students, fellow teachers, and friends of friends. No one had any expectations, yet the fire had been lit. Dreyfuss contributed detailed articles on each show. The word, somehow, got out.

Our own contribution, coming as we were from completing the construction documents for our first two Los Angeles commissions, was firmly grounded in the philosophy made famous by writer-director Bertold Brecht. We had an innate distaste for self-promotion, and decided that the only honest posture was to present exactly what we were doing as exactly as possible. By positioning a couple of long tables in the center of the storefront, and covering them with an assortment of drawings, pencils, model fragments, and references to late nights, we hoped to convey an impression of process. The hard work, attention to detail, and common materials we saw as antidotes to a more pragmatic design practice.

Predictably, the shows had little or no effect on the largely disinterested local population. After all, there were no fashionistas, no sidewalk cafes, no museums of contemporary art, and no gourmet bakeries. It was another time, a time when Case Study houses were being demolished with the same fervor that Lautner's string of tiny Naylor restaurants was being replaced with strip malls. Los Angeles was still innocent, and it would be many years before Rodney King kicked off an urban revolution.

030.3 and 030.4
Craig Hodgetts and Robert Mangurian photographed at their exhibition
at Thom Mayne's Architecture Gallery in Venice, California, November 1979.

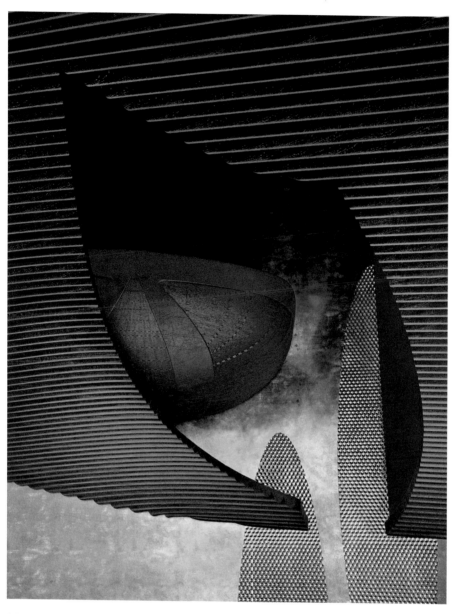

031.1
Coy Howard, *Red, Villa No. 3*, 2010.

Mystery Man

THE ARCHITECT'S NEWSPAPER (18 MAY 2015)

Hodgetts reviews Coy Howard's 2015 monograph, *The Thickening of Time*. Though he is usually skeptical of sumptuous coffee-table style books like this, Hodgetts cannot condemn the enigmatic vision and palpable passion for the mysteries of architecture of his one-time collaborator and long-time fellow traveler in Los Angeles architecture. Hodgetts is mesmerized by and lavishes his trademark exuberant description on Howard's "indulgent," even "decadent" attention to detail and allusive atmospherics.

The magical images captured on the pages of *The Thickening of Time* mark the much-delayed and nearly mythical emergence from obscurity of its author, architect Coy Howard. And much like the man himself, it presents its images cloaked in enigmatic vistas, peculiar attitudes, and piercing pictorial conundrums. This is *not* a book about architecture. This *is* a book about *Architecture*. This is *not* a book about *Architecture*, but it is a book about *Architecture* that resonates with architecture's romance with opulence, obfuscation, and metaphor. Howard's elaborate production techniques, attention to minute detail, and image density must have been quite a workout for the multiple programs one imagines he must employ. Yet the images—haunting, darkly glistening, otherworldly—are presented as documentary evidence of an imaginary yet realistic environment.

Howard, whose long tenure at SCI-Arc has been marked by an unorthodox teaching style, has mesmerized students for nearly twenty years. His emphasis on traditional skills, personal vision, and artistic rigor is legendary, and from the evidence of this book, well-deserved. The images within are simply extraordinary. They exude sophistication, erudition, and a finely honed architectural sensibility, in spite of their *tromp l'oeil* optical effects.

Take this one [031.2]. *Look hard.* That thin line far away bisecting the frame. *Look closer.* It is a finely detailed railroad track with an even more finely detailed miniature train running along the intersection of floor and baseboard. I won't hazard a guess as to what it's doing there, and I'm guessing that Howard would not ask me that question. But I am convinced that *he* knows why it's there.

Therein lies the essence of these highly controlled, hermetically sealed images.

The objects portrayed in the images—furnishings, somewhat fetishized surfaces, etc.—often refer to the actualized, functional furniture which Howard has developed for a suite of rarified architectural projects. Drawing from mostly classical sources, Howard has given a great deal of thought to the transition between, say, a cast-in-bronze detail and its carved wood receptacle. The polished results transcend mere cabinetwork and take their place alongside the extraordinary fabrications of Bugatti, Moretti, Mollino (especially), and Gaudí. These pieces, beautifully photographed and achingly detailed, form the core of Howard's architectural imagination, which, with its insistence on rigor, succeeds in joining fantasy and practice without, on the whole, sacrificing the one to the other.

His argument, insofar as he is willing to articulate it, is that "the full meaning of work that is intended as aesthetic experience is beyond explanation." Jeffrey Kipnis, who penned an introduction, compares the images to the sensations imparted by an exceptional cognac, which must be savored, but never swallowed.

031.2
Coy Howard, *Amber, Villa No. 2*, 2010.

It is we, the architects, who are frustrated by the ambiguity of the images. After centuries, eons even, of architectural representation, we who pass our professional lives parading renderings that purport to show a completed building are baffled, even angered by images that tease but refuse to reveal much. Yet it would be a blunder to demand the full Monty if it meant giving up the dark rewards of Howard's imagery.

Those images, wrought by a wicked mash-up of the hand, the eye, and the mouse, defy any effort to reverse-engineer their creation. Dot for dot and pixel for pixel they proclaim their origin as documentary evidence. Yet by their implausible point of view, their visceral texture, and their mini-Wagnerian scale, they are more painterly than Maya-ish, far more lavish than Rhino. One thinks of the exquisite draftsmanship of Dalí (minus the surrealism), or the sleek surfaces of Vermeer (minus the princelings). A rival might exist in the drawings of Syd Mead (minus the Sci-Fi), but certainly not even remotely in the architect's canon of Lebbeus Woods, Carlos Diniz, or Steven Holl. In mood, in temper, they are more Munch than Giger, more somber than headstones.

This is a big, sumptuous book, suited to pride-of-place on the coffee table or in the study. I am not a fan of such, having been on the wrong side in published comments in this very rag, but, frankly, I'm on the fence about this one. The content, which my personal philosophy would find dangerously indulgent, even decadent, is so clearly a work of passion, rather than conspicuous consumption, that I'm inclined to agree with its presentation in kind. Should still another gilded age lie ahead, Howard's work should, and probably would, be held in a kind of reverent awe that such a physical work might be produced in our *cyber-über-alles* era. And yet ... and yet ...

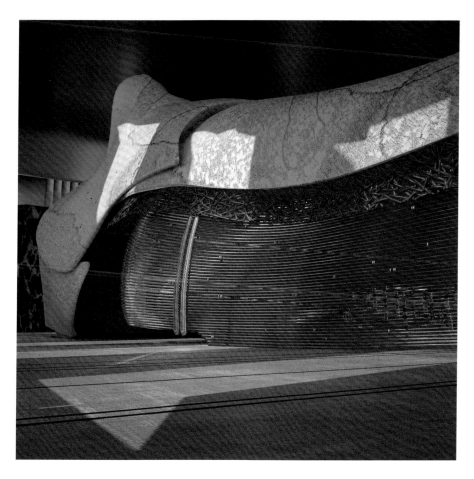

031.3
Coy Howard, *Pink and Yellow, Villa No. 5*, 2010.

The Petersen Musuem: What's Under the Hood?

FORM (10 MARCH 2016)

Hodgetts tries to give the much-maligned Petersen Automotive Museum by Kohn Pedersen Fox Associates its due. He makes a convincing case for the relevance, maybe even elegance, of the building's writhing wrapper in the legacy of googie architecture and hot rod design, but finds little to back it up in the lackluster organization of the interior. In other words, just as the museum's layout makes it difficult to get under the hood and make a real connection with the classic cars in its collection, there's nothing much 'under the hood' of the Peterson Museum.

Time was, LA was breeding 'em like rabbits. Everywhere you looked there was another one of 'em, surrounded by bright-colored tangerine metal-flake iron. Neon, too, with great big lopsided lettering and sometimes even a bow-tie-looking roof, popular with the Brylcreem set and their dolls. Serving up fries and shakes and special sauce.

They were gathering places for kids who made their own—stuffing a 283 Chevy into an old Ford, or dropping a Caddy into a Stude. Their own kind of miscegenation, snubbing their nose at the pedigreed MGs, Alfas, and Sunbeams that were beginning to make a claim on their turf.

There was even a name for them. A name named after the one at the end of the Sunset Strip, across from number 77:

"GOOGIES."

Googies (the restaurant) was a striped and angular spot that catered to the four-wheeled extravaganzas cruising by. The ones that Bob Petersen began to chronicle in a start-up magazine called *Hot Rod*. The ones the Beach Boys sing about and Tom Wolfe writes about. The ones that built an empire out of a new kind of polyglot expressionism that used the belts and springs and pipes, the valve covers and fans, those curling manifolds and gaping intakes, the sawed-off roofs and smoothed out noses to send good vibrations all across America.

Critics didn't get it. But artists did. Billy Al and Bob Irwin, Chamberlain and Valentine mined it for all they were worth, hanging hoods and crushed parts like hunting trophies on the walls of museums everywhere.

Which brings us to the Petersen Museum, many decades later. Years after McDonald's abandoned its golden arches for a tepid logo. A long time after good taste ran roughshod over the works of John Lautner and Schindler—good architects all—a vanguard doomed to obscurity and the wrecking ball. Today's anointed ones, proud in the parametric livery probably didn't notice when a museum to celebrate the cars of that era was in the making, and shrugged at the temerity of a New Yorker trying to put his stamp on the Miracle Mile. So one can understand the yowls of Main Street, the bewilderment of pundits, and the deer-in-headlights consternation of our revered tastemakers.

The shock waves from that fluorescent, zebra striped makeover—redolent of George Barris and pin-stripe shaman Ed "Big Daddy" Roth bounced off the nearby Tar Pits, and promised to tickle the underbelly of Zumthor's proposal for the Los Angeles County Museum of Art. Sporting flame-like ribbons of stainless steel, and a vivid red sheath beneath, the former Orbach Department Store, now on its third, and hopefully final bout of cosmetic surgery, draws eyes, insults, and parody in equal measure, and reaffirms the prevailing worldview that Los Angeles is a careless outlier.

But is that true? It could be argued that the Petersen Museum is a clever rejoinder to the gathering cultural consensus. As the "vulgar" County Museum of Art is poised to be replaced by Zumthor's restrained monolith, the Academy of Motion Pictures (think Oscar) is readying a glass sphere designed by Renzo Piano, and Frank Gehry is preparing a residential tower, all within a few paces of one another, the mind turns to Hollywood blockbusters—to *A Perfect Storm*, or perhaps more fittingly, to *Godzilla versus Mothra*, the '60s Japanese cult film featuring a duel between outlandish, super-scaled monsters.

To the Petersen's credit, it provides an usual insight into the mind of its architect, Gene Kohn, a genial partner in the New York firm of Kohn Pedersen Fox, which is better known for its establishment credentials than the Petersen's writhing skin would lead one to believe. That the skin is an exercise in advanced digital fabrication, applied with such élan is, in itself, a proclamation, a sort of late-career renaissance, which thrusts the firm into a next generation spotlight. Whether naively assuming (wrongly) that Los Angeles was ready for a jolt of architectural electricity, or sincerely reflecting (rightly) a populist genre, Kohn succeeded in outflanking its neighbors, and disrupting the conventions governing the museum establishment.

And that is no small accomplishment.

One might assess the strategic vision as achieving the maximum visual effect with the least. Less being way more, since the reworking of the existing building is to be found almost exclusively in the metal panels streaming around it—held together by well positioned struts—evoking the painted flames of the classic hot rods while assuming an architectural/installation art posture.

What Kohn didn't get—what so many of a Eurocentric persuasion haven't and perhaps are not capable of "getting"—is the creative depth that lurks behind the flashy skins of LA's reputation for architectural innovation, which leads to an attitude that a skin-deep project is called for, even appreciated, while nothing could be further from the truth.

Here, in a town that invented the close-up, patented the special effect, and perfected lighting, one imagined a display of automotive art bordering on the erotic, with coachwork by Falaschi, Farina, and Superleggera, the flowing lines and glossy surfaces of the Petersen's collection are voluptuous as a '50s starlet—and deserved more than a perfunctory sprinkling of downlights. As early as the '50s, GM design chief Harley Earl and Eero Saarinen dreamed up a perfect, luminous

032.1
Kohn Pederson Fox Associates, Petersen Automotive Museum, Los Angeles, 2016.

environment so that GM execs could give the nod to advanced design exercises in a secret styling dome, and cinematographers have given star treatment to everything from the Batmobile to Peter Falk's beat-up Peugeot, so its puzzling that all the flash on the Petersen's façade is wrapped around the same-old, same-old of auto museums the world over. Lined up like convicts, with little or no way for a visitor to appreciate them in the round, the display of the museum's incredible collection of magnificent, even one-of-a-kind automobiles reminded me of nothing so much as a CarMax lot, without even the satisfaction of checking out what's under the hood.

Clearly, this is not a museum for car-nuts. Its exterior, for all that writhing bravado, quickly devolves into a rude cartoon while, to the cognoscenti—that one percent that view automobiles as the ultimate twentieth century art form (think Peter Mullin whose Bugatti shares pride of place with Steve McQueen's XKSS)—it represents an opportunity to elevate the status of their passion.

To the rest of us, to the looky-loos and lurkers, it's an obligation, a chance to pay respects, but, sadly, not a chance to really connect.

Part IV
For performance

La città pulpa

1995. WITH HSINMING FUNG. PREVIOUSLY UNPUBLISHED.

It's been ten years since the big one hit Los Angeles at 2:30 PST on Memorial Day, 1996. Just about everyone was outside: at the beach, on the road, in a boat. Some said it was like the opposite of a neutron bomb. It took the buildings, even the streets and utilities, but it spared the people. Korean, Samoan, Latin, Nordic, Black, Alsatian, Slavic, Aryan, Semitic people. People who had come to a city long ago formed by a succession of merchants and entrepreneurs who'd put a definitive Middle American stamp on its desert ecology. Most had adapted to the city's strip malls and broad shouldered streets—they'd festooned otherwise bland stucco walls with neon signatures in their native languages, and stood on freeway dividers hawking oranges and roses. But it was never theirs. Many longed for streets that felt more like home.

There were others whose lives had begun to cry out for a new culture altogether. They were wired, or pumped up, or simply experimenting with relationships and lifestyles that hadn't had a place before the quake.

Suddenly they all had a chance to make something new!

Their city was to be a place which celebrated Identity and Difference.

This is the story of a visitor's experience as she searches for her own identity, in this city of differences.

SCENE 1

The folks at "locations" are helpful. She shows her picture. "Oh, I don't know, dearie." Takes it and shows to superior, who shakes her head. Suggests she browse through the pics, and if she finds one to go after it *immediately*, since things don't last.

Asks where she wants to live. She says she doesn't know, depends on where she's going to work.

Work? The attendant cracks up. You can *work* anywhere. Where do you want to *live?*

Explains that New LA is divided into seven districts. She can work anywhere, nowhere, what difference does it make? It's all electronic anyway.

SCENE 2

Cindi is aboard a train as it pulls into New Los Angeles. The reader board advises her to watch her belongings carefully, and to be sure to register the sectors she intends to visit with Traveler's Aid.

She takes a final, fond look at a photograph of a house surrounded by a white picket fence, and stuffs it into her valise.

The station is overwhelming, and confusing. Out front there is a variety of transport available, from ecological cars with strange, wing-like solar collectors, to efficient electric jobs, a few gas-guzzlers, and bicycles. Hawkers ask where she is going and offer the proper transport.

This station, as main transportation center, bullet train or intercity metro, is owned by a major commercial corporation (Swatch, Wexner, Gap, etc., not unlike a Japanese department store). There's also a combination of museum/gallery with windows showing collections by these corporations.

In the background the buildings of New LA are visible in a vibrant mix of advertising displays, retrofits, and gutted skeletons.

Contrast of exterior mix of chaotic ads with more controlled/slick interior of station which is not run by city or state but by private enterprises.

Someone approaches, hands her a flyer titled "Locations," she looks up, sees a similar sign in background. "No thanks," she says, "I know where I'm going." "Well then good luck," the person says, shaking their head in disbelief.

And she's down in the subway system which is strangely deserted, though very grand. Occupied, it seems, mainly by homeless people. She wrinkles her nose and determines to get where she's going. Interactive station on subway car is broken. Frustrating. Guy on the seat next to hers offers an insight, says no one has used the subway since it was built. Advises her to take a "Crusher" to her destination.

Maybe this subway being underground lends itself to being dilapidated, as opposed to the other transportation systems.

Outbound station is even worse, there's visible damage that hasn't been repaired, no ads in the kiosks, except for some "locations" again.

Emerging, she's pleasantly surprised. There's a thriving retail area surrounding the stop. "No time," she thinks, and goes directly to the "Crusher" line.

SCENE 3

Cop, pretty well armored, asks where she's going, advises a route that gives the area a wide berth—says it's dangerous.

Cindi rents an electric car from a lock-down recharging station, (Crusher—the name is derived by the fact that the cars "crush" to save space like shopping carts. The user simply takes the appropriate one from the head of the line, which has generally had plenty of time to recharge since spent cars are left at the "back" of the line.), by sliding her card through a reader. She thinks, "That's all there is to it?" Doesn't read the sign insisting that parking anywhere but at a recharging station is at the renter's risk.

Looks for the address of her house on the car's internal navigation system. Is surprised there are no "conventional" street numbers. Advises that the area has been "reconfigured," tries visual reference, route appears. "Aha! And everyone told her there was no way," she thinks to herself.

Whizzes through a landscape of billboards, hotels, and rest stops on a freeway we can hardly recognize. There is little view of the city beyond, just mainly freeway associated stuff. She thinks, "This feels more like a subway."

To encapsulate the car fumes which have made the city uninhabitable, freeways have been enclosed as dark tunnels with occasional skylights (which look like deep gouges through the Nervi-esque concrete enclosure) showing glimpses of the city beyond.

Arrives at destination by following map of area from subway/auto print out. Parks. Things are still pretty messed up. Not much light, it's getting dark. But there's nothing there. A sign tells her that a new development for "Fun People" will be ready for occupancy next year.

Exit signs are large reader board strolling exits, not by street name, but by sectors: ten velominutes to ID, two autominutes to ID.

She's crushed. Looks around. She is in a kind of three-dimensional Kasbah. Tiny shops, catwalks overhead, and a vigorous individuality. Different building materials make up nearly every surface, and it seems to go on forever, with, if possible, even more complexity. Signs, around here, at least, are in every conceivable language. There are signs for fortune tellers, low-rate daily insurance policies, rap clubs, cut-rate language courses, dentists, clinics, excursions, etc. and, of course, "Locations," which seems to be everywhere.

Properties here are sold by the cubic feet ... property lines vary depending on how much money you have, no irregular division, some stores are closet size.

Sees a cybercafe. Cyberjava. Enters.

Loads of people sitting around. Terminals at every table. Lots of smoke. Dingy but OK. Like old fashioned bookstore-cum-cafe.

Interactive terminal at a cybercafe. Cindi has just finished uploading a picture of her little house with a white picket fence. Waitress brings coffee, sees the pic on the screen. Says she wishes she could find something like it.

She trolls a bit, then gets a bite. A picture begins to form. Words accompany it to say they're not sure it's going to be what she's looking for, but maybe she'd like to come and take a look anyway. Or—Hey baby, I've got what you want.

Bingo! She finds something promising. A broker?

Waitress asks if she's sure she wants to go alone. Downloads map. It's in the boonies. Tells her to be careful, there are lots of house pirates out there.

Cindi, naive, says she's got a car. Goes out to get it. It's gone.

Waitress (name is Nancy) tells her the house will probably be gone too if she doesn't get there right away. Cindy's card is rejected because electronic network knows car was jacked. Looks like she's got to find it or be in big trouble.

Waitress takes pity. She's off now anyway, offers to help, asks if Cindi has ever actually seen such a house. Of course, she says. Wow, says Nancy, and asks if she can come along. Considering her blue spiked hair, nose ring, and armored car outfit, Cindi is touched. Says yes, of course. Nancy says she thinks she knows where the car may be. Will take Cindi to recycling/repo part of the city.

Waitress could be bald headed with branded design on her head, but looks very sweet and innocent like CINDI, just a different style.

SCENE 4
On a bridge overlooking the old LA river, Cindi and Nancy stop to catch their breath.

SCENE 5
A landscape of reconfigured cast-off materials stretches indefinitely towards the horizon. Furtive lights illuminate rows of what must be housing made of the shells of old refrigerators, automobiles, and industrial machinery. As they approach, a group of children politely inquire about their purpose, she shows the photo, they then volunteer advice.

Whole industry of recycled appliances and machinery, very sophisticated, clean, slick. Since this is a lucrative business it is well organized and everything is cataloged, parts and whole. Some are sandblasted to its original materials; lifts, catwalks as conveyor belts are in constant motion overhead.

The place seems amazingly benign, in spite of the radical chic of its materials. Nancy and Cindi try to guess at the origins of a storefront, crack up at traffic lights created from the taillights of wrecked cars.

As they are standing there, wondering which way to go, a band of children come by. They are like pirates of old, proud in scavenged outfits and very charismatic. They are navigating a big truck-like apparatus filled to overflowing with cans, bottles, bedsteads, etc. It looks like a kind of surreal construction as it approaches in the pre-dawn glow.

Hop on, they say.

The children take them to where they work. Brandon is making a big, kind of crazy music machine "just for fun" that everyone can bounce around on to make weird kind of bump and grind music, which comes complete with a film loop from an old X-rated movie.

His father comes in from the shop just adjacent, tells Brandon it's bed time, Brandon climbs little stair on wall of work room to his bedroom.

Father tells Cindi Brandon's a good boy, but sometimes gets too involved in fantasy world. Wishes he would focus more on something useful *like literature, a rare commodity indeed*, offers to let them stay. Grateful, they agree.

The next day, Brandon says he's located something interesting on his computer while he was supposed to be asleep. Shows it (the house!) to Cindi who says "It's perfect!" and takes them to a kind of swap meet where old and used items are bartered for new, "recycled" or remanufactured items. It's clear that there is a going economy of such transactions. Harlan, an auctioneer, points out the database generated by the systematic plotting of critical dimensions from each items as it is added to the inventory. Explains that in this way, compatibility and reuse are maximized.

They go to a *Raiders of the Lost Ark*-type storage facility. Go unerringly to a box, get it down, and voilà—Bob Stern's *Life* magazine proposal for the perfect American house. She asks if anyone's ever actually built one. They continue to sort through the box, come up with a map. It's old, water-stained, but the part of town where the house is supposed to be is torn away.

SCENE 6

The mixer is a real scene. A retro band plays in a deserted foundry, etc. There's a lot of political talk, questions about the viability of the overall system, lots of tension between the *Authentics and the Synthetics*.

Cindi wonders out loud about the fate of her house, is verbally attacked by the ringleader, who proclaims any such desire as decadent and retro. Can't stand the goody-two-shoes inhabitants of the ecological sector. Cindi breaks down. Wants to know what's so evil. He explains the over management that leads to such a good balance with scorn. Can't understand why anyone would want to live such a life.

Nancy says she doesn't see what's so great about the way LA has wound up. Shame on you too ringleader. Tries to rescue Cindi. Harlan (*Where does he come from?*) is suddenly by their side. Things are turning ugly. He leads them through narrow streets closed on both sides by corrugated metal, then under a freeway overpass.

They are just about to step from the curb to cross a street into *Lux* when a helicopter appears overhead. Amplified voice tells them not to move, that their costumes do not conform.

SCENE 7

Police station interrogation room. Cops won't believe her story, think it too naive. They imagine she is part of a notorious gang of house pirates who they are sure have a hideout in the recycling zone. Show her a map of where they strike, then a survey of a house they have completely cleaned, even to the aluminum siding, which disappeared from an estate while the owner was away in Bilbao at the opening of the new museum there.

She just wants her house. One cop believes her. Gives her the lowdown on Lux. Poo-poos the idea that there is anything like her dream house there, among the fakes. Volunteers to help them look.

She wants to look anyway. Goes with Harlan and Nancy to check it out.

Houses border golf courses, have mini shopping areas dotted throughout, kiosks where people work, no other sign of productivity. Contrast with recycling spot is profound. Entire place seems to be planned around consumption and deal-making.

Unlike other places, here there is no sign of advertising, shops have plain storefronts, all of it uniform, no name, no street address, you are supposed to know where to go if you belong. Visitors get their direction only if a map is unloaded onto their screen, and the program is immediately destroyed when they get to their destination strip.

Little concrete paths connect the periphery of golf-course-like grounds. On the grounds, cute little striped veranda/tent affairs. Everywhere she looks, people seem to be on cell phones, usually siting at a table with very nice appointments, or even shoulders deep in huge community Jacuzzis, complete with floating trays and nearby bar. It's like one of those South American resorts, but businesslike.

She spies one area that appears to be a church bingo party, approaches.

The tent is full of well-dressed women. Checks and stripes and flower corsages. Most are ample. A particularly ample one (perhaps recalling the queen in Alice) is exhorting her "troops," it's a sales meeting! For a TV marketing company introducing a new exercise machine!

A man in a black suit—security—speaks a few words into a microphone. Cindi motions to Nancy—we better get out of here.

Too late. They are surrounded by golf carts and men in black suits. Back to the same interrogation room. This time as "industrial spies." Cindi pulls out her photo. The judge—huge, female, snorts with derision. "There hasn't been one of those dinky things here since the Big One!" And the courtroom rings with laughter. "I think you'd better look elsewhere."

One of the security men, in the back seat, gives them his email number, says if they are ever in *real* trouble, to give him a call.

Black-suited security men conduct them to the border of the sector. Gates are opened, and they walk onto what appears to be a perfectly ordinary road, after the tiny paths of Lux, and breathe a sigh of relief when a huge truck zooms by.

SCENE 8

Cindi and friends queue up at the bus-stop. Others are insistent that they stay exactly in line. Looks at watch. It's a bit offensive—she's told not to worry, the bus is always on time.

While waiting they notice they're standing on a treadmill—it's hooked up, they are told, to the central power grid.

All around them, people are leaving their apartments in jogging shorts and cross-trainers. Many have big dogs. They notice that the lights in the sports stadium are burning brightly, even though it's broad day, and giant reader boards contain the names of residents and what their latest accomplishments might be. "Shades of Warhol," says Cindi, to no one in particular.

Buildings are clad with mirror and clear glass. Different activities, stock trading, body building, occupy several floors, creating large patterns of movements on buildings. Muscular buildings, Lloyd's of London/Takamatsu-type.

What did you say? Says the bus driver/monitor, and everyone stops what they are doing to wait for the answer.

I just said, "Shades of Warhol," says Cindi, as a mobile "community camera crew" passes by, and she notices that she is suddenly thirty feet high on the projection screen across the street. Then just as quickly, the image changes to that of the mayor saying that the city will no longer tolerate the incursions of residents of the repo area.

Silently, they board the bus, and are sitting deep in thought when there is a loud bang, and the bus shudders to a stop. What now? Driver says be calm, looks at smoke rising from engine compartment.

They're out on the street again. This time in front of a giant building crammed with what appears to be arcade games. Over the door it says P.S.1. What is this, some kind of joke?

Curious, they enter. Bedlam. Kids everywhere, standing in front of huge screens, frantically working joysticks. On the screen, stuff about history, finance, science. One particularly tiny kid in a leather jacket is sailing in a VR world high over a pulsing landscape. The name of the game is *Arbitrage*, suddenly, he crashes into a mountain. Shit! Everyone looks. He starts to cry.

Cop says he's heard about these schools, but never actually been in one. Says the kid was actually making trades! Was on an incredible role. Says suicide rate in score's school system is incredibly high because of what they call the "Reality Bath."

Cindi is aghast. "You mean ... well, I mean, um, what happened to their CHILDHOOD?"

SCENE 9

Cindi and friends are in the tower suite cantilevered from the side of one of the few high-rise structures left after the Big One. Immediately outside, a huge propeller is contained in the vortex of what used to be the lobby. There is one every floor, which makes use of the wind patterns created by the building. There is a video/painting on the wall of fruit trees, herbs, tomato plants, etc. Cindi remarks that they look good enough to eat. Assistant in a turban and dashiki says Mr. Leary will see her now. Nancy wishes her good luck.

Leary is sitting in a Jacuzzi in a rustic setting, earnestly trying to help. He rolls a joint, sits back. Philosophizes about the meaning of her quest. We become part of his dreamscape as he weaves images of domesticity, do-it-yourself-ness, apocalyptic world visions, peace and love, around her simple-minded desires. She is mesmerized. He offers her a toke. Then insists, inviting her to join him. As she begins to fend him off, the assistant enters, reminds him that his news conference is beginning.

He hops out of the tub, wraps towel around his waist, entire wall opens to reveal room full of shutterbugs and reporters. He, Castro-like, addresses them with big ideas that sound vaguely like the same things he was telling Cindi.

She makes a dash for the elevator thinking "narrow escape," is confronted by a bunch of weird choices on the elevator panel, can't think, punches one.

They wind up in a hydroponic garden level called a community garden. Grow lights line the ceiling. Different gardens have different names attached to them. A little video camera and bio-monitoring equipment is located near each. She picks an apple. There is a loud shriek. Sirens go off.

They zoom to the elevator, press another button. Get off on a floor filled with desks and people at work. The gardener is running after them. They make it to the elevator and another floor. It's full of books and videos. To the next and so on, always being chased by the gardener.

Finally, they reach the bottom of the building. Zoom out on the "street." It's full of strange rickshaw-like devices with elaborate fabric shades, and a canal down the center. Highly decorated boats-like cable cars float from stop to stop. Above, it's easy to see the buildings with their rustic retrofit and floor after floor of different uses.

Cindi plops into a boat, lets out a big sigh and says, "All I wanted was a bite!"

SCENE 10

The boat continues down the canal. A group of Japanese industrialists get on the boat. They are speaking and pointing at things, but we have no idea what they are saying. Cindi follows when they get out, there is some sort of a tour guide. He explains the system of rickshaws, which are a kind of community property, and the solar sensitive skin which all structures are required to be covered by. The Japanese are impressed. Then he rounds a corner to a museum.

They enter. There is a parade of antique, energy consuming devices, each one with a prominent sign indicating how much power it used to consume. There are porcelain toilets and stoplights and fire-breathing Detroit iron. There is a row of stoves. And then, the group rounds a corner, and stands while looking with approval at something Cindi can't see. She pushes her way through and there, mounted on a huge turntable, is the house with a white picket fence.

Oh my God! says Cindi, as the lecturer begins to describe the features of a bygone era.

END

Purity
A Play in One Act

2014. PREVIOUSLY UNPUBLISHED.

My thoughts on art rise toward ever the plastic, all a form, a line more esoteric. My attempts are formless, disappointing. My entire imagination is at work. I want a clarity, a sheen, a sharpness that tolerate only pure pencil, discipline and rhythm, and moderation of color. And I paint filth. My women are bestially lascivious, prurient, in heat.

— **LE CORBUSIER,** NOTEBOOK ENTRY, 12 MAY 1918.

CHARACTERS

EILEEN GRAY
The well-known Scots/Parisian designer and architect. She wears her jet-black hair in the short, cropped style fashionable in the '30s among intellectuals and artists.

LE CORBUSIER
Architect and theorist famous for stating that a house is "a machine for living." His signature circular eyeglasses complement a wiry, intense frame.

JEAN
Eileen's Paris dealer and confidant.

JOSEPHINE BAKER
The American singer/dancer who has captured the attention of Parisian audiences.

WORKMEN

FIFI
A small, fashionable dog.

SCENE ONE

Southern France, sometime in the 1930s. Crisp white room. Very modern. A rectangular window presents a view of the Mediterranean. No curtains, no carpets. Two men, both wearing French-style work trousers with suspenders. Gloved hands. They are lifting a slender chromium table, one at each end. A woman, bobbed hair, straight-cut dress, Prada-style, is pointing.

EILEEN	Towards me.
	They advance towards her slowly.
	Not so fast. Just a bit more.
	This cycle repeats several times, with increasing urgency.
MAN ONE	What about—
EILEEN	No. I've thought about it and no, I don't think so.
MAN ONE	Well, I was just thinking …
	He sets the table down. Walks to pick up a vase.
MAN ONE	If you were to—
EILEEN	But I'm not.
MAN ONE	Ma'am, excuse me. I've helped other ladies. Sometimes it's hard to decide.
EILEEN	You have, have you? And what Ex-act-ly has transpired?
MAN ONE	*(Blushing. Pokes chest à la Léger.)*
	Well, actually—
EILEEN	To get, shall we say … with it? To get … sensible? Or to perhaps get … in-ter-ested?
MAN ONE	I …
EILEEN	I'm sure you made them very happy. You're very big, you know … all that lifting …
	She bends towards him tauntingly, then prances away.
EILEEN	Let's just say I'm not into that! Now …
	Gesturing.
	Towards me! No, that won't do. That won't do at all.
MAN ONE	Ma'am, if you don't mind. My arms are getting tired. If you could just—

EILEEN	Make up my mind? Oh, that would be easy, wouldn't it? Just turn my back on the whole affair. Well, I won't. Come over here if you must. No, look. Look from corner to corner. Along the diagonal. No, not like that. Get down. Close one eye. Sight. Along. The. Diagonal. Bend. Over. Further. Further. Now … You see? It's … *To Man Two* You. You. Stand over there. Hold this. *Hands him a curtain rod.* Alright. Don't move. Stop shaking! Now. Upright! Can you please make it upright? Guides him with her hand. He flinches.
EILEEN	Up. Right. I said. *She looks around.*
EILEEN	There's a principal at stake here. You follow? None of your matrons with their crystal and lace and … but I would expect that you … *A peal of laughter.* That you … *Cracking up at a secret insight.* After all, you're workers. Just that. I must have … righto … Back to your positions. Upright, remember? Now … I want you to slowly, ever so slowly, extend your arm to the left. Hold it. H-o-l-d it. Right … there. *She bends down to sight from another angle.* I thought for a minute you might appreciate … this was just a bit … no … it's not working.
MAN ONE	What? *Eileen looks his way.*
MAN ONE	What's not working?
EILEEN	It's obvious. The hypotenuse. The structure of it all. *She hands him a feather duster.* OK. Point. Point towards the sea. Lower. L-o-w-e-r. *She walks over. Placing herself directly in line with the feather duster.* Back a bit … come towards me … stop. Right. *Steps back crosses her arms. Satisfied.* Can you feel it? Can you? *Inspecting him top to toe.* Of course you can't. Your nails are all broken. From the lifting, I mean.
MAN ONE	*(protesting)* What if I do?

EILEEN	You would know it, believe me. If you had that special something but … let me give you an example. Suppose you were a piece of string. Can you imagine that? Feel it? *(disdainfully)* Of course you can't. What a pity.
MAN ONE	Look lady …
EILEEN	Of course, of course, you would … if you could. But then I wouldn't need to tell you, would I? You'd be blabbering on about the horizon, and the alignments, all that, you see, that you don't see, do you? Oh, you're not to blame, any more than those matrons in the city with their impossibly stuffed boudoirs. Oh, you would think the sun rose and set on their chinoiserie, their antimacassars, their dining tables with little bronze antelope feet. Husbands footing it for Lord knows how many … *Man Two is fidgeting. The upright stick in his hand wavers.*
EILEEN	Say! Hey there! Steady!
MAN ONE	Yes, ma'am, but … *Eileen turns to Man One while holding out a ball of string.*
EILEEN	Here. hold it to the corner. Right here. Good! *She unrolls the string to stand parallel to the window overlooking the Mediterranean, stretching the string between them and adjusting it so that it is parallel to the horizon.* Now. You see? This is absolute! *Sights across the string to the horizon.* There can be no mistakes from here on. Now. (*To Man Two*) Hold this end … So! *At this point Man Two is struggling to hold the stick upright, the feather duster horizontal, and now the string. It's too much.*
MAN ONE	Ma'am! I need some relief.
EILEEN	I'm sure you do. Just a few moments and you shall have it. (*To Man Two*) Let go the duster. *Takes it.* Now! *Begins humming and moving about the room bending, sighting, bending.*
MAN ONE	Ma'am.
EILEEN	It's like infinity. It's endless really. This segment like every other.
MAN ONE	*(with increasing urgency, holding his crotch.)* Please may I? I can't hold out much longer.

EILEEN	*(loudly)* Well, tie it off then! I can't afford to have you running off every moment. This is important work we're doing here even if you two can't grasp it. Just tie it off and go! *Man Two half runs, half walks, off stage. The string drops to the floor.*
EILEEN	*(still louder)* I've had enough of this shit and piss and pus for a lifetime. It has no place in my work. Animal functions! Just get on with it. *We hear running water, the sound of urination. Eileen picks up the string. Ties it around a railing at approximately the correct height. Stands arms akimbo evaluating what to do next.*
EILEEN	*(to Man Two)* Ee-from! That is your name isn't it? Ee-from, well, its time you relaxed. Nothings being accomplished. Nothing at all. Just bring in the next piece. The blue one, with the cushion. You'll see it. It's out there. *High-pitched barking from outside somewhere.*
MAN ONE	Oww-ww-ww. Damn! *Sound of kicking, a squeal!* No you don't! *Limps back in, sans chair.*
EILEEN	Now what? Don't think you can slack off on me!
MAN ONE	No ma'am. 'Course not. *Eileen steps rapidly towards the door.*
EILEEN	Did you hurt her? She's quite shy, you know. Can't abide strangers. You ought to be more careful next time. Calling Little LuLu, LuLuLuU, little LuLu ... You should be ashamed ... LuLu ... LuLU ... I'm going to have to see what's become of her ... *Eileen exits.*
MAN ONE	*(Stage whisper)* What happened?
MAN ONE	*(Stage whisper)* Got teeth like needles, it has.
MAN ONE	*(Stage whisper)* Let me tend to it. Might be serious. *Eileen enters, a tiny fuzzy lap dog in her arms. Sees Man Two looking at Man One's calf.*

EILEEN	You animal! You frightened her half to death! I can't understand you. I ask you to do something quite simple—the blue settee—and it turns into this. Can you please bring it so that we can get on with it?
MAN ONE	Yes, Ma'am. After we bring it will that be all?

Ties a cloth around the wound.
Both exit, Man One limping.
Eileen sets the dog on the table. Calms her with long exaggerated strokes.
Talks to her in a sing-song.

EILEEN	Dear precious Violet Puff, Poor, poor, poor, Puff Puff, I know, I know, but men are just like that. Just barge about. Hardly conscious. Good thing you frightened them, say I.

(Cocking an ear)
I wonder what's become of them?
Wanders towards the window.
Oh!
Shrinks back.
There's that awful man again. Nearly naked! With those glasses. I wish he wouldn't sneak about.
Calls out
Jean! Jean!
Wrings her hands.
Jean!
Walks back to window. Looks long and hard. Crosses to drapes. Pulls them closed. Pensively. Steps to flowers on table. Takes one out. Pulls petals off systematically, depositing them carefully on a pad. Hums.
Jean! Please!
Jean enters from what must be the bedroom. He is in a silk dressing gown. A bit of a fop, but elegant nevertheless. He is rubbing his face with some kind of aftershave. Glances at his nails. Looks utterly nonchalant as he surveys the room.

JEAN	You've been busy. *(It's simply a statement.)*
EILEEN	*(Gazing pointedly out the window)*

I want you to do something about that man.
Men return, lugging a graceful, even feminine Bauhaus-style settee. Eileen hears them, turns, points a long arm to where it should go. The men shuffle over to the spot.

EILEEN	That's right. Put it right there. I've already marked the feet ... Balance, Jean. It all has to do with balance. One thing against many ...

She moves about the room, shifting this there, that there, stands back, looks about, moves again to make a minute adjustment
No. A bit more I think. Wait.
Walks across the room
Yes, just a bit.

JEAN	Well then. It's very orderly. Very ... clear. Just the way you like it.
EILEEN	Is it. *(A statement)* Yes, I suppose it is.
JEAN	But that's not enough?
EILEEN	To be, quote, "very orderly. Very Clear?" I don't think so. *To Men* Just slightly to the right. *To Jean* That's better, don't you think?
JEAN	What would be better?
EILEEN	I would want to deserve the word "perfect."
JEAN	But that's not attainable.
EILEEN	No?
JEAN	Not on this earth.
EILEEN	Why bring God into it?
JEAN	I didn't.
EILEEN	Well, you referred, if ever so obliquely, to an afterlife.
JEAN	But I'm an atheist. As, I imagine, are you.
EILEEN	Then ... ? *The question hangs in the air.*
JEAN	*Tapping his cigar into the ashtray.* Let's say its ... immaculate.
EILEEN	*(Angrily)* There you go again. My work is not about any of that.
JEAN	Oh, so this place, this arrangement I've been helping to organize, this is your work?
EILEEN	Only more so. It encapsulates my beliefs. It could be said that it is my only religion.
JEAN	So, you cannot be what I said you were—
EILEEN	*(completing his sentence)*

An Atheist? Of course not. That would imply I am godless, or at least bound by the here and now. Which of course is not the case. Let's say I launch my work, the objects I make, into the future, where I hope they reside for some time after I am gone.

JEAN Well, they will certainly be worth something more.

EILEEN But why should I be interested? You sound like a speculator. Already counting. Ha! Ha! And what if they are not? What if all this, all this ...
Sweeps her hand around the room.
... is worth no more than a dishrag? I can see it now. In my mind's eye. Blackish mold creeping through the cracks. Spots of ... age spots ... blistering the paint, cracking open like sores. Gulls nesting there, in the angle of that lamp, their shit littering the floor. Feathers and bones everywhere. Jagged glass out towards the sea. Is that not likely? Is that not a likely fate?

JEAN Don't be ridiculous.

EILEEN What, with no heirs? No ties?

MAN ONE *Standing awkwardly, torturing his hat.*
Ma'am.

MAN ONE *Insisting, shifting from foot to foot.*
Ma'am, If there's nothing more ...

EILEEN You're damn right. There's nothing. Nothing, nothing, nothing!

JEAN That's your choice.

EILEEN As I've told you, I have little choice in the matter. This is what I have. This (*points*), this (*points*), and of course Puff. He will shit on it as well. And those two ...
Looks at the workmen
Out! Out! Get out!
The workmen shuffle out. Man Two turns at the door, realizes he's forgotten his sling, retrieves it and leaves.

EILEEN *(She is now distraught.)*
What can I do?

JEAN Continue as you have. Wait.

EILEEN For recognition, I suppose is what you have in mind. That, and the few francs that come with it.

JEAN There's a Chinese proverb: Set a clear goal. Accomplish it. Realize it didn't matter in the first place.

EILEEN   I am the daughter of Scottish parents. My upbringing was as unremarkable as that of other girls. The weather was harsh and unforgiving and I suppose it has had some effect on my conduct but it was never the design of my parents or actually anyone in my acquaintance for my life to have been anything other than the rough duplicate of the other lives of the other persons in the other houses on the other streets that made up our village. It was in fact the realization of the other person's lives in the other houses on the other streets that first made me aware of the way in which my being was not like that of the others that it was my being itself that made marks on paper in space in my mind more than they appeared to be to the others, that is, that is, that is what brings us into this room together, Jean, you and I, together, in this incestuous merry-go-round, this battle to make, to show, to sell, to ...

Her voice is dying out to a whisper, slowing to a dirge.

Eliminate ... all ... feeling ... all ... judgment ... all ... difference ... until ... it's ... over.

Slowly as if wrapping each word in licorice

Things in life ... these things ... I'm not talking about these things in par-ti-cu-lar ... but about ... for instance food. What one places in the digestive tract. What one mast-i-cates. It must be harmonious. We look for a certain resonance when choosing to have the asparagus before the prosciutto, yes? A time when that crumb of leftover bread complements the last remaining morsel. It's that. It's intangible and mostly is taken for granted. And yet.

She looks longingly at the ever-level silhouette of the Mediterranean.

There are storms. There are storms, Jean. In my heart. In the ... You know my companions, Jean. They are pretty, yes? Elegant, yes? Oh, and they have a smooth surface, like marble, like finely honed marble.

She looks at him. He is lighting a cigar. Nods, encourages her to go on.

Yes, and they bring their perfumes, their rouge, their combs and tassels, and yes, we enjoy one another ... but where is the balance? It's all around us, me, this place.

She strides purposefully to move an abstract painting across the room and reposition it against a different wall. Voice quavering.

I try, I do, I do. Yet the touch of a different texture ... of a different ... sex. I don't know. Hard against soft. Sinews. What do the Chinese say? Ying and yang. It's not for me and yet ... where is the balance?

JEAN   Don't torture yourself. What is, is.

Looks expectantly at her.

After all—

EILEEN   After what? After wrinkles destroy my face? Even Brancusi ...

JEAN   He's a primate.

EILEEN   He's a great sculptor. You know I fell in love with Mademoiselle

Pogany. That angular smoothness. Oh! His hands must have rubbed that marble for days. Weeks. Big hands. He has dirty nails. Blunt! They are repulsive really, smoothing that marble. Caressing it! Oh, I don't know what I'm saying.

She pulls out a beautiful cloisonné modern cigarette case. Removes a cigarillo with great care, crosses to the mantle and retrieves a long cigarette holder. Inserts the cigarillo. Crosses to jean who offers her a light.

Do you think I should write to her? Would you? What would you do?

JEAN   I would do what's appropriate.

EILEEN   Damn you Jean! That's the problem! What's appropriate!

She spits out the words.

Balance. It's not nec-es-sar-ily ap-pro-pri-ate. Sometimes it's radical! Sometimes it's not obvious. Radical, down to the root. Down to the essence of things. Forget the surface. Forget the ever-so polite. Manners, vulgarity! There's a balance for you. Killing, fucking. There's another. Go down the line.

She looks at her cigarette holder with disdain.

Even this ... this ... how is it different if ...

She snaps it in two.

if my lips touch the tip ...

Sucks on the cigarillo ...

Does it give me any less pleasure? Any more? Or do I just lose an accessory?

JEAN   You ... lose ... it does not become you.

EILEEN   No? What if it transforms me? What if ... instead of these pretty feet ... encasing these pretty feet, you saw what working men wear? Then my calves would become heavy, coarse with the act of lifting heavy shoes. Perhaps, transformed, I might find a balance? A calm.

Goes to fling open a window on the Mediterranean. Shudders with what might be tears.

Even a discord can balance. Wait! I want you to hear something.

She crosses to a pile of recording discs. Pulls one from the pile

Antheil gave me this.

Pulls a cover from a very out of place looking upright phonograph machine. Opens it and places the recording on the turntable. Turns the switch. Waits.

You wonder that I keep it covered. This technical marvel! Yet it's hiding. It must be hidden. Society cannot bear to look at its mechanics, which, to me, represent beauty of the purest kind. Now. But listen.

Georges Antheil's Ballet Mecanique comes forth weakly, with scratches, pops, and hums. Eileen is transfixed.

You hear?

JEAN   *(Grunts)*

Why do you chafe so? Your work sells well. Paid for this.

He fingers his scarf.

Why? You could be off somewhere, enjoying, having pleasure. Instead you compose these lifeless trifles. Let me tell you, if I had this house, this outlook, my friends would fill it up.

EILEEN   Please. Just listen.

Turns volume up. Stands with arms crossed. Could be taunting him. Listens intently.

JEAN   *(Shaking his head.)*

Please. Turn it off. I don't like it, but I get the point.

EILEEN   Which is?

JEAN   I can't really put it into words.

EILEEN   Why not, Jean?

JEAN   *(Trailing off)*

It's ... something ...

EILEEN   Crazy? Is that what you think? Now she's done it? She's out there? While you, you are so certain, with your patrons, and artist puppies, and salons that I wear a coat and tie to attend? That I'm not like the others? Of course I'm not. Nor was I meant to be. Sometimes, usually, almost always, it repels me.

JEAN   The last time ... you seemed so ... sullen. Far away.

EILEEN   I was thinking about Damia. How she didn't belong. We had a row. We always do, but that time, oh, she got to me. It was as I was draping the pearls, lapping the strands as I do, and she, she in her chinois, looking at me when I asked, "Why, why do you look at me in that way," and her pursed lips. I slapped her. The pearls were swinging, she caught them and ... poof! And as I was on the floor gathering them she mocked me.

JEAN   I've said she's not good for you. It's your life. Your career.

EILEEN   *(Stops in her tracks)*

Of course. You are of course offering good advice. Advice I reject at my peril, I might add ... and yet ... do you not think, at those soirées, those salons, those endless parades, surrounded by my work, on the walls, lighting the room, under someone's ahem, bottom, at those soirées – do I not pervade the room? Like perfume? and having done so, are there not those that come simply to partake?

I'm not naïve. Don't tell me that those ever so stylish swans don't yearn to be in my bed!

JEAN	You amaze me.
EILEEN	*(the coquette)* Of course. *She returns to the window. Steps back suddenly.* He's out there.
JEAN	Who?
EILEEN	You know, it was you that introduced us. He's building that dreadful shack, the one with logs. Oh, and he's ... I think he knows I'm here ... he must ... there he goes, diving in without a stitch. It's not civilized. *She pulls the curtain across with a jerk.* I don't want him up here Jean. Do you hear? He can take those curious spectacles and ... *Opens window, calls out.* Scat! Scat! There, take your ridiculous eyewear and ...
JEAN	*(Gravely)* He's said how impressed he is ...
EILEEN	With this house! With its white walls. Its pure ... white ... walls. Well, he's not coming in here to drip seawater all over the place. I know what's up and I won't have any of it. Mr. Le Corbusier. Mr. Crow or whatever you claim to be, I'm sick of your propaganda, sick to death of you r... machines for living ... your ... utopias. They're never going to be. Never! I would as soon ... wait! There's someone with him ... *Thinks a moment. Changes her mind. A gleam in her eye.* Jean! You've got to go down and speak to them. Here. Give him this and tell him ... tell him ... *She crosses to a slim table, picks up a magazine and tears a sheet out of it.* ... it's from an ... admirer ... of sorts ... who would love to meet his companion.
JEAN	Oh no you don't. You don't put me in the middle.
EILEEN	Jean, please. He'll understand. He might even, well, he might even glance up. He's got to be consumed with envy. Envy! That would be perfect.
JEAN	Be assured, my dear.
EILEEN	Please Jean. Just do it. For me. This once.
JEAN	I will, but I don't like it. It won't come out right.
EILEEN	There you go again. Right! Right! Right! You'll ruin it for everyone. Just see what happens. If he breaks a smile, it will be his first. Then we'll see. We'll see if they are good company or ...

The door closes behind Jean. She crosses to the window. Looks out stealthily.
Time passes. She taps her foot. Moves a vase. Infinitesimally. Pricks her
finger on a rose thorn.
Ohhh.
Sucks on it.

CURTAIN

SCENE TWO

A rooftop terrace overlooking the Mediterranean. A pure white wall at railing height
defines the edge. Late afternoon with strakes of orange sunlight. A table is set with liquor,
aperitifs, some glasses. Otherwise empty. Eileen is pacing back and forth nervously.
Distracted. She clutches her cigarette holder like a spear, one stiff arm oscillating by
her side as she circumnavigates the roof—at times staring directly out at the audience.
After a time, voices emanate from behind a curved wall, which we guess shields a spiral
staircase from view.

JOSEPHINE   Not so quickly. My umbrella!

CORBUSIER   Damn the umbrella.

JOSEPHINE   It's caught.

CORBUSIER   Well pull it.

JOSEPHINE   No. It's my favorite. I won't be seen without it.

CORBUSIER   We haven't been here for a moment and already you act like a child.
...
I'll get you a new one. Come along.
Eileen puts her head out from behind the wall and calls out.

EILEEN   Yoo-hoo. Down there. Is something the matter?

JEAN   *(from below)*
They are with me.

EILEEN   Who?

JEAN   You asked me to bring them.

EILEEN   Yes, I did.

JEAN   Well, they are with me.

EILEEN   Then bring them up.

JOSEPHINE	My umbrella!
JEAN	*Offering a hand to an invisible Josephine* Madam. *Without answering, Josephine hands him the umbrella as well as the huge beach bag she's been carrying. Languidly adjusts her enormous hat.* Please see to it that it's hung properly ... now ... indulge me ... *She walks around the perimeter of the terrace, taking everything in. Then stops with her back to the audience, enjoying the vast view. Eileen, Jean, and Corbusier stand awkwardly, scattered around the rooftop. No one speaks. Finally, Josephine snaps her fingers. Gestures. Corbusier walks to her, fumbles in his pockets, brings out a cigarette holder. Lights a long thin black one for her. She takes a puff.*
JEAN	*Gazing at the Mediterranean* Nothing out there.
JOSEPHINE	As it should be.
EILEEN	Nothing to distract us ... Snot green, isn't that what he said? ... Daedalus. The Greeks ... *Watching Josephine with interest* Oh, my dear, you must be exhausted with all this talk. I'm sure you simply can't bear any more. You look all done in.
JOSEPHINE	Well, I did wonder when you'd ask.
EILEEN	About?
JEAN	*Offering a tall glass* I'm sure Miss Gray is very happy you could visit.
EILEEN	*(Imperiously)* Jean! Leave the young lady alone. Refreshments are for later. Now ... *Looks pointedly at Corbusier.* You two were out there.
CORBUSIER	Where is that?
EILEEN	In the water—nothing on you but those spectacles you've always got on. Mind you don't lose them.
CORBUSIER	Certainly not!
JOSEPHINE	*(Laughing)* Sometimes ... he even wears them when ... *Looks shyly at Le Corbusier.* Sometimes ... we ... it's not natural, but—

CORBUSIER *(Cutting her off)*
Surely there are other subjects Cherie, please

JOSEPHINE *(Looking at Eileen)*
You had a good look, eh?

CORBUSIER *(Awkwardly)*
The view. Yes. Your project makes good use of it. My poor little cabin has only a small window.

EILEEN But surely, that was your choice.

CORBUSIER *(Reluctantly)*
Yes.

EILEEN *(Sarcastically)*
Also you must admire the home of the American President ... Lincoln, I think.

JEAN *(Sternly)*
Eileen!

EILEEN Well why else ... Really ... Did you think those rough boards would disappear? From L'esprit nouveau to a cabin in the forest ... It is a wonderful transformation, no?
Sardonically
So ... novel.

JOSEPHINE *(Gulled)*
It is, it is. And it's cozy ...
Glances haltingly at Eileen then, trailing off.
It is cozy. More than here.

JEAN *(Relieving the tension)*
Well, what will you have? Nothing too ... complicated.

JOSEPHINE *(Laconically, a bit disappointed.)*
There's no breeze.

EILEEN I love it up here.

JOSEPHINE Something cool then.

JEAN Pernod? We have no ice.

CORBUSIER So be it. We are not, after all, in a café. We are here, on an island ... a bare island without so much as a twig. It's no wonder there is no ice. The wonder is that we are here at all.

JOSEPHINE It's so still ... and empty.

Walks to the balcony. Stands, back to the audience and opens her robe wide. It hangs loosely, the setting sun silhouettes her body through the cloth.

You see? No breeze.

EILEEN   My dear. We can't just order one up. Jean, see to Mr. Corbusier ... perhaps ... perhaps he can. After all, his prescriptions—hah—I should say his grand visions, seem to have no boundaries. Maybe he ...

JOSEPHINE   Watch!

JEAN   Unprecedented.

JOSEPHINE   Watch.
She cartwheels around the terrace, stops in front of Eileen.

CORBUSIER   *(Relieved)*
Exhilarating! Superb!
Josephine does a backflip to the balcony, does a handstand atop it, exposing her bloomers.

CORBUSIER   Ah, my coquette, have a care. We don't want your black blood on our hands. Come down, I beg you. What will Paris be if you pass? Their favorite negress? Come, just do a dance if you can.
Jean walks towards her. Extends his hand to be her partner. She twists away, sashays deliberately towards Eileen.

JOSEPHINE   Dance with me.
Provocatively. Teasingly.
Come.

EILEEN   I ... don't know.

JOSEPHINE   Of course you do. Come.

EILEEN   It's ...

JOSEPHINE   *(Commanding)*
Dance with me!
She twirls. Comes uncomfortably close. Jean and Corbusier watch spellbound.
I'm not good enough for you?
I'm just an American with big ideas? I do have big ideas. I'll have a club! Wanna make a plan for it? Wanna be my co-co architecto? Wanna? Wanna smoke with me? Huh!
Eileen shrinks away. Josephine is in heat. She advances.

CORBUSIER   Remarkable! What tension. The space between. The energy! But her best, her best is what you cannot see. Her breasts. They are like figs!

No, ripe figs!

EILEEN   But if I could just ... touch ... her.

CORBUSIER   *Interrupts himself in mid-sentence.*
Go on. Go on. ... Arrange her. Compose what you like. This is what
she does. She lives for it. Symmetry! Legs like so!
He demonstrates.
Like any other arrangement. Of rooms. Of teacups. She lives for it.

JOSEPHINE   *Following Eileen's direction*
I can't ... quite ... There, I've got it!

CORBUSIER   Just as I thought.

EILEEN   *(Pausing)*
May I ask?

CORBUSIER   So strict. Only with the horizontal, the vertical. No curve. No ...
discontinuity.

EILEEN   *Giving in. Begins a languid Biguine.*
Your ... movements ... I ... like two ... I feel the space ... never before ...
Josephine continues her gyration. Her arms weave a complex pattern.
Big ideas. Big ideas. A club ... blue light ... electric light. ... Can you
see it? None of these empty walls, these virginal walls enclosing ...
nothing. ... A band ... me ... singing ... hatchi hatchi hatchi boo, hatchi
hatchi boo boo, hatchi boo ... and you ... you-oo-oo will drape it ...
you-oo-oo will rouge it ... you-oo-oo will make it sweat, make it ...
They are close now, swirling, Eileen is losing her balance.
Smoke.
Jean grabs Eileen, catches her waist in his arm. She pushes him away.

EILEEN   No! We're not finished! Go away!

JEAN   You've had enough!

EILEEN   You! Always telling me what to do!
Almost strutting.
I'm the one you all want. I'm the one with what counts. Without me,
you'd be selling rugs. Rugs! Do you hear! On an alley somewhere
in Montparnasse. Bit of Turkish, Moorish, whatever they call it.
Something to throw down to show what? Money? Hah! Good sense!
Hah hah! I'm not sure you could sell even one!

JOSEPHINE   Oh ... but he could. He could! With those fine eyes. That moustache!
Squeals.
Uh ... The boys would be crazy! Let me take you to Broadway, no, to

the top of the tallest building ... The Woolworth ... We could dance ... I would make you ...

EILEEN   You, you guttersnipe, we know where you came from, and it's not so nice. So hands off!

CORBUSIER No, Miss Gray. No. No. You go too far. There is a place for these things.

EILEEN   (*Stopping suddenly*)
           Where? Some horrible ornamental place? In a bordello? Sorry, I thought we were comrades. I thought, from the house ... the one for Stein. ... So ... white.

CORBUSIER A canvas only. Not meant to be that. But here, with what you've made, it might be more than that. It might be ...

EILEEN   A rival? A shot over the bow? I'm hardly fool enough to pray that my poor skills might engage you, much less play the bully. But if you'd like ... I can tell you that this house is just what it is. No more, no less. Nothingness pleases me. A mark would spoil it. Sometimes ... sometimes in the morning the sun makes a mark, and I curse it. I curse it and finally it moves. It makes no sound. Just ...*[giggles]*... moves ...
           Lights a cigar.
           For me!

CORBUSIER Yes, yes, I see, nothing extra. Not even a brick.

JEAN   I knew you would appreciate this especially. Note the fine relations. A real jewel. Careful of the dog! She gets wild up here.

EILEEN   Poor Choo-choo. Did he hurt you? You stay there now.

CORBUSIER A place for everything! I noted the shelves, the cubicles, the small niches, the cupboards. Is it enough, I ask? Is it enough? The man in the street, does he have a use for all this? His undergarments, his sweat-stained blouse, those thick shoes. Where is the place to feed his cat?

JEAN   Eileen! Where do you feed Choo-choo?

CORBUSIER Not only that. Hygiene in general is denied to those who cannot afford it. White and light should dominate! Nothing to hide. Everything in sight. Is that not so?

EILEEN   Yet it is—how would you say—a kind of purity. In spite of ...

CORBUSIER Bah! I speak of ... of ... cheese and she, she speaks of feathers. Of course it's empty. So that it can be filled. So that man can live life!

I'm not speaking of the pure white of angels, of a dove, but the white of a canvas ready to paint. The white of notepaper about to become a love letter. My good lady, I speak of white as anathema to the white you impose. I speak of a white in readiness, a white to be sullied, but I do not think that is your white. Your white is scrubbed white. Not to be snubbed white. It's a white that erases, eliminates the—

EILEEN   Oh come now. Isn't that going a little bit too far? I'll admit I have little appetite for common ways. I cannot say I am moved, as you say you are by the reek of the street, but don't you have some secret desire? Some—

JOSEPHINE   *(To Corbusier)*
My dear! Be careful!

CORBUSIER   Damn you woman! You don't get it. You don't see? This is nonsense!
To Jean
How can you ... are you blind? Here I've come some distance, assured that there might be some ... corr-es-pond-ence and I find not a bully ... no ... I find a pretender!
A pretender who would ...
A bow heavy with sarcasm.
Madame, it is I who should be counted as one among many of your devotees. Please, tell me all about your aesthetic system. I am longing to hear it from your lips.

JOSEPHINE   Cornichon!

CORBUSIER   No! The slender, oh-so-well-appointed mademoiselle must be accorded the honors she so richly deserves.
To Eileen
Do you dare to say it? Will you admit that these ... poses ... are those of a pretender? That the "oh so white" is no thicker than a coat of paint ... and a thin one at that!

EILEEN   And that parti-colored harlequin of yours? That "rustic" little cabin. Is that one of your "machines for living?"

CORBUSIER   Exactly. A machine for LIVING! Madam. A "machine" for a life that reeks of everything you find vile and repulsive. A "machine" that brings out the sweat, the nighttime emissions, the aroma of garlic and last night's crusted wine-glasses. A machine where the noises from the peddlers and streetwalkers assault those from the gramophone.

EILEEN   This is too much! I have tried, in earnest, to put up with your silly round eyeglasses, your smirk, the evil thoughts that lurk just behind your lips. You and your oh-so-exotic Amazon, nothing but an American, and a black one at that!
To Jean

Jean, I beg you, show Mr. Corbusier out.

JOSEPHINE   I'm staying put!
Looks to Eileen. Sultry.
That is, if you want me to.
After a piercing look, Jean and Le Corbusier exit, leaving Josephine and Eileen alone.

EILEEN   I don't understand. You ...

JOSEPHINE   Me? Just a secret. In the boat. On the sea ... you and me ...
Eileen looks intently at Josephine.

CURTAIN

SCENE THREE

Same room, early evening.
Eileen, Le Corbusier, and Jean are seated rather stiffly around a low table. When they speak it is in the clipped, formal language of academia. Josephine reclines somewhat apart, clad in a ravishing silk robe.

EILEEN   *(Icily)*
I understand that you've gotten your permissions for the house at Garches. You must be quite pleased.

CORBUSIER   That's something I don't allow to myself. It serves a purpose. That's enough.

EILEEN   Nothing more?

CORBUSIER   Nothing more.

EILEEN   But what of ...

CORBUSIER   Madame Stein? She will walk the floors. Perhaps indulge in a bit of Turkish schmatta. Who cares?
He gets up, goes to the stack of tubes and sticks he has propped against a wall.
Look! I haven't come to mine the past. It's over. Done. I have something new. Something to reveal ... to you. It concerns you.
He unfolds a wooden easel. Places it directly in front of Eileen. Slowly reveals a drawing and places it on the easel directly in front of Eileen. Points towards the audience.
Up there ... just near the tracks. Here, let me show you. There will be these six spots for vacationers. Red, Yellow, Green, Blue, all the colors of the rainbow. You don't face in that direction. They are above

you. Like birds.

Glances at Eileen. She is stony. In shock.
Well, the proprietor has struck a deal you see. A deal is a deal.
To Jean
It's what I told you. What do you make of it?
All are silent.
I admit there will be ... in-con-veniences. Perhaps you will want to erect a screen? A barrier of some sort? I mean at your discretion, of course ...
He is flummoxed by their reaction. Goes on.
He, the proprietor, of course he's aware ... you have guests ... you have ...

JEAN   Please! You needn't continue.

CORBUSIER But.

EILEEN No. Just get on with it.

CORBUSIER Well, I imagine a modularity. To govern the composition, you see. And to direct the views ... towards the water ... towards the horizon.

EILEEN Ah! There it is again. The hor-i-zon!
Sarcastically
How original! Wouldn't you say that's a breakthrough? And what about the view, eh? We don't all drop our gaze on cue. And when you do—when THEY do—it's my bare backside ... mine and anyone else who is on this very deck that's going to be parading in front of their eyeballs. Erect a screen, you say? Hah! More like a wall, more like ... Jean, you must not let him do this!

JEAN   Monsieur!

CORBUSIER Interesting! I find it interesting that you, Madame, you who have so much in reserve ... you harbor your thoughts, your desires ... what a curious state? I would have thought you'd relish such an opportunity. White skin. White where the sun hasn't touched even a hair. White where the dancer's bindings criss-cross ... I would have thought that you, of all people, you would find the possibilities delicious.

EILEEN I'd be mortified! The very thought ... and what if I were, as you say ... curious ... playing to those weekenders? Do you think they merit so much as a fart from my naked ass? No. I won't have it! You must not build anything of the sort.

CORBUSIER But, dear lady, I haven't a choice.
Stony silence. No one moves.

CORBUSIER	Well then, I suppose that you must devise some sort of a screen ... as you've done before. I've heard you've a knack for that. *Looks at her.* All that peek-a-boo. That's something all the ladies must appreciate. Think of it as an opportunity.
EILEEN	*(To Jean)* Must I put up with this, this insult!
JEAN	Eileen. Really. I'm sure he means no harm.
EILEEN	Of course he does. You don't know him. This is a campaign. It amuses him to imagine my distress. And just like you to side with him. *Looks at Josephine, walks over to her. Puts an arm around her waist. Whispers in her ear. Josephine giggles. Nods excitedly. Elaine speaks languidly.* When we take the sun ... *Josephine begins a slow striptease. Hands her clothing bit by bit to Eileen.* When we take the sun ... we take it all over. We bury ourselves in it. We lather it, spread it like butter. It invades even the smallest, most se-cret ... places. It ... *She is watching Corbusier, pacing her speech to his rising discomfort. Josephine is removing her elaborate lace pantaloons. Strides to him and extends her arm to demand that he receive them.*
EILEEN	*(Coos)* It requires total exposure. *Turns violently to Corbusier with sudden hardness in her voice. Gestures towards an imaginary hill positioned where the audience is sitting.* And it cannot tolerate the eyes you intend to put up there!
JEAN	*(Embarrassed)* See what you've done!
CORBUSIER	What's all the fuss? So I made a deal. I am an architect, not a social secretary. Her liaisons are her responsibility. Mine is to build. Besides, those ... cabins ... what do you think will be going on up there? You think they are not ... busy up there as well? *Scoffs, tosses the pantaloons to Josephine.* You forgot the bananas. Here, put these on. Where's my pipe? *To Eileen* You, dear lady, have talent, and would do well to apply it. *He bends to light his pipe.*
JEAN	I'm sure she didn't mean, I mean, she has only the greatest respect. Don't you? *Looking at Eileen* She has great admiration for your contributions, it's just ...

EILEEN	An invasion, that's what it is. This has been my private place, my private view, my dear forest of birds, and trees, and animals, and soon, soon, if he does this, this senseless thing. ... Oh, what's the use? He'll only ...
CORBUSIER	What? Make a place for a few campers? I'm afraid you take yourself altogether too seriously madam. What you do, what we do, we architects, is to put together a few sticks and stones.
JEAN	*Trying to make peace.* It's such a beautiful evening. Let us enjoy what light remains.
EILEEN	If this is evening, midnight can't be far off. Soon there will be nothing to enjoy. Monsieur, I beg you.
JOSEPHINE	*Beckoning to Eileen* Cheri, come with me, we will watch the sunset. Together.
CORBUSIER	Yes, yes, go. At once. *Josephine and Eileen make their way to the spiral stair. Half way up they pause.*
JOSEPHINE	I have an idea. *They exit, leaving Corbusier and Jean alone.*
JEAN	*In a confidential tone* So ... how is it?
CORBUSIER	What? Oh, ... you mean?
JEAN	Yes ..., with her.
CORBUSIER	Like any other. ... An animal function ... no, it's mechanical, like a piston.
JEAN	It can't be!
CORBUSIER	Oh, I assure you.
JEAN	But we've seen you. On the boat. In the sea.
CORBUSIER	Oscillation, you mean. Oh yes. The jitterbug. The black skin glistening. Jazz. ... They have skyscrapers, you know, in New York. Big ones. Made of steel. Jazz. Not like these overwrought chateaus. Thinks. French women. They're like that. Perfumes. Lace undergarments ... with wires! Bits peeking through.
JEAN	*(Approvingly)*

Yes!

CORBUSIER   Well, I've none of it. Honesty! Reality! Rivers of sweat! Hair! Black flesh like ebony. She's a dancer you know, but …
Searches for the right word.
… en pointe. Not en pointe. Barefoot, with big thighs.
He gestures with his hands, makes an approximation of the diameter.
The frills worn by your French dancer would burst at the seams.
Laughing and gesturing to the door through which Eileen and Josephine have left.
And to think of the two of them … in this house … so white. So … clean.

JEAN   This is her way. I find it refreshing.

CORBUSIER   *(Right back at him)*
Re-*pressing* you say? Repressing. I should say so. There's a desert between us. A desert of her making. When I move through it it's as though the Mistral has been here! Look! Look there! It sucks the life from your eyes. Here, help me.
He moves towards the table Eileen has just positioned.

JEAN   What are you doing?

CORBUSIER   Help.

JEAN   Not an inch. Not a fraction. It would distress her.

CORBUSIER   So much? Think of it as a game. A subtle one, but a game nonetheless.

JEAN   To what end?

CORBUSIER   A cor-rec-tion then. A parry.
His voice gets very soft, to a whisper.
A message! A primer for Ms. Gray. Come. Help me.
Lays down his cane.
A fresh wound.
He moves to lift the table.
The width of a finger.
Jean lunges towards him.

JEAN   No! Are you crazy?
They struggle, knock into the table, which wobbles precariously, then rights itself as the empty vase tumbles down and smashes on the floor.

JEAN   Now you've done it!

CORBUSIER   *Watching the table closely*

You mean ... progress ... of a sort.

JEAN   *(Angrily)*
        Nothing of the sort.

EILEEN *(Offstage)*
        Jean! Jean! I heard something.

JEAN   *(Calling out)*
        It's nothing.

CORBUSIER   Is that so? It's that fraction, is it? Moved heaven and earth have we?
            He sights along the table.
            Alright then, here. Close one eye. Look here, along the edge. It's
            obvious. The hypotenuse. The structure of it all.
            He hands him his cane.
            OK. Point. Point towards the sea. Lower. L-o-w-e-r.
            He walks over. Placing himself directly in line with the cane.
            Back a bit ... come towards me ... stop. Right.
            Steps back, crosses his arms. Satisfied.
            Can you feel it? Can you?

EILEEN *(Offstage)*
        Is everything all right?

JEAN   *(Calling out. Annoyed.)*
        Not to worry.
        Jean kneels to sight along the table

CORBUSIER   *(Stage whisper)*
            Imagine it's a weapon. You've got the target in your sights.

JEAN   Oh, this is preposterous. No one would ...

CORBUSIER   *Stands at the focus of Jean's sight line. Removes his glasses.*
            Perhaps these would help.

JEAN   I couldn't.

CORBUSIER   Of course you can.
            Hands him the glasses, which he puts on.
            Is it off? Do you have any idea what you're looking at?
            Well then. It can't matter all that much.

JEAN   Her eye ...

CORBUSIER   Save it for her customers. What about yours? Your eye!
            Pauses. There's no answer.

I thought so. You're both … the two of you … like gypsies … reading palms, delivering utopias as flimsy as they are enticing. If I had only a few hours … you don't suppose … that wretched place of mine … oh you can say it is of my own making. A bad bargain with a bad cook.

JEAN   But you swim, you paint, you read.

CORBUSIER It fills the hours.

JEAN   And now …

CORBUSIER Now I need something more. You can go back to your soirées, your endless dances, the rites of Paris … Diaghilev alone will keep you entertained. But I … I am alone here with my thoughts, my paintings … my … visitors. That cabin of mine she so despises … it's like a ship. A ship adrift on a hillside, and there I am the captain. I can see almost across to the desert. I long for the desert. Flat. Unbroken. Waiting. Waiting as the sun rises and sets.
Musing. Abruptly.
But you are not interested in this. You and Madam Gray, you prefer your orgies surrounded by the ornaments of the bourgeoisie. It's not for nothing that those fancy screens of hers – look at this one.
He points to the screen with his cane.
It reeks of opulence. One imagines one of those flat-chested odalisques to appear from behind it, with little pearls dripping to the waist.

JEAN   But you, Monsieur, you have no heart. Those words cannot convince me. If I did not know better …

EILEEN   *Entering from above, speaking over her shoulder to Josephine.*
No. No, no, no, no. My mind is set.
Sees the broken vase,
What is this?

JEAN   *(Perspiring)*
An accident.

EILEEN   Well, what of it. It was out of place in any case. I say good riddance.

JEAN   But …

EILEEN   Then pick. It. Up. … Now.
Looks to Josephine.
My black jewel has agreed to watch over Fifi.

CURTAIN

SCENE FOUR

The white room again, but now enveloped in hanging, paint-spattered drop cloths. An assortment of ladders, painter's planks, and buckets clutter the space among the ghost-like cloth covered silhouettes of furniture. The sound of someone humming emanates from behind the curtain, which is occasionally moved by the activities going on behind it. This goes on for some time, an abstract ballet. Josephine, in a highly decorated silk kimono, bare feet, and hair wrapped in a towel, enters holding a demitasse.

JOSEPHINE   Where shall I put it?
The humming stops.

CORBUSIER   (*From behind the curtain*)
Near the Victrola ... while you are there—

JOSEPHINE   Again?

CORBUSIER   You'll need to take off the cover, and the recording is right there. ...
See it?
I was referring to the coffee I've brought for you.

CORBUSIER   First things first. Please.
Josephine sets demitasse on the floor, goes to a shrouded shape and removes the cover to reveal the Victrola from Scene One.

JOSEPHINE   You know I don't like it. All that noise ... gives me a headache.

CORBUSIER   All the same. ... Damn.
A great clattering crash. Hastily.
Not you ... I've just ... Can you get me a rag?
Josephine rummages around. Finds a cloth. Disappears behind the drop cloth. Empty stage.

CORBUSIER   There! You'll have to bend over. That's more like it.
The drop cloth drapes her protruding backside as she wipes up a spill on the floor.

JOSEPHINE   Edouard? Pet? I'm looking at the sea. It's very calm. There's the sun. No clouds.

CORBUSIER   Please. I've asked you not to call me that.

JOSEPHINE   Sorry. Which?

CORBUSIER   Neither. Just ... well, alright, pet will do.

JOSEPHINE   It looks warm enough for a swim.

CORBUSIER   No, not now, can't you see I'm in the middle of something?

JOSEPHINE	I can't see anything. It's been a week since we've taken up here and I haven't seen or touched anything.
CORBUSIER	(*Muffled*) What did you have in mind? I take good care of you, don't I? You're not in need of anything?
JOSEPHINE	Jean is on his way …
CORBUSIER	With her? I can only hope he knows what he's doing. … Over there, there's another spot. *His arm describes an arc in the cloth.* It's true my coquette. This will put us at odds.
JOSEPHINE	I'm imagining her face.
CORBUSIER	Well, I'm sure of one thing … you will not be seeing anything else, eh? After this? All your games will come to an end. You'll have no one but this one. The one on the ladder, eh? Hmm! She is, you know, not likely to be happy.
JOSEPHINE	She'll get used to it.
CORBUSIER	Jean is not sure. He has, I might say, an axe to grind. *The drop cloth parts as Corbusier, clad only in paint-covered swimming trunks and smeared with great swaths of bright paint descends a ladder and crosses to the Victrola, bending to pick up the demitasse on the way, then placing a record on the turntable. The Antheil Ballet Mecanique starts out. Corbusier raises the volume until it is at its max.*
CORBUSIER	(*Loudly*) Come. Let's have some help with this. *He ascends a ladder to untie the knots on the drop cloth. Then, seeing an opportunity, grabs a large brush and plunges back at the fresh paint on the now revealed mural covering the walls. Like an animal trainer, he brandishes the brush, swiping at the mural with great, lunging gestures. Josephine stands, transfixed.*
CORBUSIER	Bon-bon. *Gestures towards the knots, continues to paint.* What are you waiting for? *Josephine stands still. Looks as though she will break out in sobs at any minute.*
CORBUSIER	(*Consolingly*) Bon-bon …
JOSEPHINE	I didn't expect … I mean … Oh my god … She trusted me …

CORBUSIER   With the dog! Some things ...
             Another swipe at the wall ...
             Must take first ...
             Another!
             ... place. There! Is it not fitting? No more of that ...
             Searches for the words
             ... it cried out for color, for shape. It's as though some secret ... urge ...
             some buried ... lust ...
             Another swipe, this time with the finality of a conductor's final stroke.
             ... has been fulfilled. The walls ...

CORBUSIER   *(Quietly)*
             Violated. They've been violated, that's what.
             A loud knocking at the door. A pause. Repeat. A longer pause.

JEAN   *(Outside and muffled.)*
             Shit! Will you open? I'm alone.
             *More pounding. Corbusier climbs down. Anthiel continues to play on the
             phonograph.*

JEAN   *(Still outside)*
             Look, I've come a long way. I was hoping I could change your mind.

CORBUSIER   *(Shouting)*
             It's too late.

JOSEPHINE   *(To Corbusier)*
             He needs to come in.
             To Jean
             Just a moment.
             *Josephine crosses to the door. Jean explodes through it. Stops wide-eyed at
             the center of the room.*

JEAN   Shit!

CORBUSIER   Dear Jean. You are just in time.

JOSEPHINE   I could not make him stop.

JEAN   Shit! Do you know what you've done?

CORBUSIER   That woman! You cannot put a stop to history! So. We must have a
             record. Please. It is more beautiful than before. You can only say that
             it was an empty canvas. Empty! Empty no more.
             He pulls a tripod and four-by-five camera from the debris.

JEAN   You were a guest.

CORBUSIER   So I am. One who pays his bills.

Extends the camera towards him.
Please. Some clicks. Eh?
The Antheil record has finished. The rhythm of its rotation repeats throughout the scene.
Jean looks at him as though he is insane.

JOSEPHINE   He's been like this. It's been non-stop.

CORBUSIER   *(To Josephine)*
Bon bon, stay out of this. Its' not the cootchy cootchy!
To Jean
Its better off for it, don't you think? Just look! I'm always thinking about this. Breasts! Thighs! Its architecture! I have sketchbooks full but here ... here they've jumped off the page!

JEAN   You have no idea ...

CORBUSIER   *(Suddenly pensive)*
So often my attempts are formless. Disappointing. But here ... my entire imagination is at work. I want a clarity, but I paint filth. My women are bestially lascivious. They're lascivious, prurient, perpetually in heat.
Proffers the camera once more.
Here. You can do me a great favor.

JEAN   *(Nodding reluctantly)*
What is it you want of me?
Josephine watches Corbusier climb back on the scaffold, shakes her head. Thoroughly numbed by events. Tries to hand him a towel.

CORBUSIER   No bananas!
He assumes a lunging pose, one naked leg extended behind, the other bent at the knee, arm with a brush extended. He could be a hood-ornament on a car of the period.
To Jean
Focus!

JEAN   I've never—

CORBUSIER   Pretend. Shove your head under the skirt!
Jean puts his head beneath the black velvet shroud hanging from the camera.

CORBUSIER   Snap it.

FINAL CURTAIN

Afterword

CRAIG HODGETTS

It's now 2018, nearly fifty years since a party conversation with Gloria Steinem led to our speculation about a liberated community for *Ms. Magazine Number One*, in which "computers replace commuters; downtown offices dissolve into a million crossing circuits; garages turn into galleries, metal-working shops, and organic restaurants." Those were heady days that careened into an immersion in the avant-garde culture of the California Institute of the Arts, Walt Disney's extraordinary "community of the arts," where I met and became friendly with a burgeoning group of artists and musicians committed to a new, mostly electronic future.

Looking back, I am struck by how imminent it all seemed, with not a hint of the slow pace of the societal and technological evolution that would lead to our present state, here in the second millennium, where such ideas are commonplace, if not downright ordinary.

The propositions and observations that compose the body of this book are rooted in my personal worldview, forged at CalArts, that the highest calling of the designer is to conjure an appreciation of future potential, to seed the imagination with images and text meant to flower with the passage of time, and to bring awareness of radical change to the physical world.

My interests have always veered towards the eclectic, and many of the texts here began with chance thoughts that arose from my encounters with an array of objects and events. A Fellini movie inspired "Object Lesson: Four Short-end Views" for *Progressive Architecture*. A visit to Syd Mead's exhibition led to comments for the *Architect's Newspaper*. The Los Angeles riots prompted a reaction piece for the *Los Angeles Times*. Essays on James Stirling and on Charles and Ray Eames celebrate a "damn the torpedoes" ethos I've always found attractive. In each case, I try to piece together a meaningful, highly personal commentary, which sates my curiosity in a way that straightforward reportage could never replace.

On reflection, those modes of thought are difficult to bring to bear on the practice of architecture. The long slog through regulations, reviews, and markets inexorably reflects the centerline of social and cultural norms, and too often has exiled my speculation to the realm of fiction, or worse, *fantasy*, which I can assure you was and is not the case.

Theoretical work such as *La città pulpa*, developed with my wife and partner, Hsinming Fung, explores alternative urban structures that nurture idiosyncratic enclaves designed to embody different traits and lifestyles. Created for the 1996 *Milan Triennale* and inspired by the formation of the stand-alone city of West Hollywood, we adopted the *manga* format as a way to foreground *lifestyle*, that crucial ingredient so often missing in city planning.

That work takes its place alongside the images of the secessionist *State of Ecotopia* that I proposed for a film based on Ernest Callenbach's novel of the same name, which now, in an odd twist of fate, is echoed in my involvement with the Hyperloop, which is fast becoming a reality. Of course, those ideas did not come from nowhere. I must acknowledge my considerable debt to the Archigram Group, Cedric Price, and of course Jim Stirling, whose mentorship still inspires me even now, so many years since his death.

I suppose it's obvious that my preoccupation with the future and the impact of design on individual lives has a quixotic overtone. Some might argue that the boundaries of architectural practice make it a poorly equipped medium for the promulgation of such ideas, and they would be right. Architecture is the servant, not the master, of society. The presence of buildings, while all-encompassing and functionally indispensable, can do nothing but follow the dictates of forces far more powerful than the spaces they contain.

Thus my reluctance to operate within the constraints deemed important within academia. Looking forward towards the tumult of social media, disruptive technologies, and environmental challenge, it seems to me that it's the stuff *outside* of architecture that begs for scrutiny. One cannot—must not—limit critical comment to a description of physical features and ignore political and social consequences.

Today, with the profusion of media platforms and the drumbeat of today's events, the luxury of reflection has become just another perfume. Architecture, that most elusive of the arts, is now represented by glowing images which confirm the thousand-word adage. Those relatively passive interventions that we call buildings require a voice, an interpretive language able to articulate the meanings buried in the stone and steel from which they are made. These essays are my attempt to provide that voice, and this compilation, inspired by late-night conversations with Ming and carefully assembled by my friend Todd Gannon, has finally put those adventures in context. My thanks to them both, and to all those who have allowed me the privilege of appearing on their pages.

Acknowledgements

A hearty thank you goes out to all of the colleagues, friends, and co-conspirators who helped us bring this project to fruition. We are especially grateful to our dear friends at SCI-Arc and to the Graham Foundation for Advanced Studies in the Fine Arts for generous financial support of the project.

In addition, we wish to thank our project assistants, Zaid Kashef Alghata and Erika Viado; Laura Allen, Allie Bogle, Natalie Egnatchik, Lisa Lang, Dana Nichols, and the rest of the team at Hodgetts + Fung; Jake Anderson and Gordon Goff at ORO Editions; Hernan Diaz Alonso, Antonio Amado, Iwan Baan, Barbara Bestor, Mike Cadwell, Meara Daly, Cynthia Davidson, Joe Day, Eames Demetrios, John Enright, Sarah Herda, Coy Howard, Pablo Mandel, Robert Mangurian, Syd Mead, Bill Menking, Nina Rappaport, and Mohamed Sharif, who each made important contributions; and, in particular, Ming Fung and Yumna Siddiqi.

Credits

We gratefully acknowledge the following sources for permission to reprint copyrighted material. All reasonable efforts have been made to trace the copyright holders of the visual materials reproduced in this book. Please report any errors or omissions to the publisher for correction in future editions.

Texts. All texts © Craig Hodgetts except as follows:

"Biography of a Teaching Machine" © *Artforum,* September 1973, and reprinted by permission.

"Object Lesson: Four Short-end Views" reprinted courtesy of Hanley Wood.

"Behind the Action," reprinted courtesy of California College of the Arts.

"Heretical Remarks on Architecture and Photography" reprinted courtesy of *Architecture California.*

"Rubbing Out the Craft" reprinted courtesy of *Architecture California.*

"Role Reversal" reprinted with permission of *Contract* magazine, contractdesign.com.

"Inside James Stirling" reprinted courtesy of Walker Art Center.

"All the Ideas" reprinted courtesy of Lapis Press.

Review, Eames Design, © Architectural Association, London. Reprinted by permission.

"Requiem for a Heavyweight" reprinted with permission of *Blueprint* magazine.

"Big Jim" reprinted courtesy of Hanley Wood.

"Corb's Car" reprinted courtesy of *The Architect's Newspaper.*

"The Future According to Mead" reprinted courtesy of *The Architect's Newspaper.*

"Architects' Statement for A Confederacy of Heretics" reprinted courtesy of SCI-Arc.

"Mystery Man" reprinted courtesy of *The Architect's Newspaper.*

"The Petersen Museum" What's Under the Hood?" reprinted courtesy of *Form* magazine.

IMAGES. All images © Craig Hodgetts except as follows:

Figs. 4.1–4.6: Photo by Benjamin Lifson

Fig. 5.1: Courtesy of Craig Hodgetts and Robert Mangurian

Fig. 5.2: Photo by Holger Elgaard

Fig. 8.1: Courtesy of Hodgetts + Fung

Figs. 8.2–8.3: © Constantinos and Emma Doxiadis Foundation

Fig. 9.1: Collection, the J. Paul Getty Museum. © Estate of T. Lux Feininger

Fig. 9.2: New York, the Metropolitan Museum of Art. Gilman Collection, Purchase, Ann Tennenbaum and Thomas H. Lee Gift, 2005. © Henri Cartier-Bresson/Magnum

Fig. 9.3: Photo by Julius Shulman. © J. Paul Getty Trust. Getty Research Institute, Los Angeles (2004.R.10)

Figs. 14.1–14.3: Photo by Robert Mangurian

Fig. 15.1: Courtesy of the Los Angeles Forum for Architecture and Urban Design

Figs. 18.1–18.2: Courtesy of Hodgetts + Fung

Fig. 19.2: Photo by NotFromUtrecht

Fig. 19.4: Photo by Cmglee

Fig. 19.5: Reproduced from Anthony Vidler, *James Frazer Stirling: Notes from the Archive* (New Haven: Yale, 2010): 64.

Fig. 19.6: Arcaid Images / Alamy Stock Photo

Figs. 19.7–19.8: Photo by Clay Tudor

Fig. 20.1: Photo by Tim Street-Porter/OTTO

Figs. 21.1–21.2: Courtesy of Robert Mangurian

Figs. 22.2; 25.1–25.5: © 2018 Eames Office, LLC (eamesoffice.com)

Figs. 23.1–23.2: Photo by Woolf Haxton, www.thevhf.com

Fig. 23.3: Photo by Iwan Baan

Fig 24.1: Arcaid Images / Alamy Stock Photo

Figs. 26.1–26.3: Courtesy of Alexis Rochas

Figs. 28.1–28.2: Courtesy of Antonio Amado

Figs. 29.1–29.4: Courtesy of Syd Mead

Fig. 30.1: Photo © 1980 Ave Pildas

Fig. 30.2: Photo by David Tritt

Figs. 30.3–30.4 : Photo by Mary Frampton. Los Angeles Times Photographic Archive, Library Special Collections, Charles E. Young Research Library, UCLA

Figs. 31.1–31.3: Courtesy of Coy Howard

Fig. 32.1: Photo by David Zaitz

ORO Editions
Publishers of Architecture, Art, and Design
Gordon Goff: Publisher
www.oroeditions.com
info@oroeditions.com

BOOK DESIGN: Pablo Mandel / circularstudio.com
EDITOR: Todd Gannon
MANAGING EDITOR: Jake Anderson

Typeset in Lyon Text and HongKong

Generous support for this project was provided by the Graham
Foundation for Advanced Studies in the Fine Arts

Color Separations and Printing: ORO Group Ltd.
Printed in China

ISBN: 978-1-940743-74-5
10 9 8 7 6 5 4 3 2 1 First Edition

For more information on our distribution, please visit our website
www.oroeditions.com/distribution